Escovitz · THE OFFICE OF QÂḌÎ AL-QUḌÂT

ISLAMKUNDLICHE UNTERSUCHUNGEN · Band 100

herausgegeben von

Klaus Schwarz

KLAUS SCHWARZ VERLAG · BERLIN

ISLAMKUNDLICHE UNTERSUCHUNGEN · BAND 100

Joseph H. Escovitz

THE OFFICE OF *QÂḌÎ AL-QUḌÂT* IN CAIRO UNDER THE BAḤRÎ MAMLÛKS

KLAUS SCHWARZ VERLAG · BERLIN · 1984

ISBN 3-922968-42-2
Druck: aku-Fotodruck GmbH, Eckbertstr. 19, 8600 Bamberg

In memory of my father, Maurice Escovitz.

Acknowledgments

I would like to thank all those who helped in the formulation and execution of this study. I benefited from conversations I had with my fellow students at the Institute of Islamic Studies, McGill University: Linda Northrup, S.S.K. Hussaini, and Hasan Murâd; as well as conversations with Professors Michael Winter of the University of Tel Aviv, David Ayalon of the Hebrew University of Jerusalem, and Ulrich Haarmann of the Orientalisches Seminar (Freiburg). I owe special thanks to my supervisor, Dr. Donald P. Little, for his suggestions and advice. I was supported during much of my studies by the McConnell Foundation, which also was generous enough to provide me with a travel grant to consult manuscript collections in Europe and the Middle East. I would like to thank the Publication Grants Committee of the Faculty of Graduate Studies and Research, McGill University for their financial support to publish this book. I also wish to thank Zayn Kassam for her efforts in preparing the final draft.

Finally, I wish to thank my wife for her immeasurable help and encouragement at all stages of preparing this work.

Of course, I bear the responsibility for any omissions and errors.

A Note on Transliteration and References

It has been my general policy to follow the Arabic transliteration system of the International Journal of Middle Eastern Studies. However, I have anglicized many words which I felt have almost become part of the English vocabulary; e.g., sultan, Sufi, and the like. It has also been my policy to capitalize as few Arabic words as possible, especially when they form part of a direct quote or the name of a book. In such cases I have capitalized the first word, and left the rest in lower case letters. Honorifics and bureaucratic titles, such as *qâḑî al-quḑât*, have been left in lower case letters in all instances. Technical considerations have forced me to replace the dot below the emphatics with a cedilla, such as under the *d* in *qâḑî*.

In addition I have used Hijrî dates almost exclusively. For the years which concern us they correspond almost exactly (with the addition of 600 years) to the dates of the Common Era, especially once we enter the eighth century A.H.; e.g., 709 A.H. equals 1309 C.E. When discussing the ages of the judges and the lengths of their terms of office, etc., Hijrî years have also been used. The Muslim year is a lunar year of 354 days; 12 months of twenty-nine and thirty days. Thus, it is slightly shorter than a solar year, but close enough to be meaningful for readers accustomed to solar years, and certainly more meaningful for the present study, since the sources use Hijrî years.

Most of the judges under study had jurisdiction over both sections of Cairo as well as Upper and Lower Egypt. On a few occasions this jurisdiction was split, and one judge was given authority over al-Qâhira and al-Wajh al-Baḥrî (Lower Egypt) and another over Fusṭâṭ and al-Wajh al-Qiblî (Upper Egypt). Alexandria and the nearby coastal region were under the control of separate chief judges. When necessary, I have referred to the appropriate section of Cairo (al-Qâhira or Fusṭâṭ), otherwise the name Cairo has been used meaning the entire city. For the purposes of the present study I have not differentiated between the chief judges with a half jurisdiction and those with jurisdiction over all Cairo and the related provinces during this time period.

Finally, this work was completed prior to the publication of Carl Petry's The Civilian Elite of Cairo in the Later Middle Ages (Princeton, 1982). Although his work deals with the subsequent Burjî Mamlûk period, it is an extremely valuable study for anyone interested in bureaucrats, biographical dictionaries, and medieval Middle Eastern social history.

Table of Contents

CHAPTER I

Introduction

Legal systems of one form or another are necessary for all states in order to prevent chaos and insure the smooth running of government, commerce, and society in general. Islamic civilization developed its own legal system, the *sharîʿa,* and one of the principal officers concerned with its administration was the judge or *qâḍî.* Yet even before the *sharîʿa* had evolved, arbitrators or judges were needed to resolve legal disputes. The first *qâḍî* of Islam, in fact if not in name, was the Prophet Muḥammad himself. Right from the beginning he was faced with a number of legal problems arising not only out of the natural frictions and conflicts of any community, but also out of the terms of the Quran itself; for example, problems of inheritance.[1] The early caliphs continued to exercise such functions, but other close associates of the Prophet were probably called upon to settle disputes as well, since at this stage no special body of judicial officers existed.[2]

As the Islamic empire expanded under the Umayyads, a *qâḍî* was appointed as the delegate of the local governor to settle disputes. At first this was only a part-time job, usually combined with some other bureaucratic function, but by the end of the Umayyad period judges were "exclusively concerned with judicial business."[3] More importantly, "the *qadis* came to have a general judicial competence which cut through the subsidiary administrative divisions of the state, and by the end of the Umayyad period they had become the central organ for the administration of law," although they still depended upon their political superior for the enforcement of their decisions.[4]

The coming of the ʿAbbâsids marked a period of centralization in the judicial administration. The ʿAbbâsids, perhaps following a Persian model, established a *qâḍî al-quḍât* (chief judge) in the capital at Baghdad to head the judiciary.[5] He was chosen by the caliph, as were the provincial judges.[6] The first judge in Egypt was chosen by the ʿAbbâsid caliph al-Manṣûr (ruled 136-158/754-775), although a judge in a province like Egypt must have selected his own deputies and assistants.[7]

When Egypt broke away from the suzerainity of the caliph in Baghdad under the Ṭûlûnids (ruled 254-292/868-905) and later regimes, the new rulers chose their own judges, but the one *qâḍî al-quḍât* was in Baghdad.[8] However this changed with the Fâṭimids (ruled in Egypt 297-567/909-1171), who established their own chief judge in the second half of the 4th/10th century, and other provinces, which were only nominally under the control of the caliph in Baghdad, also started to apply this title to their own head judge.[9]

Towards the end of the year 663 the Mamlûk sultan Baybars al-Bunduqdârî (ruled 658-676) established four chief judgeships in the capital of his empire, Cairo, and the next year established a similar system in Damascus and elsewhere in Syria. Whereas previously there had only been a Shâfiʿî chief judge, there were now chief judges for the Ḥanafîs, Mâlikîs, and

Ḥanbalîs as well. These four *madhâhib* had not been given this sort of equal status in Egypt previously, and from this time onwards the administration of justice there entered a new phase. More importantly, members of the other three schools of law were able to pursue careers which could culminate at the highest levels of the judicial bureaucracy.

The purpose of this study is to examine the office of *qâḍî al-quḍât* in Cairo and the men who held it from the establishment of the four chief judgeships in 663 until the end of the Baḥrî period in 784. The present work does not continue into the Burjî period, because the judiciary of that era has already been the object of some major studies.[10] Greater Syria (i.e., roughly the modern states of Syria, Lebanon, Israel and Jordan) was the other major area of the Mamlûk empire, and there were four chief judges appointed by the sultan in all its principal cities (Damascus, Aleppo, Tripoli, and Ḥamâ).[11] Neither the appointments of the Syrian judges nor their decisions were subject to the approval of the Cairene chief judges, and they should be seen as separate and autonomous units, deserving a separate study.[12]

The four chief judges of Cairo were the principal interpreters of the Islamic law in the capital of what was probably the most powerful and influential Islamic state of the time. Thus their relevance for that state is undeniable. A discussion of their careers is important not only in order to study their activities within the framework of Mamlûk society and politics, but also to assess their role and functions as officers of an Islamic state.

A. Sources

This study is based on the Arabic chronicles and biographical literature dealing with the Baḥrî Mamlûk period. These sources have been supplemented by the relevant secretarial literature, such as al-Qalqashandî's Ṣubḥ al-aʿshâ[13] and Gaudefroy-Demombyne's study of the Mamlûk bureaucracy, La Syrie à l'époque des Mameloukes; and for geographical details by al-Maqrîzî's Khiṭaṭ.[14] No single source provided all the necessary information, and it was necessary to read widely in the original sources to assemble the necessary data. The following discussion attempts to characterize and evaluate the principal literary sources which have been used in this study.[15]

Biographical Literature

The biographical dictionaries and the necrologies in the chronicles are the purest examples of Arabic biographical literature and are extremely rich sources of information.[16] For example, the manner in which the individual's name is listed, A the son of B the son of C, etc., usually going back a number of generations allowed us to construct genealogical tables for some of the chief judges under study. Since many of the fathers and grandfathers were also to be found in these biographical collections, it was possible to make some observations concerning their family background, and, where places of birth were indicated as well, their geographic background. The biographical literature also supplied information on the judges' education, but this is a problematical area. Data on education are provided by lists of subjects and/or teachers with whom the judge had studied. However, there is hardly ever an indication of the time frame in which these studies took place nor their extent. The purpose of these lists was probably to impress the reader with the names of these, usually, famous teachers. All the future judges studied *fiqh*, *tafsîr*, Arabic, etc., and the evidence available is not sufficient to meaningfully distinguish the education of one judge from that of another.

The one biographical dictionary which, perhaps, should have been the best source was Raf' al-iṣr 'an quḍât miṣr by Ibn Ḥajar al-'Asqalânî,[17] which is supposed to list all the judges of Egypt from the Islamic conquest down to the author's own day. Ibn Ḥajar (d. 852/1449) was a famous Shâfi'î author, teacher, and himself a chief judge. He became a chief judge for the first time in 827/1423. Those who have used this dictionary for studying earlier periods of Egyptian history have found it not always reliable,[18] perhaps because Ibn Ḥajar was never able to make a final copy.[19] One major problem is that several biographies are missing. These omissions may be explained by the fact that a final copy was never made. The author certainly knew the names of almost all the judges, because they are mentioned in a poem with which the dictionary begins.[20]

There is some evidence of Shâfi'î favoritism. This prejudice surfaces in the description of the establishment of the four chief judgeships in the biography of Tâj al-Dîn Ibn Bint al-A'azz, the first Shâfi'î chief judge under study, and during whose tenure the other chief judgeships were established. (The establishment of the four chief judgeships will be discussed in detail in the next section.) Ibn Ḥajar avoids using the term *qâḍî al-quḍât* and rather says the three men who had earlier been deputies of the Shâfi'î chief judge now became deputies of the sultan, rather than saying that all now bore the title of chief judge. He then calls Ibn Bint al-A'azz *al-qâḍî al-kabîr,* thus avoiding the term *qâḍî al-quḍât* altogether, and also avoiding any description of a decline in the status of his own *madhhab.*[21] However, there is no evidence that favoritism to his own Shâfi'î *madhhab* was a major characteristic of this biographical dictionary as a whole.

Ibn Ḥajar's other biographical collection which is important for this study is his famous al-Durar al-kâmina.[22] This is an alphabetically arranged centenary biographical dictionary devoted to the most important people who died in the eighth Islamic century, and who lived mainly in Egypt and Greater Syria. This work is indispensable not only because it supplies biographies of many of the chief judges under study, but also because the wide scope of this dictionary helps us trace back a judge's ancestry to determine his family background and to study his progeny. It is easier to learn about ancestors than descendants. The manner in which the name is listed (A son of B, etc.) provides information on ancestors, but the names of children (and wives, cousins, etc.) are rarely to be found anywhere in the biography.

Comparing the biographies in Raf' al-iṣr and al-Durar, we find that they are very similar, but those in Raf' al-iṣr tend to be more detailed. There is some evidence that al-Durar was written later, and it may be that Ibn Ḥajar sometimes abridged the entries from Raf' al-iṣr for his biography of a given judge in al-Durar.[23] Certainly, Raf' al-iṣr often provides better biographies. For example, in the biography of the Ḥanbalî judge

Sharaf al-Dîn al-Ḥarrânî (in office 696-709) as presented in al-Durar we learn that he was born in 645 or 646, taught at al-Ṣâliḥiyya *madrasa*[24] and elsewhere, that he was *nâẓir al-khizâna*[25] for a long time, then became Ḥanbalî chief judge of Egypt.[26] The account in Raf⁽ al-iṣr is more detailed. Only the year 645 is given as the date of birth, and although this is not critical, the fact that he was born in Ḥarrân in upper Mesopotamia (now Turkey) where his great-grandfather had been a *qâḍî* is important. Then Ibn Ḥajar gives a fuller title of his office as *nâẓir al-khizâna al-sulṭâniyya* and that the office of (chief) judge was added to this other bureaucratic post *(uḍîfa ilayhi qaḍâ' al-ḥanâbila)*. We learn again that he taught at al-Ṣâliḥiyya, but, more importantly, he did not assume that post until after the death of his predecessor, the chief judge ʿIzz al-Dîn Ibn ʿAwaḍ, in (6)96 during the sultanate of Lâjîn.[27] Sometimes, however, al-Durar can be more informative, but in a different way. The biography of the Ḥanafî chief judge Sirâj al-Dîn al-Hindî (in office 769-773) as given in Rafʿ al-iṣr[28] does not include the story of this judge's attempt to upgrade the position of the Ḥanafî chief judge by allowing him certain prerogatives which had been reserved for the Shâfiʿî chief judge for many years. This report is contained in al-Durar's biography of this judge.[29] Thus, neither are these two biographical collections identical nor are they complementary; rather, both must be consulted because they often contain different or differently worded reports.

Probably the most famous biographical dictionary, and surely the longest, produced in this period was al-Wâfî bi-al-wafayât by Khalîl ibn Aybak al-Ṣafadî (d.764/1363).[30] Al-Ṣafadî was of

Turkish descent, and although it is said that he did not begin his education until the age of twenty, he was one of the most famous and prolific authors of his time, as well as being an employee of the Mamlûk chancery. This biographical dictionary comprises some forty volumes in manuscript, of which nine have so far been published.[31] This work is meant to deal with notable individuals of the entire Islamic world from the dawn of Islam to the author's own time, but the emphasis seems to have been on the contemporary Mamlûk empire. Regrettably the biographies of chief judges in this collection tend to be very meagre. For example, the biography of Zayn al-Dîn Ibn Makhlûf, the Mâlikî chief judge of Egypt for more than thirty years (in office 685-718), a major opponent of Ibn Taymiyya, and a man of considerable power, is dismissed with only a six-line biography, indicating the names of his predecessor and successor as chief judge and his own date of death.[32] Not all the biographies are this short and useless, but the biographies here do tend to be rather sketchy.

Al-Ṣafadî wrote another biographical dictionary entitled A'yân al-'aṣr, which contains the biographies of men who died between 696 and 763.[33] The biographies of judges in this collection are usually longer than those in al-Wâfî. Thus, the biography of the same Mâlikî judge, Ibn Makhlûf, in A'yân al-'aṣr includes some information on his short deposition from the chief judgeship in 711.[34] This incident is omitted from al-Wâfî as we have noted.

F. Krenkow has charged in an article written a number of years ago that Ibn Ḥajar al-'Asqalânî relied almost exclusively on A'yân al-'aṣr in writing al-Durar al-kâmina.[35] Although it is beyond the scope of the present study to discuss this problem in general, this accusation is certainly not valid for the particular biography of Ibn Makhlûf. In al-Durar[36] this biography is much fuller, and includes the fact that Ibn Makhlûf had held the post of *amîn al-ḥukm*[37] and something about his role in the affair of Bint al-Ashraf.[38] Although al-Şafadî is frequently cited by later writers, including Ibn Ḥajar, his biographies of the chief judges of Egypt are disappointingly brief, and even though he was a contemporary of many of the judges under study, his biographies are not to be preferred to the later biographies of Ibn Ḥajar.

Another general biographical dictionary is al-Manhal al-şâfî by Ibn Taghrî Birdî.[39] Although he does include many biographies of *ʿulamâʾ* and judges, they usually rely heavily on other earlier sources which are available to us.[40] For example, the biography of Taqî al-Dîn Ibn Bint al-Aʿazz, a Shâfiʿî chief judge (in office 684-686, 693-695), is drawn from al-Asnawî (see more below on this biographer),[41] as is the biography of the Shâfiʿî Badr al-Dîn Ibn Jamâʿa (in office 690-694, 702-710, 711-727).[42] The biographies of al-Manhal al-şâfî usually add little or nothing to those written by more contemporary observers or to the works of Ibn Ḥajar.

Finally, there is a later source by Ibn al-ʿImâd al-ʿAkarî (1032-82/1623-79) entitled Shadharât al-dhahab.[43] This eight volume work, arranged chronologically, covers all the years down to 1000 A.H. Since it is a late work, it has drawn on many earlier sources. Franz Rosenthal says of this dictionary, "the author intended it to be a help to impecunious scholars like himself."[44] This helps explain its scope and pithy biographies.

Two more contemporary observers wrote *ţabaqât* devoted to the

Shâfi'î *madhhab.* The first of these, Ţabaqât al-shâfi'iyya, was written by Jamâl al-Dîn al-Asnawî (d.772).[45] He was both a native Egyptian and the contemporary of many of the judges in our study as well as a source for later writers including Ibn Taghrî Birdî (as noted above) and Ibn Ḥajar al-'Asqalânî.[46] This edition is extremely well edited with many cross references and excellent indexes. It is also unique, and helpful for our purposes, in that biographies of sons immediately follow that of their father; e.g., the biographies of Şadr al-Dîn and Taqî al-Dîn immediately follow that of their father, Tâj al-Dîn Ibn Bint al-A'azz.[47]

The Ţabaqât al-shâfi'iyya by Tâj al-Din al-Subkî (d.771)[48] is also important, but al-Subkî, a famous *'âlim,* was a Syrian, not an Egyptian like al-Asnawî. The question of residence is not as important, however, as being able to establish a more definite link between the two of them. Yet this is no easy task. Both men were contemporaries, but, according to the editor of al-Asnawî's *ţabaqât,* al-Subkî finished his own book in 766, and al-Asnawî not until 769.[49] Al-Subkî certainly did not mention al-Asnawî in his listing of other Shâfi'î *ţabaqât* which he knew about.[50] Comparison of biographies does not supply evidence of any borrowing. There are biographies presented in al-Subkî's work which are missing from al-Asnawî and vice-versa.[51] Also, the biographies in al-Subkî's collection tend to be longer. For example, the biography of Jalâl al-Dîn al-Qazwînî (in office 727-738) is about twice as long in al-Subkî, and he also mentions several sources including al-Şafadî.[52] Al-Asnawî does not refer to any other sources. Although both mention some of the offices which al-Qazwînî held, only al-Asnawî mentions that he was deposed from office as chief judge of Egypt along with the Ḥanafî and Ḥanbalî judges, because of some matters which were made generally known about them; whereas al-Subkî skims over the incident even more severely, only noting that he was removed from the judgeship of Egypt, and made judge of Damascus, while ignoring the removal of the other judges. Even in the biographies of native Egyptians who spent their entire lives in Egypt (al-Qazwînî spent most of his life in Damascus), al-Asnawî is no great improvement over al-Subkî. Such an Egyptian was Ṣadr al-Dîn Ibn Bint al-Aʿazz (in office 678-679). Both biographies of this man are rather short.[53] Al-Asnawî does not even bother with the date of his birth, which al-Subkî does provide. More importantly al-Subkî claims that Ṣadr al-Dîn resigned from office, whereas al-Asnawî says that he was deposed. Additional details on this point would have been of some interest, since other sources do not indicate why Ṣadr al-Dîn's tenure ended. In short, there is no evidence that one borrowed from the other, and that one of these Shâfiʿî *ṭabaqât* should be preferred for that reason. Furthermore, the fact that al-Asnawî was an Egyptian does not seem to have given him any special status as an observer of Cairene chief judges, and his biographies are usually more cursory than those of his Syrian counterpart. Both also seem to be guilty of trying to suppress, to a greater or lesser extent, incidents which were unflattering to the Shâfiʿî *madhhab*, such as the deposition of al-Qazwînî, which was a scandal of some note.

There are a few other biographical dictionaries devoted to individual schools of law which should also be noted. Dhayl ʿalâ ṭabaqât al-ḥanâbila by Ibn Rajab (736-795/1335-92)[54] is the only Ḥanbalî biographical dictionary relevant to the chief judges of

Baḥrî Egypt, and the author was a contemporary of many of these judges. He also tries to minimize the incidents which were unflattering to members of his own *madhhab.* His biography of the first Ḥanbalî chief judge, Shams al-Dîn Ibn al-ʿImâd (in office 663-670), is reasonably detailed and many sources are indicated. He goes so far as to note that Ibn al-ʿImâd was deposed from office and imprisoned, but ignores the reason for the imprisonment; viz., his being found guilty of holding deposits of money which no longer should have been in his keeping (see details in Chapter VI).[55] Ibn Rajab provides biographies of only the first four of the seven Ḥanbalî judges; the more contemporary ones are missing: Taqî al-dîn Ibn ʿAwaḍ (738); Muwaffaq al-Dîn al-Maqdisî (d. 790); and Nâṣir al-Dîn Naṣr Allâh (d. 795).

The Ḥanafî *ṭabaqa,* al-Jawâhir al-muḍîʾa, by Ibn Abî al-Wafâʾ (d. 735)[56] supplies extremely short and cursory biographies. A very late collection, al-Fawâʾid al-bahiyya,[57] by al-Lakhnawî (d. 1290/1873) provides fuller biographies, but obviously relies on contemporary or more contemporary sources, most of which are available to us; e.g., al-Ṣafadî is the primary source for the biography of Ṣadr al-Dîn al-Adhraʿî (in office 663-677).[58]

Chronicles

In discussing the contemporary Syrian historians whose writings included the reign of al-Malik al-Nâṣir Muḥammad Ibn Qalâʾûn, Professor Little has written, "The Syrians...write from a local vantage point and...being religious scholars, devote more attention to the activities of the religious institution" than to political affairs.[59] This interest in the activities of the members of the religious institution is undeniable, but it is heavily weighted in favor of local Damascene affairs with the result that events in Egypt, at least those relating to chief judges, are ignored or reports of them are severely condensed. A greater problem is that since the Syrian historians were religious scholars, they often shape or suppress incidents which were unflattering to fellow Syrian *ʿulamâʾ*. The most blatant example of this is the deposition of Jalâl al-Dîn al-Qazwînî from the Shâfiʿî judgeship in 738. We have mentioned the cursory treatment of this scandal by al-Asnawî and al-Subkî above. The Syrian chronicler Ibn Kathîr, a well known *ʿâlim* (d. 774), in his al-Bidâya[60] deals with this matter in a somewhat similar fashion. In his listing of the events for the year 738, he notes al-Qazwînî's deposition without an explanation, as well as that of the Ḥanafî and Ḥanbalî chief judges. He notes that the son, Ṣadr al-Dîn, of the Ḥanbalî chief judge, Taqî al-Dîn Ibn ʿAwaḍ (in office 712-738), had to pay the sum of nearly 300,000 (dirhems?) in recompense[61], but ignores the fact that al-Qazwînî's family had to pay 230,000 dirhems.[62] In his obituary of al-Qazwînî Ibn Kathîr excuses himself from explaining al-Qazwînî's deposition by saying it was because of matters whose explanation is (too) drawn out *(bi-sabab umûr yaṭûlu sharḥuhâ)*.[63] Yet he did not find it too tedious to record the teaching and bureaucratic posts which al-Qazwînî's three sons received when they were exiled to Damascus with their father.[64] Surely the events in Egypt leading to this judge's dismissal were more spectacular than these minor appointments, yet it is typical of this Syrian historian to portray a contemporary fellow Damascene Shâfiʿî in the best possible light as well as to pay very close attention to local affairs.

Another Syrian *ʿâlim* and historian, Shams al-Dîn al-Jazarî (d. 730),[65] suffers from the same provincial viewpoint. One indication of this attitude is that he begins the events of each year by giving the names of the caliph, sultan, and governor of Damascus, as well as the names of the four chief judges there, but does not mention the chief judges of Egypt or any other Cairene officials.[66] This is not to say that al-Jazarî completely ignores the chief judges of Cairo, but his interest in them is not very great, unless an incident occurs which is relevant to Damascene society or politics. Thus he notes the appointment of Taqî al-Dîn Ibn Daqîq al-ʿÎd as Shâfiʿî chief judge in 695,[67] but ignores this judge's argument with an *amîr* which led to Taqî al-Dîn's resignation, albeit temporary, from the chief judgeship; an incident which later Egyptian writers describe in some detail.[68] On the other hand, al-Jazarî does devote considerable space, both in the events and obituary sections of his chronicle, to the swindle of Sayf al-Dîn al-Surramarî (or al-Samarrî) and others who had purchased properties from the daughter of the Ayyûbid prince al-Malik al-Ashraf. The swindle was contrived by a Damscene official named Ibn al-Maqdisî, but events were centered in Cairo, where the *wazîr* was deeply involved and the Mâlikî chief judge Ibn Makhlûf helped legitimize the fraud.[69] Such an event greatly interested al-Jazarî, because Sayf al-Dîn was a Damscene and the land involved was in Syria, but al-Jazarî is of little value as a source for events more wholly concerned with the judiciary of Cairo.

Still another Syrian historian is Quṭb al-Dîn al-Yûnînî (d. 726),[70] who wrote Dhayl mirʾât al-zamân.[71] This is a continuation of Sibṭ Ibn al-Jawzî's (d. 654/1256) universal history.[72] Al-Yûnînî is mainly interested in biography, and shares the provincial viewpoint of his fellow Damscene historians. Dhayl mir'ât al-zamân consists of more necrologies than events; e.g., in the printed edition, the events section of the year 672 consists of only five pages while the necrologies amount to fifty pages.[73] These necrologies are usually quite detailed, but some obituaries of chief judges are missing and some note-worthy events and incidents are omitted.[74] All this seems to indicate a less than thorough interest in the affairs of the Cairene judiciary. For example, the biographies of the Mâlikî Taqî al-Dîn Ibn Shâs (in office 680-685) and the Shâfi'î Wajîh al-Dîn al-Bahnasî (in office 680-685) are missing from the obituaries for 685; the omission of the latter's obituary is somewhat strange since al-Yûnînî does mention that al-Bahnasî split the jurisdiction with Ibn al-Khuwayyî in 681, although he does not go into details.[75] Like al-Jazarî, he ignores the dispute between the Shâfi'î chief judge Ibn Daqîq al-'Îd and an *amîr* which led to the judge's resignation. More disappointing is the fact that he ignores the reasons for the deposition of Taqî al-Dîn Ibn Bint al-A'azz from the Shâfi'î chief judgeship in 690,[76] and further ignores all the trials and tribulations which this judge suffered at the hands of the *wazîr*, only mentioning his return to office in 693.[77]

The really important chronicles for the present study are al-'Aynî's 'Iqd al-jumân and al-Maqrîzî's Sulûk. Al-'Aynî (d. 855/1451) and al-Maqrîzî (d. 845/1442) were contemporaries and both were religious scholars who wrote universal histories.[78] In those cases where each reports the same incident, al-'Aynî's account is always more detailed, usually because he carefully and fully cites al-Yûsufî (d. 759), the author of a chronicle, now almost entirely lost, entitled Nuzhat al-nâẓir.[79] For example, al-ʿAynî's account of the deposition and trial of Taqî al-Dîn Ibn Bint al-Aʿazz in 690 is extremely long and detailed, and even includes an eyewitness account by al-Yûsufî himself or his father.[80] However, there are many other incidents relevant to the activities of the chief judges which are only to be found in Sulûk. This may be due, in part, to the fact that al-ʿAynî seems to have stopped relying on al-Yûsufî for events after 741;[81] yet there are deficiencies even earlier. For example, al-ʿAynî does not mention the appointment of Taqî al-Dîn Ibn Bint al-Aʿazz as judge of Fusṭâṭ in 685,[82] nor the fact that earlier, in 681, Wajîh al-Dîn al-Bahnasî resigned half of his chief judgeship, keeping only that of al-Qâhira, because he was too weak to carry out his judicial duties in all of Cairo.[83] Therefore, it is necessary to consult both these chronicles to study the relevant incidents.

The Târîkh of Ibn al-Furât[84] (d.807/1405) is, by and large, simply a duplication of al-Maqrîzî's chronicle. Little has shown that al-Maqrîzî has relied on Ibn al-Furât.[85] In any case, this Târîkh does not add much to the information to be found elsewhere, especially in al-Maqrîzî's Sulûk.[86] Since Ibn al-Furât was a source for al-Maqrîzî, we might have expected fuller accounts in the Târîkh, but this is not the case.

Ibn Ḥajar al-ʿAsqalânî wrote a chronicle entitled Inbâʾ al-ghumr bi-abnâʾ al-ʿumr fî al-târîkh.[87] It is supposed to be a continuation of Ibn Kathîr's chronicle, which ended in 766, but it devotes more attention to obituaries than Ibn Kathîr ever did.

It actually begins with the year 773, and continues well into the Burjî period. The biographies in Inbâʾ al-ghumr are often shorter than those in al-Durar al-kâmina, but sometimes the reverse is true. Yet even at its best the biographies of Inbâʾ al-ghumr are inferior to those of Rafʿ al-iṣr.[88] The real value of this work, however, is as a check on al-Maqrîzî's Sulûk, since al-ʿAynî's ʿIqd is much less useful for the years after 741, according to Little, and more importantly I have not been able to consult al-ʿAynî for the last years of the Baḫrî period.[89]

Finally, mention must be made of Shihâb al-Dîn al-Nuwayrî (d. 732), a contemporary of much of the time period under study. Al-Nuwayrî was an official in the Mamlûk bureaucracy, and it is the last section of his encyclopaedia, Nihâyat al-arab, which deals with the history of the Mamlûk empire, that interests us.[90] Although al-Maqrîzî seems to have relied on al-Nuwayrî for certain events (e.g., the establishment of the four chief judgeships; see more below), there are incidents which are only to be found in al-Nuwayrî; such as the reasons behind the appointment of Ibn Makhlûf to be chief judge in 685,[91] and the plotting of Taqî al-Dîn Ibn Bint al-Aʿazz to be chief judge of both al-Qâhira and Fusṭâṭ in 686.[92] For these reasons, it is an invaluable source, although it does end some fifty years short of the end of the Baḫrî period.

In conclusion, both the biographical literature and the chronicles are important for the study of the Egyptian chief judges of the Baḫrî Mamlûk empire, because each provides information that the other does not. Some of the sources are more valuable than others, and it is necessary to consult a wide range of sources in an attempt to acquire the best possible picture of the careers of these chief judges.

Before leaving this discussion of the sources, however, there are two historiographical observations worth noting. The first concerns the relationship between the writings of Ibn Ḥajar al-ʿAsqalânî and al-Yûsufî. Little has called al-Yûsufî's work "one of the three key sources for the early reign of al-Malik al-Nâṣir"; he has also pointed out that Franz Rosenthal had recorded five references to al-Yûsufî's Nuzhat al-nâẓir in Ibn Ḥajar's al-Durar al-kâmina.[93] Yet Ibn Ḥajar relied on al-Yûsufî's work even more heavily than that, but he mentioned al-Yûsufî by name only rarely because he greatly summarized al-Yûsufî's accounts. Evidence for this theory is to be found in Ibn Ḥajar's biography of the Shâfiʿî chief judge Taqî al-Dîn Ibn Bint al-Aʿazz. Since this judge died in 695, his biography is not in al-Durar al-kâmina, but it is in Rafʿ al-iṣr. As mentioned above, this dictionary of judges was probably written before al-Durar al-kâmina, and its biographies were sometimes abridged for the latter work. During the years 690 to 693 Ibn Bint al-Aʿazz suffered persecutions at the hands of the *wazîr*, who accused him or had him accused of many things, including the charge that Taqî al-Dîn was a Christian. In his last trial, Ibn Bint al-Aʿazz stood up and denied this charge, saying, "I am so and so, the son of so and so, (etc.) and there is no Buṭrus nor Jirjis in my *nisba*." He then went on to deny another charge, that he drank wine. I have found this sentence only in Rafʿ al-iṣr[94] and in al-ʿAynî,[95] where al-Yûsufî is cited as the original source for the account of this incident.[96] Ibn Ḥajar does not mention any sources at all in this biography, although he does cite sources in other biographies. Al-ʿAynî, thanks to al-Yûsufî, goes into great detail concerning the sufferings of this chief judge, and Ibn Ḥajar's account is a severely condensed version of it. However, these lines of direct quotation are virtually identical in the two sources, and since we know that Ibn Ḥajar mentioned al-Yûsufî in al-Durar al-kâmina, it may very well be that he relied on this author elsewhere, either directly or through another source, summarizing al-Yûsufî's account and not showing his indebtedbess to him.

The other observation is that, assuming Ibn Ḥajar depended on al-Yûsufî's chronicle for some of his biographies, it is necessary to modify Little's contention that "a compiler of biographical dictionaries did not rely heavily on annals as a source for his biographies."[97] Of course, for the biography of Ibn Bint al-Aʿazz, the information on the persecutions of this chief judge is put together under one entry (at least in al-ʿAynî's recension), even though the events actually happened over the space of a few years.[98] This might satisfy Little's contention that it was too cumbersome for biographers to search the annals for information,[99] but it certainly contradicts his view that annalists and biographers were reluctant to cross the line into the territory of the other.[100] To this must be added the evidence from the biography of the Ḥanafî judge Sharaf al-Dîn Ibn Manṣûr in Rafʿ al-iṣr, where Ibn Ḥajar mentions al-Maqrîzî as his informant. There is no doubt that here Ibn Ḥajar has drawn from al-Maqrîzî's Sulûk.[101] We cannot reach any final conclusions on the extent to which biographers borrowed from annalists and vice-versa from these few references, but some borrowing certainly did occur, and we should therefore avoid thinking of biography and annals as two distinct genres.

B. The Establishment of the Four Chief Judgeships

Towards the end of the year 663 Sultan Baybars ordered the establishment of the four chief judgeships.[102] The sources blame this move on the hesitation *(tawaqquf)* of the Shâfiʿî chief judge, Tâj al-Dîn Ibn Bint al-Aʿazz, in executing legal decisions, and the pressure exerted by the *amîr* Jamâl al-Dîn Aydughdây al-ʿAzîzî.[103] These are the two basic reasons, but the sources vary somewhat in the details. Shâfiʿ ibn ʿAlî in his biography of Baybars says it was due to the judge's hesitation in accepting testimonies as well as his stubborness,[104] whereas Ibn Kathîr[105] says that this hesitation was only in matters not relating to the Shâfiʿî *madhhab*. Al-ʿAynî,[106] Ibn al-ʿImâd,[107] Ibn Taghrî Birdî,[108] and al-Yûnînî[109] simply refer to the judge's hesitation in making judgements. The *amîr* also plays an important role in all these accounts as the one who suggested the creation of the other three judgeships.[110]

The accounts in al-Nuwayrî[111] and al-Maqrîzî[112] are virtually identical. Here the emphasis is placed on the fact that Aydughdây hated Tâj al-Dîn and he constantly berated him before the sultan for the severity of his judgements and, according to al-Maqrîzî, his slowness or hesitation in making decisions which did not conform to his *madhhab*.[113] Three cases came before the sultan in a session of the *dâr al-ʿadl* in late 663. The first was a complaint by the daughters of al-Malik al-Nâşir (probably the Ayyûbid Şalâḥ al-Dîn al-Nâşir II; ruled in Damascus and Aleppo 648-58) who explained that they had purchased a house from the former chief judge Badr al-Dîn al-Sinjârî,[114] and after his death his heirs said that this house was part of a *waqf*. This prompted Aydughday to start criticizing judges. The sultan turnd to Ibn Bint al-A'azz and asked him how could judges act in this way. The judge avoided a direct answer, but did say that the money should be refunded. The sultan then asked the procedure if al-Sinjârî's heirs had no money. The judge replied that the *waqf* remained inviolate, and the money could not be reimbursed. This greatly angered the sultan, but before the matter could be concluded an envoy of the *amîr* of Medina appeared complaining about Ibn Bint al-A'azz. The envoy said that he had asked the judge for one quarter of the value of a *waqf* which was under his control, because the *amîr* of Medina wanted to distribute the money to the poor of that city, but the judge had refused to surrender any money. The judge explained that he was not willing to hand over such money to someone he barely knew, but he was willing to comply if the sultan so instructed. The sultan told him to act as he saw fit. Finally, one of the *umarâ'* stepped forward, saying that Ibn Bint al-A'azz had refused to accept his testimony. When asked to explain his refusal, the judge said that it was not necessary for him to explain. The *amîr* Aydughday spoke up and said let him judge according to the Shâfi'î *madhhab* and we will establish a judge for each of the other three *madhâhib*. This was pleasing to the sultan and the new arrangement was soon enacted.

A more partisan interpretation is supplied by the Shâfi'îs al-Asnawî and al-Subkî in their *ṭabaqât*.[115] According to this version, Ibn Bint al-A'azz was asked to turn over a case to his Ḥanafî deputy *(nâ'ib;* more on this office below), but the chief judge did not want to transfer this particular case, so he refused to let the case be heard. At that point the *amîr*

Aydughday suggested the establishment of the four chief judgeships and the sultan agreed.

Whatever story or combination of stories is really true, there is no question of the importance of the *amîr* Aydughdây nor with Tâj al-Dîn Ibn Bint al-Aʿazz's reluctance to deal with at least certain cases.

However, the events of 663 should not be seen in isolation, and the establishment of full chief judgeships for each of the four *madhâhib* was not a revolutionary occurrence, but rather it evolved from earlier events in Egypt. At the end of the Ayyûbid period, al-Malik al-Şâliḫ Najm al-Dîn Ayyûb founded al-Şâliḫiyya *madrasa*. It was completed in 648, but even before that date, in 641, professorships of *fiqh* were established for each of the four schools of law.[116] The equalizing of the four *madhâhib* entered a new phase when, in 661, Sultan Baybars ordered the Shâfiʿî chief judge, the same Ibn Bint al-Aʿazz, to choose deputies *(nuwwâb)* from the other three *madhâhib*, and he chose those who were his three fellow professors of *fiqh* at al-Şâliḫiyya.[117] However, it is highly likely that there was no Ḫanbalî *nâʾib* appointed, but rather the Ḫanbalî professor was given the lower ranking office of *ʿâqid al-ankiḫa* (binder or registrar of marriages), which was also subordinate to the Shâfiʿî chief judge.[118]

This establishment of the three *nuwwâb* (or two *nuwwâb* and an *ʿâqid)* is obviously significant, but most of the sources do not explain the reason for it or give many details of how it came about. Instead, they say only that the sultan ordered Ibn Bint al-Aʿazz to appoint *nuwwâb* from the three *madhâhib*,[119] although Ibn Ḫajar al-ʿAsqalânî implies that this move was Tâj al-Dîn's own idea and was carried out by permission of, not at the order of, the sultan.[120] Ibn Ḥajar also says that the *nuwwâb* were created so there would be more judges for the people.[121] This explanation of the appointments of 661 is unique to Ibn Ḥajar and its flattering attitude towards Ibn Bint al-Aʿazz is very likely an attempt to minimize the importance of an act which was certainly a blow to his own Shâfiʿî *madhhab*. (We have mentioned in our earlier discussion on sources, Ibn Ḥajar's circumlocutions when it came to describing all four judges by the title *qâḍî al-quḍât*.) Ibn ʿAbd al-Ẓâhir, a more contemporary source, says the events of 661 occurred because the sultan saw the great number of people (in the city); that Cairo had become the seat of power *(dâr al-mulk)* and that scholars of different *madhâhib* congregated there.[122] These last explanations seem more likely, since we do know that the population of Cairo had been increasing,[123] and at least part of this expansion was due to the influx of refugees fleeing the Mongols.[124]

In addition, we should remember that Nûr al-Dîn Zangî (ruled 541-569/1146-74) had established four chief judges in Syria during his reign,[125] but there had not been four chief judges in Cairo since the Fâṭimids, and even then there had been two Shîʿî judges (an Imâmî and an Ismâʿîlî), a Mâlikî and a Shâfiʿî, not one from each of the four recognized Sunnî schools of law. When the Ayyûbids came to power they changed the system back to a single Shâfiʿî chief judge.[126] What is most interesting, however, is that the sources do not indicate any oppostion to the developments of the early Baḥrî period, either in 661 or 663.[127] In fact, Ibn ʿAbd al-Ẓâhir says that the selection of the *nuwwâb* brought relief *(râḥa)* to the people.[128] Certainly, the establishment of the four professorships of *fiqh* at al-Ṣâliḥiyya during the Ayyûbid period and the continuation of these appointments into the Mamlûk period prepared the ground for the later changes in the organization of the judiciary by making some equalization of the four *madhâhib* acceptable.

On the other hand, the Shâfiʿî chief judge was able to remain a notch above the others throughout the Baḥrî period, despite some attacks on the superiority of his status. The first challenge came in 663, at the time of the establishment of the other three chief judgeships when all the judges were allowed to appoint deputies in the districts of Egypt.[129] Yet this situation lasted only for fifteen years and in 678 the right of appointing deputies outside the capital was reserved for the Shâfiʿî chief judge.[130] Even in 663, however, the Shâfiʿî judge was put in charge of the moneys of the orphans, as well as verifying *waqfiyyât* and legacies.[131] These duties, as embodied in the office of *nâẓir al-aḥbâs*, were lost to the Shâfiʿî chief judge at Ibn Bint al-Aʿazz's death. However, in 698 the Sultan Lâjîn established a new deposit *(mawdaʿ)* for the orphans of *umarâʾ* and decreed that anyone who died and had heirs who were minors would have their estates transferred to this *mawdaʿ al-ḥukm,* which would be under the supervision of the Shâfiʿî chief judge.[132] This depository continued at least until the end of the Baḥrî period. The Ḥanafî chief judge, Sirâj al-Dîn al-Hindî (in office 769-73), tried to establish a similar depository for the funds of Ḥanafî orphans. This was granted, but he died before it could be implemented.[133] According to Ibn Ḥajar, his timely death was through the intervention of the Imâm al-Shâfiʿî.[134] Another attempt by the Ḥanafî Jalâl al-Dîn Jâr Allâh in 781 met with more success, but pressure from the Shâfiʿî chief judge, Burhân al-Dîn Ibn Jamâ'a, eventually forced its cancellation.[135]

The Shâfi'î chief judge may well have enjoyed the unique prerogative of approving wills. This may have been the right which Tâj al-Dîn Ibn Bint al-A'azz was granted in 663, although it may have been connected to his duties as *nâẓir al-aḥbâs*. We do know that at the time Lâjîn established the *mawda' al-ḥukm*, the Shâfi'î chief judge was to establish notaries (*'udûl*) for those deceased who had written wills to insure that they were executed properly.[136] Also, one of the reasons given for the deposition of the Mâlikî chief judge 'Alam al-Dîn al-Bisâtî in 779 was the fact that he had approved a will before the Shâfi'î chief judge, Burhân al-Dîn Ibn Jamâ'a, had seen it.[137]

Finally, the Shâfi'î chief judge had precedence over the other chief judges in the sessions of the *dâr al-'adl*. He sat to the right of the sultan in these sessions, followed by the Ḥanafî, Mâlikî, and Ḥanbalî judges. The order was changed after the days of al-Malik al-Nâṣir Muḥammad, probably in the middle years of the 8th century A.H., and the Ḥanafî chief judge, followed by the Ḥanbalî, was moved to the sultan's left.[138] It is difficult to assess the importance of this change. It seems to have been an upgrading of the status of the Ḥanafî judge, because now he was closer to the sultan, but being on the sultan's left was still probably inferior to being on his right.

There is little doubt that the Shâfi'î was the highest ranking *madhhab* and the Ḥanbalî the lowest. After all, the Ḥanbalîs were, probably, only assigned an *'âqid* and not a *nâ'ib* between 661 and 663, and in the next chapter we shall see that the Ḥanbalîs were without a chief judge for several years after the deposition of Shams al-Dîn Ibn al-ʿImâd in 670. However, the ranking of the Ḥanafî and Mâlikî chief judges is more difficult to ascertain, and it seems that during the Baḥrî period the Ḥanafîs gained power at the expense of the Mâlikîs. As the various schools of law had begun to take shape in the early years of Islam, it was the Mâlikî school which was dominant in Egypt, but it lost this leading position after al-Shâfiʿî came to Egypt in 198 A.H. We have seen that during the Fâṭimid period only these two schools were represented in addition to the Shîʿîs, and the Ayyûbids established only a Shâfiʿî chief judge during their years of control in Egypt. According to al-Maqrîzî, the Ḥanafîs were numerous in Syria, thanks to the efforts of Nûr al-Dîn Zangî, but it was only towards the end of the Ayyûbid period that the Ḥanafî, as well as the Ḥanbalî presence became larger in Egypt.[139] The Ḥanafîs came from Syria and further east,[140] where they had always enjoyed dominance.[141] Therefore, the new seating arrangement in the *dâr al-ʿadl,* with the Mâlikî sitting next to the Shâfʿî, may have been an attempt to reestablish an older hierarchy. We also know that in the year 690 there was a procession in honor of the installation of a new *wazîr,* and al-Maqrîzî says that the two persons closest to him (i.e., in the positions of the greatest honor) were the Shâfiʿî and Mâlikî chief judges.[142] On the other hand, the Mâlikî chief judge in that year was Zayn al-Dîn Ibn Makhlûf, one of the most powerful judges of the Baḥrî period (as we shall see in more detail in later chapters), and this place in the procession may have been more in the nature of a personal honor than an acknowledgement of the status of his *madhhab.* Certainly the briefly successful attempts by the Ḥanafî chief judges al-Hindî and Jâr Allâh to gain certain privileges, which had been reserved for the Shâfiʿî, for themselves and their successors show the increased influence of this *madhhab* towards the end of the Baḥrî period. This small amount of data indicates that the Mâlikîs were superior to the Ḥanafîs in the earlier Baḥrî period, and the Ḥanafîs superior to them in the later years of that era. The rise of the Ḥanafîs may have been due to the fact that many of the Mamlûks were Ḥanafîs, and they became more "religiously" active in the later Baḥrî period; e.g., in the year 767 the *amîr* Yalbughâ al-Khâṣṣakî al-ʿUmarî endowed seven posts for the teaching of Ḥanafî *fiqh* at the mosque of Ibn Ṭûlûn. According to al-Maqrîzî this induced many Shâfiʿîs to change *madhhab*.[143] It is not possible to carry the discussion of this point any further, and its resolution probably lies in a detailed study of the *ʿulamâʾ* of this period.

In conclusion, the establishment of the four chief judgeships was more evolutionary that revolutionary. Earlier events had set the scene for the judicial reorganization of 663, and it may well be that the really significant event in the judicial history of the Baḥrî period occurred in 661 when the Ḥanafîs, Mâlikîs and Ḥanbalîs were given a place in the judicial bureaucracy. Looking at developments from this point of view, there was not so much a reorganization of the judiciary in 663 as there was the promotion of three lower ranking judicial officers to a higher rank. Thus the events of 661 were more revolutionary than those of 663, although then too an earlier basis had been established for that change with the establishment of the four professorships at al-Ṣâliḥiyya. Nevertheless, one cannot help but be struck by the almost total silence of the sources as regards opposition by the Shâfiʿî chief judge or anyone else to either judicial reorganization. The explanation for this apparent lack of opposition may well be that this change was both necessary and generally welcome.

ENDNOTES

[1]N.J. Coulson, A History of Islamic Law (Edinburgh, 1964), pp. 21-22.

[2]Ibid., pp. 25-26.

[3]Ibid., pp. 28-29.

[4]Ibid., p. 121.

[5]Ibid.; E. Tyan, Histoire de l'organization judicaire en pays d'Islam (Leiden, 1960), p. 124.

[6]Tyan, Histoire, p. 124.

[7]Cf. ibid., p. 127.

[8]Ibid., p. 136.

[9]Ibid., pp. 137-38.

[10]A. Schimmel, "Kalif und Kadi im spätmittelalterlichen Aegypten," Die Welt des Islams, XXIV (1942), 1-128; Carl Petry and Stanley Mendenhall, "Geographical Origins of the Civil Judiciary of Cairo in the Fifteenth Century," Journal of the Economic and Social History of the Orient, XXI (January, 1978), 52-74.

[11]W. Popper, Egypt and Syria under the Circassian Sultans, 1382-1468 A.D.; Systematic Notes to Ibn Taghrî Birdî's Chronicles of Egypt (Berkeley, California, 1955-57), I, 108, 110. M. Gaudefroy-Demombynes, La Syrie à l'époque des Mamelouks (Paris, 1923), pp. LXXVII, 160, 209, 224, 231; hereafter cited as La Syrie.

[12]The work has already begun for the Burjî period. See J. Mandaville, "The Muslim Judiciary of Damascus in the Late Mamlûk Period," (unpublished Ph.D. dissertation, Princeton University, 1969).

[13]Shihâb al-Dîn Aḥmad ibn ʿAlî al-Qalqashandî, _Ṣubḥ al-aʿshâ fî ṣinâʿat al-inshâʾ_ (Cairo, 1963), 14 vols. For biographical details, see C.E. Bosworth, "al-Ḳalḳashandî," _Encyclopaedia of Islam_, 2nd edition, IV, 509-11. Hereafter cited as EI-2.

[14]Taqî al-Dîn Aḥmad ibn ʿAlî al-Maqrîzî, _al-Mawâʿiẓ wa-al iʿtibâr bi-dhikr al-khiṭaṭ wa-al-âthâr_ (Bûlâq, 1853); hereafter cited as _Khiṭaṭ_. For biographical details, see C. Brockelmann, "al-Maḳrîzî," _Encyclopaedia of Islam_, 1st edition, III, 175-76. Hereafter cited as EI-1.

[15]I have avoided the technique of evaluating a number of sources on the basis of their treatment of one or several incidents as, for example, Little has done in his _Introduction to Mamlûk Historiography_ (Montreal, 1970). I myself used a somewhat similar approach in the evaluation of biographical sources for my "Study of _al-Durar al-kâmina_ as a Source for the History of the Mamlûk Empire," unpublished M.A. thesis, McGill University, 1974, pp. 12-33). However, I did not think that this method was as useful now, because in the present study I have been concerned with a fairly long time period. More importantly I felt that this type of comparison would be too limited, and would prevent me from showing various examples that would be more illustrative of the value of a given source than the comparison of one or two incidents or biographies would allow.

[16]See my "Vocational Patterns of the Scribes of the Mamlûk Chancery," (_Arabica_, XXIII, (1976), 42-62.) for an example of a study based only on these types of sources.

[17]Aḥmad ibn Ḥajar al-ʿAsqalânî, _Rafʿ al-iṣr ʿan quḍât miṣr_ (Cairo, 1957-), 2 vols. to date. Hereafter cited as _Rafʿ_. The last part is avilable only in manuscript; I have used Bibliothèque Nationale (hereafter BN) MS Arabe 2149, hereafter cited as _Rafʿ_ MS. For biographical details, see F. Rosenthal, "Ibn Ḥadjar al-ʿAsḳalânî," EI-2, III, 776-78.

[18]R.J. Gottheil, ed., _The History of the Egyptian Cadis...by...al-Kindi_ (Paris, 1908), p. XIX.

[19]R. Guest, ed., _The Governors and Judges of Egypt_ (Leiden, 1912), p. 43.

[20]The following judges are missing. The Shâfiʿîs: Ṣadr al-Dîn Ibn Bint al-Aʿazz (in office 678-679), see _Rafʿ_, I, 12, note 14; Jalâl al-Dîn al-Qazwînî (in office 727-38), see _ibid._, p. 14, note 2. The Ḥanafîs: Ṣadr al-Dîn al-Adhraʿî (in office 663-677), see _ibid._, p.17, note 2; Muʿizz al-Dîn al-Khaṭîbî (in office 677-92), see _ibid._, note 3; Jalâl al-Dîn Jâr Allâh (in office 778-82), see _ibid._, note 17. Only the Ḥanafî Sirâj al-Dîn al-Râzî is not mentioned in the poem.

[21]Ibid., II, 381.

[22]Aḥmad ibn Ḥajar al-ʿAsqalânî, al-Durar al-kâmina fî aʿyân al-mi'at al-thâmina (Cairo, 1966-67), 5 volumes. Hereafter cited as Durar. For some general comments on this work, see F. Krenkow, "The Hidden Pearls concerning the Notables of the Eighth Islamic Century," Islamic Culture, II (1928), 527-39.

[23]See the biography of Burhân al-Dîn Ibn Jamâʿa (Durar, I, 40).

[24]Khiṭaṭ, II, 374. A detailed architectural study of this *madrasa* is to be found in K. A. C. Creswell, The Muslim Architecture of Egypt (Oxford, 1959), II, 94-100. Some of the unique features of this *madrasa* will be discussed in more detail below.

[25]See chapter V for a discussion of this office.

[26]Durar, II, 499.

[27]Rafʿ, II, 365.

[28]Rafʿ MS, fols. 87a-b.

[29]Durar, III, 230-31.

[30]For details of his life and works, see F. Krenkow, "al-Ṣafadî," EI-1, IV, 52-54.

[31]Ṣalâḥ al-Dîn Khalîl ibn Aybak al-Ṣafadî, al-Wâfî bi-al-wafayât. Only part of this work has been published so far, (Istanbul, Damascus, Wiesbaden, 1931-), 9 volumes to date. I have consulted a number of different manuscript collections for the remaining volumes. Hereafter cited as Wâfî.

[32]Wâfî, Ahmet III MS 2920/22, fol. 71a.

[33]I have consulted a microfilm copy of the Istanbul MS, Emine Hazine 1217; hereafter cited as Aʿyân. See also D.P. Little, "Al-Ṣafadî as Biographer of his Contemporaries," in D.P. Little, ed., Essays on Islamic Civilization Presented to Niyazi Berkes (Leiden, 1976), especially pp. 197 ff.

[34]Aʿyân, fol. 347b.

[35]Krenkow, "al-Şafadî," p. 53.

[36]Durar, III, 202.

[37]The *amîn al-ḥukm* was an official of the judge's court who dealt with financial matters, especially that of funds for orphans; EI-2, I, 437.

[38]This affair will be discussed in more detail in chapter IV. See also below, note 69.

[39]Abû al-Maḥâsin Ibn Taghrî Birdî, al-Manhal al-ṣâfî (Cairo, 1956-), 1 volume to date. Hereafter cited as Manhal. For the remaining volumes I have consulted Arab League MS 841 (photocopy of Topkapi Ahmet III 3018); hereafter cited as Manhal MS. THe summary outline of this work, Les Biographies du Manhal Sâfî, by G. Wiet (Cairo, 1932) is also important. For his biography, see W. Popper, "Abû'l Maḥâsin," EI-1, I, 138.

[40]Ibn Taghrî Birdî is also prone to making mistakes in his biographies of *ʿulamâʾ*. See the discussion in my "Study of al-Durar...," p. 25, and see below chapter III, notes 61 and 64.

[41]Manhal MS, fols. 437b-438a.

[42]Ibid., fols. 630a ff.

[43]Ibn al-ʿImâd al-ʿAkarî, Shadharât al-dhahab fî akhbar man dhahab (Cairo, 1931-32), 8 vols. Hereafter cited as Shadharât. For biographical details, see F. Rosenthal, "Ibn al-ʿImâd," EI-2, III, 807.

[44]Rosenthal, "Ibn al-ʿImâd," ibid.

[45]Jamâl al-Dîn ʿAbd al-Raḥîm al-Asnawî, Ṭabaqât al-shâfiʿiyya (Baghdad, 1390/1970), 2 vols. For his biography see ibid., I, 11-46. Hereafter cited as al-Asnawî.

[46]E.g., Durar, II, 373; the biography of the Shâfiʿî chief judge Bahâʾ al-Dîn Ibn ʿAqîl.

[47]Al-Asnawî, I, 147-53.

[48]For biographical details, see J. Schacht, "al-Subkî," EI-1, IV, 494.

[49]Al-Asnawî, I, 32.

[50]See Tâj al-Dîn al-Subkî, Ṭabaqât al-shâfiʿiyya al-kubrâ (Cairo, 1964), I, 217, where this listing ends.

[51]The biographies of Wajîh al-Dîn al-Bahnasî, Burhân al-Dîn al-Sinjârî, and Jamâl al-Dîn al-Zarʿî are in al-Subkî's collection, but missing from al-Asnawî's. The biography of Shihâb al-Dîn Ibn al-Khuwayyî is in al-Asnawî, but missing from al-Subkî, as is the biography of Bahâʾ al-Dîn Ibn ʿAqîl. However, the latter chief judge died in 769, which, if al-Subkî did finish writing in 766, would make his inclusion highly unlikely.

[52]Al-Asnawî, II, 329-30; al-Subkî, Ṭabaqât al-shâfiʿiyya (Cairo, 1906), V, 238-39. Hereafter cited as al-Subkî.

[53]Al-Asnawî, I, 150; al-Subkî, V, 131.

[54]Zayn al-Dîn ʿAbd al-Raḥmân ibn Aḥmad Ibn Rajab, Dhayl ʿalâ ṭabaqât al-ḥanâbila (Cairo, 1952), 2 vols. in one. Hereafter cited as Ibn Rajab. For biographical details, see J. Schacht, "Ibn Radjab," EI-2, II, 901-902.

[55]Ibn Rajab, II, 294-95.

[56]Muḥyî al-Dîn ʿAbd al-Qâdir Ibn Abî al-Wafâ', al-Jawâhir al-muḍîʾa fî ṭabaqât al-ḥanafiyya (Hyderabad, 1332/1913), 2 vols. See also G. Brockelmann, Geschichte der arabischen Litteratur (Leiden, 1945-49), II, 80, and Supplement II, 89.

[57](Cairo) 1324/1906. See also Brockelmann, Geschichte, Supplement II, 857.

[58]Al-Lakhnawî, pp. 80-81.

[59]D.P. Little, Mamlûk Historiography, p. 95.

[60]This is ʿImâd al-Dîn Ismâʿîl ibn ʿUmar Ibn Kathîr. For his biography, see H. Laoust, "Ibn Kathîr," EI-1, III, 175-76. His chronicle, al-Bidâya wa-al-nihâya fî al-târîkh (Cairo 1932-39), 14 vols., is a universal chronicle from the creation to the year 767. Volumes thirteen and fourteen are of importance to the present study. Hereafter cited as Ibn Kathîr.

[61]Ibn Kathîr, XIV, 180-81.

[62]Taqî al-Dîn Aḥmad ibn ʿAlî al-Maqrîzî, Kitâb al-sulûk li-maʿrifat duwal al-mulûk (Cairo, 1934-73), II, 442; hereafter cited as Sulûk. Al-ʿAynî, ʿIqd al-jumân, MS Ahmet III 2911/c34, fol. 63a.

[63]Ibn Kathîr, XIV, 185.

[64]Ibid., p. 181.

[65]For his biography, see A.S. Bazmee Ansari, "al-Djazarî," EI-2, II, 522-23.

[66]See, for example, J. Sauvaget, La Chronique de Damas d'al Jazarî, Années 689-698 H. (Paris, 1949), infra, which is a summary translation of Jawâhir al-sulûk fî al-khulafâ'. BN MS Arabe 6739.

[67]Sauvaget, La Chronique, p. 48.

[68]This incident will be discussed in more detail in chapter VI. Ibn Kathîr (XIII, 352) on the other hand, says only that Ibn Daqîq al-ʿÎd became angry, left the judiciary for a short while, then finally returned. The Egyptian al-Maqrîzî spends almost two pages in the printed edition describing this incident(al-Maqrîzî, Sulûk, II, 848-49. Al-ʿAynî (ʿIqd al-jumân, Ahmet III 2912/4, fol. 181b) also describes this incident in some detail.

[69]I shall discuss this incident in more detail in chapter IV. J. Sublet has devoted an article to this entitled "La Folie de la Princesse Bint al-Ashraf," Bulletin d'Etudes Orientales, XXVII (1974), 45-50. Al-Jazarî devotes considerable space to it under the events of 680; see U. Haarmann, Quellenstudien zur frühen Mamlukenzeit (Freiburg, 1970), Arabic text, pp. 90-91. It is also mentioned in his obituary of al-Surramarî (J. Sauvaget, La Chronique, p. 64).

[70]For biographical details, see Durar, IV, 382.

[71]Four volumes have been published, ending with the year 686/1287 (Hyderabad, 1954-). For the years 690-697 I have consulted MS Ahmet III 5803. Hereafter cited as al-Yûnînî.

[72]See EI-2, III, 752-53.

[73]See al-Yûnînî, III, infra.

[74]See, for example, the biography of the Shâfi'î Taqî al-Dîn Ibn Razîn (al-Yûnînî, IV, 124).

[75]Ibid., p. 144.

[76]Al-Yûnînî, Ahmet III 5803, fol. 6a.

[77]Ibid., fol. 48b.

[78]For biographical details, see W. Marcais, "al-'Aynî," EI-2, I, 790-91. For the years 660-678, I have used BN MS Arabe 1543; for 679-686, hand copy of Dâr al-Kutub MS 1584; for 689-736, Ahmet III 2912/4; and for 736-745, Ahmet III 2911/c34. Hereafter cited as al-'Aynî, and the appropriate MS.

[79]For biographical details of Mûsâ ibn Muḥammad al-Yûsufî, see Durar, IV, 381. The importance of this historian has been the subject of several studies by D.P. Little: "An Analysis of the Relationship between Four Mamlûk Chronicles for 737-745," Journal of Semitic Studies, XIX (Autumn, 1974), 252-68; "The Recovery of a Lost Source for Baḥrî Mamlûk History: al-Yûsufî's Nuzhat al-Nâẓir fî Sîrat al-Malik al-Nâṣir," Journal of the American Oriental Society, volume 94, pp. 42-54; and his Introduction to Mamluk Historiography, especially pp. 81-87, 95.

[80]Al-'Aynî, Ahmet III, 2912/4, fols. 158a-159b. Cf. the shorter version in Sulûk, I, 771-73.

[81]Little, "Analysis," p. 265.

[82]Cf. Sulûk, I, 732.

[83]Cf. Sulûk, I, 706.

[84]Muḥammad ibn 'Abd al-Raḥmân Ibn al-Furât. Volume 6 is available only in MS, and I have used MS Vienna Flügel 814; volumes 7, 8, and 9 have been published (Beirut, 1936-42). For biographical details, see Cl. Cahen, "Ibn al-Furât," EI-2, III, 768-69.

[85]Little, Mamlûk Historiography, p. 78.

[86]Cf., for example, Sulûk, I, 539-40 and Ibn al-Furât, Târîkh, Flügel 814, fols. 89b-90a.

[87]Hyderabad, 1967- ; 4 vols. to date. Hereafter Inbâʾ al-ghumr.

[88]Cf. the biography of the Ḥanafî judge Sharaf al-Dîn Ibn Manṣûr in Durar, I, 234; Inbâʾ al-ghumr, I, 93-94; and Rafʿ, I, 89-90.

[89]Cf. the account of the Ḥanafî judge Jâr Allâh's attempt to gain an improved status for his *madhhab* in Sulûk, III, 358-59, and Inbâʾ al-ghumr, I, 302-303.

[90]For biographical details, see I. Kratschkowsky, "al-Nuwairî," EI-1, III, 968. The section of this work which interests us is available only in MS. For the years 659-688 I have consulted BN MS Arabe 1578; for 678-700 BN 1579; for 701-720 Leiden MS Or. 20; and for 721-730 Leiden MS Or. 19b. Hereafter cited as al-Nuwayrî, and the appropriate MS.

[91]Al-Nuwayrî, BN 1578, fols. 86a-b.

[92]Ibid., fols. 63a-64b.

[93]Little, "Lost Source," p. 43.

[94]Rafʿ, II, 328.

[95]Al-ʿAynî, Ahmet III 2912/4, fol. 159a.

[96]Ibid., fol. 158b.

[97]Little, Mamlûk Historiography, p. 134.

[98]See chapter VI, notes 61-63.

[99]Little, Mamlûk Historiography, p. 134.

[100]Ibid., p. 135. See also the comments in my "A Lost Arabic Source for the History of Early Ottoman Egypt," Journal of the American Oriental Society, volume 97 (1977), especially pp. 517-18.

[101]Cf. Rafʿ, I, 90 and Sulûk, III, 240.

[102]Al-Maqrîzî places their formal investiture on Monday, 19 Dhû al-Hijja (Sulûk, I, 538); Ibn Taghrî Birdî says the decision grew out of a *majlis* which was held on Monday, 18 Dhû al-Hijja (al-Nujûm al-zâhira (Cairo, 1929-72), VII, 121). Another late historian, al-ʿAynî, simply credits the events to the year 663 (BN 1543, fol. 188a) and Shadharât (V, 312) places it sometime at the end of this year. The more contemporary Syrian historians place the appointment of the other three judges on Tuesday 22 Dhû al-Hijja (Ibn Kathîr, XIII, 245; al-Yûnînî, II, 324). A more contemporary Egyptian historian refuses to be more specific than the year 663 (Shâfiʿ ibn ʿAlî, Ḥusn al-manâqib (Riyad, 1976), p. 103) and al-Nuwayrî places the events in the month of Dhû al-Qâʿda (BN 1578, fol. 29b). There is a lacuna in the biography of Baybars by Ibn ʿAbd al-Ẓâhir at about that point, so we do not know his opinion on the matter (Ibn ʿAbd al-Ẓâhir, al-Rawd al-ẓâhir (Riyad, 1976), p. 243; F. Sadeque, Baybars I of Egypt (Dacca, 1956), p. 74.)

[103]Jamâl al-Dîn Aydughday ʿAbd Allâh al-ʿAzîzî. He died in 664. See al-Yûnînî, II, 354; Wiet, Manhal, no. 588.

[104]Shâfiʿ ibn ʿAlî, Ḥusn al-manâqib, p. 103.

[105]Ibn Kathîr, XIII, 245.

[106]Al-ʿAynî, BN 1543, fol. 188a.

[107]Shadharât, V, 312.

[108]Ibn Taghrî Birdî, al-Nujûm, VII, 121. He also says there were numerous complaints about this.

[109]Al-Yûnînî, II, 324. The account in al-Nujûm is almost identical to this one.

[110]He is credited with this role in the accounts supplied by Shadharât, al-Nujûm, Ibn Kathîr, al-ʿAynî, and Ḥusn al-manâqib as given in the previous notes. See also al-Asnawî, I, 147.

[111] Al-Nuwayrî, BN 1578, fols. 29a-b.

[112]Sulûk, I, 538-39.

[113]Ibid., p. 538.

[114]Ibn al-Ṣuqâʿî, Tâlî kitâb wafayât al-aʿyân (Damascus,

1974), no. 105.

[115]Al-Asnawî, I, 149; al-Subkî, I, 134.

[116]Khiṭaṭ, II, 374.

[117]Tâj al-Dîn was appointed to al-Ṣâliḥiyya in the year 660 (al-Yûnînî, II, 174; al-Nuwayrî, BN 1578, fol. 36a), and the post was given to his son, Ṣadr al-Dîn, upon his father's death in 665 (al-Nuwayrî, BN 1578, fol. 36a).

The Ḥanbalî Shams al-Dîn Ibn al-ʿImâd was among the first appointees to this *madrasa* (Khiṭaṭ, II, 374; Wâfî, II, 10) and remained teaching there until his death in 676, except for the two years of his imprisonment, 670-672.

The first Mâlikî chief judge, Sharaf al-Dîn al-Subkî, also taught at al-Ṣâliḥiyya, but the date of his appointment is uncertain; but, at least, he seems to have held the judgeship and this teaching appointment simultaneously; see al-Yûnînî, II, 669; Ibn al-Sâbûnî, Takmilat ikmâl al-ikmâl (Baghdad, 1956), p. 235; al-ʿAynî, BN 1543, fol. 206a; Wâfî, Ahmet III 2920/22, fol. 188b.

The first Ḥanafî chief judge, Ṣadr al-Dîn al-Adhraʿî is called *mudarris al-madrasa* al-Ṣâliḥiyya (Sulûk, I, 539).

[118]Ibn ʿAbd al-Ẓâhir says that the Ḥanbalîs were given only an *ʿâqid* because there were so few of them (al-Rawd al-ẓâhir, p. 182; Sadeque, Baybars, p. 197, Arabic text, p. 89). Others indicated that each of the other three *madhâhib* was given a *nâʾib* (al-Nuwayrî, BN 1578, fol. 16b; al-ʿAynî, BN 1543, p. 173a; al-Yûnînî, I, 496). Ibn al-Furât presents both stories, but is unable to say which is correct (Flügel 814, fol. 35b). It seems almost certain, however, that there was no Ḥanbalî *nâʾib*, because in 662 the future Ḥanbalî judge Ibn al-ʿImâd was accused of plotting against Sultan Baybars, because the sultan had not appointed a judge (i.e., deputy judge) for the Ḥanbalîs (Ibn ʿAbd al-Ẓâhir, al-Rawd al-ẓâhir, p. 183; Sadeque, Baybars, p. 199; Sulûk, I, 503).

[119]See the references in the previous note. They all use the phrase *amara* or *amara al-sulṭân*.

[120]Rafʿ, II, 381.

[121]Ibid.

[122]Sadeque, Baybars, p. 197; Ibn ʿAbd al-Ẓâhir, al-Rawd al-ẓâhir, p. 182.

[123]J. Abû Lughod, Cairo: The City Victorious (Princeton, 1971), especially pp. 30-32.

[124]H. Laoust, "Le Hanbalisme sous les Mamlouks Bahrides," Revue des Etudes Islamiques, XXVII (1960), 6. This migration must have occurred among more than just the Ḥanbalîs.

[125]N. Elisséef, Nûr al-Dîn (Damascus, 1967), III, 826.

[126]Khiṭaṭ, II, 343.

[127]Ibn Ḥajar tries to play down this new judicial organization by calling the new judges *"nuwwâb ʿan al-sulṭân,"* instead of chief judges, while still referring to the Shâfiʿî as *al-qâḍî al-kabîr* (Rafʿ, II, 381). He also claims that as long as Ibn Bint al-Aʿazz was alive, none of the other judges spoke in a *majlis* of the sultan, and further that the Mâlikî chief judge would not render a judgement until he had shown it to Ibn Bint al-Aʿazz (ibid., pp. 381-82). I cannot find any evidence to contradict these statements, but in the year 662 the sultan received *fatâwin* from the Shâfiʿî chief judge and his Ḥanafî *nâʾib*, Ṣadr al-Dîn al-Adhraʿî, on the matter of an inheritance, and the sultan chose the Ḥanafî interpretation (Shâfiʿ ibn ʿAlî, Ḥusn al-manâqib, p. 74). This incident does not really contradict what Ibn Ḥajar said, but it does indicate that the Shâfiʿî rule was not absolute, and it is support for the idea that the establishment of the four chief judgeships was not revolutionary.

According to al-Subkî, hardly an unbiased observer, Baybars later regretted this action, and even saw the Imâm al-Shâfʿî in a dream, criticizing the sultan for his action (al-Subkî, V, 135).

[128]Sadeque, Baybars, p. 199.

[129]Al-Nuwayrî, BN, fol. 29a; al-ʿAynî, BN 1543, fol. 188a; Rafʿ, II, 381; Sulûk, I, 539.

[130]Sulûk, I, 668.

[131]Although the description of these duties varies in the sources (cf. the references in note 129 and al-Subkî, I, 134), he was probably given only the office of *nâẓir al-aḥbâs*, which left the hands of the Shâfiʿî chief judge at the time of Tâj al-Dîn's death (al-Nuwayrî, BN 1578, fol. 36a). On this office, see Popper, Notes, I, 101; La Syrie, p. LXXIX.

[132]Sulûk, I, 864.

[133]He also asked for the privilege of appointing *nuwwâb* in the provinces and wearing the *ṭarḥa*, a ceremonial scarf, like the Shâfiʿî chief judge (Sulûk, III, 196).

[134] _Durar_, III, 230.

[135] _Inbâʾ al-ghumr_, I, 302; _Sulûk_, III, 359.

[136] _Sulûk_, I, 864.

[137] _Rafʿ_, II, 249.

[138] _Khiṭaṭ_, II, 209.

[139] _Ibid._, p. 343.

[140] _Ibid._

[141] EI-2, III, 163.

[142] _Sulûk_, I, 761.

[143] _Khiṭaṭ_, II, 268-69.

CHAPTER II

Appointments

The reasons for an individual's appointment to the chief judgeship were varied and sometimes complex, but four basic ones emerge: merit, nepotism, patronage and *nâʾib* succession. Often some combination of these factors contributed to an individual's appointment, as when a man who had been deputy judge as well as a son or son-in-law of the preceding *qâḍî al-quḍât* took over the judicial duties when his predecessor left office. Similarly, a man might be chosen for the chief judgeship because an *amîr* or influential bureaucrat nominated him; this is an example of patronage. Of course, there are a number of cases in which it has not been possible to determine why an individual was selected for chief judgeship. In general, it is not very helpful to explain such cases by simply referring to the man's qualification, since most of the judges were fairly equal in this area, and certainly there were many qualified *ʿulamaʾ* within the Mamlûk empire who were never even offered the chief judgeship. Rather than speculate too widely on the reasons for such appointments, I have preferred to leave the matter open, although I will indicate any circumstantial evidence I have been able to gather.

The appointment of a new chief judge often involved the

deposition of predecessor, and the two events were sometimes closely linked. However, in order to make the present discussion more manageable, there are separate chapters on appointments and depositions. Likewise, the questions of social and geographic origins may have some relevance to the individual's appointment, or may be of interest or significance in their own right. However, in order not to clutter the section on appointments with extended descriptions of family background, this matter will be discussed separately as well.

The present chapter is devoted to the reasons for the appointments of the chief judges. What is interesting is that although there are more Ḥanafîs, for example, to study than there are Ḥanbalîs, the reasons for appointments transcend *madhhab* affiliation, and all of the basic reasons for an appointment can be found in some form in the discussion of each *madhhab*.

Ḥanbalîs

Ḥanbalî Chief Judges

1. Shams al-Dîn Ibn al-ʿImâd	663-670
2. ʿIzz al-Dîn Ibn ʿAwaḍ	678-696
3. Sharaf al-Dîn al-Ḥarrânî	696-709
4. Saʿd al-Dîn al-Ḥârithî	709-711
5. Taqî al-Dîn Ibn ʿAwaḍ	712-738
6. Muwaffaq al-Dîn al-Maqdisî	738-769
7. Nâşir al-Dîn Naşr Allâh	769-795

This school of law was the least important one in Egypt.[1] We have seen earlier that when Baybars ordered the Shâfiʿî chief judge to choose *nuwwâb,* the Ḥanbalîs, in all likelihood, were given only an *ʿâqid.* We have also seen that the Ḥanbalî chief judge sat in the lowest ranking position of the four judges in the *dâr al-ʿadl.* There are fewer Ḥanbalî chief judges to discuss, and they tended to last longer in office than their contemporaries in the other *madhâhib.* These are indications of the stability of the Ḥanbalî regime during the Baḥrî period, and there is little evidence of the struggles and intrigues to attain the chief judgeship which sometimes occurred in the other *madhâhib.*

In the discussion of the establishment of the four chief judgeships in 663, we have mentioned how Shams al-Dîn Ibn al-ʿImâd rose from his teaching post in al-Ṣâliḥiyya to become Ḥanbalî *qâḍî al-quḍât.* It is said that he agreed to accept the office of judge only on condition that he receive no salary for those duties.[2] His later imprisonment for mishandling funds entrusted to him makes this pre-condition seem ironic in retrospect, but we must not forget that it may have been a pious invention by later writers. Although he came from a distinguished Ḥanbalî family of Damascus,[3] there is no evidence that this played any role in his appointment to the chief judgeship or his earlier appointment to al-Ṣâliḥiyya. We do know that he was well liked by Sultan Baybars, who refused to turn against him in spite of the efforts of Bahâʾ al-Dîn Ibn Ḥannâ, his sometime *wazîr,*[4] nor would Baybars believe a sealed letter brought to him in the year 662 by a black slave charging Shams al-Dîn with plotting against the sultan, because the sultan had not appointed a Ḥanbalî to his new *madrasa*[5] nor nominated a *nâʾib* for the Ḥanbalîs.[6] However, the sultan was probably very angry with him over the incident of mishandling of funds, and no one rose to the judge's aid.

Following the deposition of Shams al-Dîn in 670, the Ḩanbalîs were officially without a chief judge, but his *nâʾib* and son-in-law, ʿIzz al-Dîn Ibn ʿAwaḑ, carried on the necessary judicial tasks at Shams al-Dîn's urging.[7] Ibn ʿAwaḑ was officially appointed chief judge in 679, and held this office until his death in 696.[8] The next Ḩanbalî chief judge was Sharaf al-Dîn al-Ḩarrânî, and he is the most mysterious of the Ḩanbalî judges under study. According to al-Nuwayrî, he was originally a Shâfiʿî, but during the last days of the reign of Sultan al-Ashraf (ruled 689-93), he became a Ḩanbalî[9]; this was shortly before he became chief judge. More importantly, he held the office of *nâẕir al-khizâna al-sulţâniyya,*[10] and continued to hold that office after he had become chief judge.[11] His closeness to court circles as *nâẕir al-khizâna al-sulţâniyya* may have helped him to move into the judgeship at Ibn ʿAwaḑ's death, inasmuch as he certainly did not enjoy a scholarly reputation.[12]

When al-Ḩarrânî died the judgeship passed to Saʿd al-Dîn al-Ḩârithî. He is unique among the Ḩanbali judges, both because his tenure in office was only two years and because his father was a merchant.[13] Here again, it is not possible to determine why he was appointed, although he had held a number of teaching posts in Damascus and Cairo earlier. The reason for the appointment of Taqî al-Dîn Ibn ʿAwaḑ at al-Ḩârithî's death is not clear either, but we must remember that he was both the son and grandson of previous Ḩanbalî chief judges of Egypt, and his good name, and perhaps a friendship with those in court circles might have been factors in his appointment. On the other hand, there may have been some trouble in finding a replacement, since there was an interval of about two months between al-Ḥârithî's death and Ibn ʿAwaḍ's appointment.[14] There is no evidence that either Ibn ʿAwaḍ or the sultan was anywhere but in Cairo during that interval, and such a long delay in appointing a new judge is difficult to explain. Perhaps no one could be found to fill the vacancy, so the authorities looked for a Ḥanbalî of good stock.

The end of Ibn ʿAwaḍ's tenure is easier to explain; he and the Shâfiʿî and Ḥanafî chief judges were all deposed at about the same time because of the corruption of themselves and their sons. The *amîr* Badr al-Dîn Jankalî Ibn al-Bâbâ[15] denounced them to the sultan, and, perhaps as a result, he was instrumental in choosing a new Ḥanbalî chief judge; he nominated Muwaffaq al-Dîn al-Maqdisî, and was supported in this by a number of *umarâʾ*.[16] Al-Maqdisî's term of office was the longest of any Ḥanbalî judge, some thirty-one years. According to Ibn Ḥajar, during this judge's tenure the Ḥanbalî *madhhab* expanded in Egypt.[17] This is interesting, but details are lacking, and there is no indication whether Muwaffaq al-Dîn played a part in this expansion. When he died in 769, he was succeeded by his *nâʾib* and son-in-law, Naṣr Allâh. This judge served a long apprenticeship, beginning at the age of thirty-one, prior to which he had been *qâḍî* in Nablus. His term of office would extend well into the Burjî period.[18]

The Ḥanbalî regime during the Baḥrî period was not dominated by any single family, but evidence of nepotism is very strong. Ibn al-ʿImâd, his son-in-law ʿIzz al-Dîn Ibn ʿAwaḍ, and ʿIzz al-Dîn's son Taqî al-Dîn held the Ḥanbalî judgeship for a total of fifty-three years. If we add the eight years when ʿIzz al-Dîn was de facto and not official *qâḍî al-quḍât*, the new total is sixty-one years. Muwaffaq al-Dîn al-Maqdisî and his son-in-law kept the chief judgeship in their family for forty-one years. Naşr Allâh's tenure extended even longer. Thus these two extended families had control for about three-quarters of the period under study. The accession of Taqî al-Dîn Ibn ʿAwaḍ is an example of nepotism of a kind different from the one we mentioned at the beginning of this chapter, since a certain amount of time had elapsed since any relative of his had held the chief judgeship. Discussing an earlier period and a different office, D. Sourdel wrote in his work on the ʿAbbâsid vizirate, "'fils de vizirs'...constituaient alors une veritable caste...paraissent souvent avoir été choisis de préférence aux autres."[19] This observation seems to have applied to the Mamlûk judiciary of Cairo also, as we can see in the case of Taqî al-Dîn ibn ʿAwaḍ, and as we shall see in more detail below in other *madhâhib*. To Sourdel's comments we can only add the supposition that sons or other relatives of earlier chief judges, once introduced to court circles, were often able to maintain some contacts which they could use to their own best advantage. Or, at the very least, a good family name always carried some prestige and could be helpful to anyone interested in the chief judgeship.

The selection of Muwaffaq al-Dîn al-Maqdisî for the Ḥanbalî judgeship is somewhat difficult to characterize. On the one hand, he was nominated by a Mamlûk *amîr* and supported by other *umarâʾ*, but on the other hand, we must remember that the sultan solicited nominations at that time, and he was presented as being the most worthy candidate.[20] This raises the possibility that merit was a real factor in his appointment. Certainly, his nomination was not the blatant sort of patronage whereby some individual worked for the appointment of his protégé, regardless of the latter's qualifications. This judge's appointment has been classified as an example of merit, but his case is an example of how this classification process can become complicated. Nevertheless, the four factors mentioned earlier can be found in the appointments of the Ḥanbalî judges, as well as in the appointments of the chief judges of the other schools of law.

Mâlikîs

Mâlikî Chief Judges

1. Sharaf al-Dîn al-Subkî	663-669
2. Nafîs al-Dîn Ibn Shukr	669-680
3. Taqî al-Dîn Ibn Shâs	680-685
4. Zayn al-Dîn Ibn Makhlûf	685-718
5. Taqî al-Dîn al-Akhnâʾî	718-750
6. Tâj al-Dîn al-Akhnâʾî	750-756
7. Nûr al-Dîn al-Sakhâwî	756
Tâj al-Dîn al-Akhnâʾî	756-763
8. Burhân al-Dîn al-Akhnâʾî	763-777
9. Badr al-Dîn al-Akhnâʾî	777-778
10. ʿAlam al-Dîn al-Bisâṭî	778-779
Badr al-Dîn al-Akhnâʾî	779
ʿAlam al-Dîn al-Bisâṭî	779-783
11. Jamâl al-Dîn Ibn Khayr al-Anṣârî	783-786

The Mâlikî chief judges present a different picture from their Ḥanbalî counterparts. Firstly, there were more Mâlikî chief judges than Ḥanbalî ones in this period, and their terms of office were generally shorter. Also, several of the Mâlikî chief judges were deposed and then reappointed to office, a move which can sometimes be interpreted as an attempt to humble the individual or remind him he is at the mercy of the sultan. Here again, the evidence of nepotism is quite pronounced. Four of the eleven judges were from the extended family of al-Akhnâʾî. They managed to succeed each other, except for two very short intervals, for a period of sixty years, which is about half the time span of the present study.

Shams al-Dîn al-Subkî (no relation to the famous Shâfiʿî family), became chief judge like the others in 663 when the former *nuwwâb* of Ibn Bint al-Aʿazz became chief judges themselves. He was probably teaching at al-Ṣâliḥiyya then as well, and had held the post of *muḥtasib* of al-Qâhira during the days of the Ayyûbid al-Malik al-Kâmil (ruled 615-635), as well as that of *ʿâqid al-ankiha* at some point. According to Ibn Kathîr, he accepted the post of judge only under compulsion, and with the stipulation that he receive no salary. He was among the oldest of all the chief judges to ever have been chosen, being seventy-eight years old in 663. Nevertheless, he managed to stay in office for six more years, until his death in 669.[21]

Al-Subkî's successor, Nafîs al-Dîn Ibn Shukr, had started his career as a judge in Dimyât, where he had been *nâʾib* to Tâj al-Dîn Ibn Bint al-Aʿazz; this was obviously prior to 663.[22] He and the Ḥanafî chief judge were deposed from office briefly during the short reign of Salâmish, but both were returned to office at the accession of Sultan Qalâʾûn the next year (679)[23] It is not clear what happened to the offices of Mâlikî and Ḥanafî chief judges during that time, but Taqî al-Dîn Ibn Shâs, Ibn Shukr's ultimate successor may have been chief judge during that interval.[24] More likely, there was only a Shâfi'î chief judge then. In any case, Ibn Shâs did become Mâlikî chief judge in 680, but we are not aware of any special circumstances surrounding his appointment.

When Ibn Shâs died, he was replaced by Zayn al-Dîn Ibn Makhlûf, who is a much more interesting character than any of his predecessors. At the time of his appointment he was *nâẓir al-khizâna al-sulṭâniyya,* but earlier in his career he had held the post of *amîn al-ḥukm.* At that time, the then *amîr* Qalâ'ûn had purchased from him some properties which he controlled in his capacity as *amîn al-ḥukm.* When Qalâ'ûn delayed in paying for the properties, Ibn Makhlûf demanded them back and even went so far as to complain to Sultan Baybars about the problem. Qalâ'ûn remembered him when he became sultan, and he made Ibn Makhlûf *nâẓir al-khizâna al-sulṭâniyya* and then Mâlikî chief judge as well. He eventually became the tutor of Qalâ'ûn's son, the future sultan, al-Malik al-Nâṣir Muḥammad.[25] He enjoyed the longest tenure of any chief judge and died in office after having served a little over thirty years.

Ibn Makhlûf nominated his *nâ'ib,* Taqî al-Dîn al-Akhnâ'î, the first of this family to hold the office, to succeed him. Taqî al-Dîn enjoyed a fine reputation for scholarship, piety, and asceticism, and the sources say that Ibn Makhlûf chose him as his *nâ'ib* because he was amazed to find someone with such qualities. Ibn Makhlûf himself had a reputation as a poor scholar.[26] Al-Akhnâ'î was also liked by the Sultan al-Malik al-Nâṣir Muḥammad,[27] but the judge's contemporary, the Ḥanafî *qâḍi al-quḍât*, Ibn al-Ḫarîrî, thought little of al-Akhnâ)î, because he was the youngest of the Mâlikî *nuwwâb*. He even wrote a letter against the Mâlikî, charging that he was inept. When he had completed the letter, he took it and rode to the citadel, but his donkey fell, and the judge suffered some broken bones. This accident incapacitated him, and he could not perform his duties for a while; his tenure as chief judge ended soon after as well.[28]

Taqî al-Dîn al-Akhnâ)î managed to stay in office almost as long as his predecessor, and his successor, Tâj al-Dîn al-Akhnâ)î, was his nephew and his *nâ)ib*. Tâj al-Dîn held office for twenty-three years, except for a few months in 756.[29] What is interesting about these two members of the al-Akhnâ)î clan is that both were originally Shâfi(îs who later changed *madhhab*.[30] Even more striking is that Taqî al-Dîn's brother (Tâj al-Dîn's father) was Shâfi(î *qâḍî al-quḍât* of Damascus.[31] Tâj al-Dîn was removed from the chief judgeship in 756,so that he could assume the post of *nâẓir khizânat al-khâṣṣ*,[32] but his successor, Nûr al-Dîn al-Sakhâwî, died after only seventy-two days in office, and al-Akhnâ)î was given back his old job and allowed to keep the new one as well. He held both posts until his death in 763.[33]

Although al-Sakhâwî was chief judge only briefly, his appointment was a clear example of patronage and was due to the intervention of the *amîr* Shaykhû[34] He had known al-Sakhâwî for many years and had even given the future judge an appointment in his *madrasa*, al-Shaykhûniyya.[35] After he began to serve as chief judge, he became ill, but Shaykhû urged him to remain and even gave a banquet in honor of his recovery a few days before the judge died.[36]

Tâj al-Dîn al-Akhnâʾî was followed by his brother, Burhân al-Dîn, who had also changed his *madhhab*. Burhân al-Dîn had been *nâʾib* to his brother and had even taken over the duties of chief judge, at least on occasion; he is called his brother's *khalîfa*.[37] When Tâj al-Dîn held both the offices of *nâẓir khizânat al-khâṣṣ* and *qâḍî al-quḍât* during his second term, he made Burhân al-Dîn his deputy in the *naẓar al-khâṣṣ*.[38] In 762 Burhân al-Dîn was made *muḥtasib*, but he had to give it up the next year when he became chief judge.[39] We also know that he had been *nâẓir al-mâristân*,[40] which he also had to relinquish when he became chief judge.[41] Ibn Ḥajar says that he faced some opposition to his appointment from a number of Maghribis. He responded by having some of them tortured, while other fled the city.[42] Unfortunately, there are no further details available concerning this incident, and the reason for this opposition is unknown.

The last member of the al-Akhnâʾî family to concern us is Badr al-Dîn, who was the nephew of both Tâj al-Dîn and Burhân al-Dîn. He was appointed *muftî* in the *dâr al-ʿadl* in 772[43], and at some earlier point in his career he had also been *nâẓir khizânat al-khâṣṣ*.[44] Like the other members of his family who became chief judges, he had also changed his *madhhab*.[45] His term as chief judge was very short. He was appointed in 777, but lost office after the death of Sultan al-Ashraf Shaʿbân in 778. He was reappointed in 779, but lost office again in the ensuing struggle for power.[46]

Badr al-Dîn was succeeded, both in 778 and 779, by ʿAlam al-Dîn al-Bisâṭî, who had been *nâʾib* both to Badr al-Dîn and his uncle Burhân al-Dîn.[47] Al-Bisâṭî was aided in obtaining the judgeship through the efforts of the *amîr* Qaraţây and the *shâhid* of the amîr's *dîwân,* Burhân al-Dîn Ibrâhîm Ibn al-Labbân. The latter had grown up among Mâlikî *fuqahâ'* and had studied Mâlikî *fiqh.* When the change in the sultanate occurred in 778, Qaraţây made Ibrâhîm his *shâhid al-dîwân* and one of the scribes. When the people came to Qaraţây soliciting favors, al-Bisâţî was among them, and he spoke about the chief judgeship. Qaraţây arranged for his appointment, and made Ibn al-Labbân al-Bisâţî's *nâ'ib.*[48]

Al-Bisâţî was driven from office after a dispute with Burhân al-Dîn Ibn Jamâ'a, who was then allowed to choose a new Mâlikî judge. He chose Ibn Khayr al-Anşârî, who had been one of al-Bisâţî's *nuwwâb.*[49] He was originally from Alexandria, where he had been a notary, scribe in the courts, and a *nâ'ib* to the chief judge. He then went to Cairo, being first a scribe, again, and then *nâ'ib,* and finally chief judge. He held office from 783 to 786, and was reappointed in 789, but this falls too far into the Burjî period to concern us here.[50] We do not know of any special friendship between him and Ibn Jamâ'a, and perhaps he was chosen simply because he was one of the deputy judges.

In conclusion, the appointments of the Mâlikî chief judges can be explained by several factors. On the one hand there was the influence of the al-Akhnâ'î family, which managed to keep the office to itself for many years, and on the other hand there was the influence of powerful *umarâ',* such as in the cases of al-Sakhâwî and al-Bisâţî. The original appointment of Ibn Makhlûf was due to the high regard in which Sultan Qalâ'ûn held him, and the appointment of the first member of the Al-Akhnâ'î family, Taqî al-Dîn, was likewise due to the respect which Ibn Makhlûf felt for him. Almost all the judges had previous judicial experience, and most had been *nâʾib* to the preceding judge, although in a number of cases the predecessor had also been a close relative.

Ḥanafîs

Ḥanafî Chief Judges

1. Ṣadr al-Dîn al-Adhraʿî	663-677
2. Muʿizz al-Dîn al-Khaṭîbî	677-692
3. Shams al-Dîn al-Sarûjî	692-696
4. Ḥusâm al-Dîn al-Rûmî	696-698
Shams al-Dîn al-Sarûjî	698-710
5. Shams al-Dîn Ibn al-Ḥarîrî	710-717
(al-Qâhira only)	717
6. Sirâj al-Dîn al-Râzî (Fusṭâṭ only)	717
Shams al-Dîn Ibn al-Ḥarîrî	717-728
7. Burhân al-Dîn Ibn ʿAbd al-Ḥaqq	728-738
8. Ḥusâm al-Dîn al-Ghûrî	738-742
9. Zayn al-Dîn al-Bisṭâmî	742-748
10. ʿAlâʾ al-Dîn Ibn al-Turkumânî	748-750
11. Jamâl al-Dîn Ibn al-Turkumânî	750-769
12. Sirâj al-Dîn al-Hindî	769-773
13. Ṣadr al-Dîn Ibn al-Turkumânî	773-776
14. Najm al-Dîn Ibn Abî al-ʿIzz	777
15. Ṣadr al-Dîn Ibn Abî al-ʿIzz	777
16. Sharaf al-Dîn Ibn Manṣûr	777-778
17. Jalâl al-Dîn Jâr Allâh	778-782
18. Ṣadr al-Dîn Ibn Manṣûr	782-786

The first in the line of the Ḥanafî chief judges of the

Baḫrî period was Şadr al-Dîn al-Adhra(î. As with the other chief judges appointed in 663, he had been *nâ)ib* to Ibn Bint al-A(azz. Şadr al-Dîn enjoyed an excellent relationship with Sultan Baybars. He accompanied the sultan on the pilgrimage to Mecca and on his military campaigns, acting as a sort of *qâḍî al-(askar,* although Ḥanafîs were not officially appointed to this office until later. The sources say that the sultan allowed him to judge wherever the riders dismounted.[51] Şadr al-Dîn had established a strong reputation for himself in Damascus even before he came to Egypt. He held quite a few teaching posts there, and upon his departure for Egypt was able to pass some of them on to his sons.[52] He was also an early member of the extended family of Ibn Abî al-(Izz, but was probably only very distantly related to the two Ḥanafî judges who would not assume office until one hundred years after his own departure from that post.

Al-Adhra(î was followed by Mu(izz al-Dîn al-Khaţîbî, who had been his *nâ)ib,* and who had also held some other judicial posts earlier. He was deposed briefly in 678, along with the Mâlikî chief judge, but returned to office the next year when Qalâ)ûn became sultan.[53] At al-Khaţîbî's death, Shams al-Dîn al-Sarûjî became chief judge. He had originally been a Ḥanbalî, and was the only Ḥanafî chief judge not born into the *madhhab.*[54] His tenure in office was quite long, and was interrupted only during the short sultanate of Lâjîn, at whose death al-Sarûjî was returned to office.[55] During that interval, the chief judgeship was held by Ḥusâm al-Dîn al-Rûmî. He had been chief judge in Malatya in Anatolia for more than twenty years, when he fled to Syria in 675 out of fear of the Mongols, and became chief judge of Damascus in 677. At that time he became friendly with Lâjîn, who was then governor of Syria, and when Lâjîn became sultan, Ḥusâm al-Dîn gave the judgeship of Damascus to his son Jalâl al-Dîn and went to assume his new duties in Egypt. He held the post until Lâjîn's assassination.[56]

After Shams al-Dîn al-Sarûjî was deposed at the end of his second term, another former *qâḍî al-quḍât* of Damascus was summoned to fill the vacancy in Cairo. This was Shams al-Dîn Ibn al-Ḥarîrî, who had held the chief judgeship of Damascus from 699 to 705.[57] All went well in Egypt until 717, when Ibn al-Ḥarîrî was asked to approve the transfer of certain *awqâf* lands. He refused, but Sirâj al-Dîn al-Râzî, one of al-Sarûjî's *nuwwâb,* let it be known that he would approve the action if appointed chief judge. As a result of this offer the judgeship was split; Ibn al-Ḥarîrî was assigned the judgeship of al-Qâhira, and Sirâj al-Dîn that of Fusṭâṭ. Sirâj al-Dîn died after only sixty-odd days in office, and Ibn al-Ḥarîrî regained his former power.[58]

Another Syrian, Burhân al-Dîn Ibn ʿAbd al-Ḥaqq, was summoned to fill the vacancy left by Ibn al-Ḥarîrî's death in 728. He was from a distinguished Syrian family, and was teaching in several colleges in Damascus at the time of his appointment.[59] According to Ibn Kathîr, Ibn ʿAbd al-Ḥaqq had recommended Ibn al-Ḥarîrî for the judgeship of Cairo earlier, and was a worthy successor to him.[60] Unfortunately, this glowing praise did not apply to Burhân al-Dîn's children, who became so involved in corrupt and illegal financial dealings that their father was deposed because of them.[61]

After Ibn ʿAbd al-Ḥaqq was exiled to Syria, the sultan appointed Ḥusâm al-Dîn al-Ghûrî. He was unlike any other Ḥanafî judge, because he was a Baghdâdî, who had fled Egypt in the company of two other important political figures as a result of troubles in Iraq. He had been born and educated there, rising to the post of judge and *muḩtasib* of Baghdad.[62] THe other two received important posts in the Mamlûk empire,[63] and the sultan was probably well disposed towards bringing "new blood" into the judiciary after having been forced to depose three chief judges at once. Al-Ghûrî's colorful activities in office will be discussed in a later chapter. He eventually returned to Baghdad, and was replaced by Zayn al-Dîn al-Bisţâmî, who was the maternal grandson of Shams al-Dîn al-Sarûjî.[64] It is difficult to know if this relationship had any effect on his appointment since al-Sarûjî had died some thirty years earlier, but perhaps his ancestry was a factor in his appointment.

He was followed by ʿAlâʾ al-Dîn Ibn al-Turkumânî, the first of three members of this family to hold the office of chief judge. His term of office was cut short by his death in the plague of 750, but he seems to have been well connected to some of the Mamlûk *umarâʾ*. Al-Maqrîzî says that al-Malik al-Nâşir Muḩammad disliked him because of his meetings with *umarâʾ*.[65] In 730 he was placed in charge of the teaching and was named shaykh of the Sufis at the *madrasa* al-Jamâliyya, which had just been completed by the *amîr* ʿAlâʾ al-Dîn Mughulţay al-Jamâlî and was devoted exclusively to the Ḩanafîs.[66]

Ibn al-Turkumânî's son, Jamâl al-Dîn, succeeded him in the judgeship, and was apparently a very popular figure. The Ḩanafî *fuqahâʾ* were in favor of his appointment, and they even urged the *amîr* Shaykhû to support their choice. Their backing must have been very strong, since Jamâl al-Dîn was only thirty-five years old at the time, the youngest chief judge to be appointed during the Baḥrî period.[67] Even more fascinating is that the Shâfiʿî chief judge at the time, ʿIzz al-Dîn Ibn Jamâʿa, married his daughter to Jamâl al-Dîn.[68] He may have been *nâʾib* to his father previously as well.[69]

After the death of Jamâl al-Dîn the reign of this family was broken by the installation of Sirâj al-Dîn al-Hindî. As his name indicates, he was from India, where he was born and educated. In the year 740, at the age of thirty-five, he arrived in Egypt and took up residence in various Ḥanafî *madâris*, where he both studied and related Traditions. Al-Hindî was a clever man, and he worked to establish a strong position for himself among the high ranking *ʿulamâʾ* as well as with the sultan and Mamlûks. At first he attended the lectures of the *qâḍî al-quḍât* Zayn al-Dîn al-Bisṭâmî, then those of ʿAlâʾ al-Dîn Ibn al-Turkumânî when he became chief judge. The latter made him an *ʿâqid* at a shop in Bayn al-Qaṣrayn.[70] When Jamâl al-Dîn succeeded his father, ʿAlâʾ al-Dîn Ibn al-Turkumânî, as chief judge, he made al-Hindî his only *nâʾib*.[71] At the same time al-Hindî had achieved some status with the leading *umarâʾ*. When the office of *qâḍî al-ʿaskar* fell vacant in 758, al-Hindî went to Shaykhû, asking him for it, but Shaykhû offered him an *iqṭâʿ* instead. Al-Hindî was not easily put off, however, and he next went to the *amîr* Ṣarghitmish, who did arrange for him to receive it.[72] Shaykhû's death was a boon to al-Hindî, and gave him greater status with Ṣarghitmish; he was also well liked by Sultan Hasan (ruled 748-52, 755-62).[73] Al-Hindî's fortunes took an abrupt turn for the worse when Ṣarghitmish was jailed. One of al-Hindî's adversaries, al-Hirmâs,[74] convinced Jamâl al-Dîn Ibn al-Turkumânî to depose him as *nâ)ib,* and al-Hindî removed himself from public life, staying at home and teaching, although he remained *qâḍî al-(askar.*[75]

However, al-Hindî was not by nature passive, and it was not long before he moved, albeit obliquely, against his enemy al-Hirmâs. Al-Hindî became friendly with a certain Ibn Naqqâsh, who was also at odds with al-Hirmâs.[76] Both went on the pilgrimage with Sultan Ḥasan in 760, and worked to turn the sultan against al-Hirmâs, who, as it happened, had not joined that pilgrimage.[77] They were successful in their activities to the extent that the sultan sent al-Hirmâs into exile.[78] Although Sultan Ḥasan was deposed two years later, al-Hindî was clever enough to gain new friends among the *umarâ).* Finally he became Ḥanafî *qâḍî al-quḍât* in 769, along with appointments to several teaching posts.[79]

When Sirâj al-Dîn died in office in 773, the chief judgeship returned to the family of Ibn al-Turkumânî in the person of Jamâl al-Dîn's son, Ṣadr al-Dîn. He was only about forty years old at the time and had already been passed over once when his father died, because he was too young and inexperienced.[80] Instead, he had taken al-Hindî's place as *qâḍî al-(askar,* having previously served as *nâ)ib* to his father. He was certainly not much older when the chief judgeship fell vacant at al-Hindî's death, but he was appointed nonetheless.[81] A famous family name must have been a major factor in the appointment of someone so young, but he obviously had a good deal of support, because he had been considered for the post at the time of his father's death.

In any case Ṣadr al-Dîn survived only a few years, and died a very young man in 776. The Shâfi(î chief judge in Cairo,

Burhân al-Dîn Ibn Jamâ(a, nominated a Damascene, Sharaf al-Dîn Ibn Abî al-(Izz, also known as Ibn Manşûr, to succeed him.[82] Sharaf al-Dîn soon arrived in Cairo, was summoned to the palace, and was sitting near the door of the *khizânat al-khâşş* when the *amîr* Ţashtamur passed by in the company of some other *umarâ)*. Ţashtamur greeted him and invited him to his home for a meal. Afterwards the *amîr* told him to return to the *madrasa* where he had been residing since he had come to Cairo until the sultan called for him.[83] However, the *amîr* was interested in recommending someone else for the judgeship, and he (or the *amîr* Nâşir al-Dîn Âqbughâ Âş) nominated[84] Jalâl al-Dîn Rasûlân (or Rislân) al-Tabbânî instead.[85] He refused the nomination, saying that a non-Arab (or Persian; *al-(ajam)*, like himself, did not know the practice or customs of the people of Egypt, and the sultan accepted that excuse.[86] Some *umarâ)* then began to speak about Majd al-Dîn Ismâ(îl ibn Ibrâhîm, but this idea was soon dropped.[87] Then some people at court mentioned Najm al-Dîn Ibn Abî al-(Izz, known also as Ibn al-Kishk. There was agreement on this and he was summoned from Damascus.[88] The office of Ḩanafî chief judge was vacant for two and a half months between the death of Ibn al-Turkumânî and the appointment of Ibn al-Kishk.[89]

Najm al-Dîn lasted in office only about one hundred days. He kept on asking to be relieved of his office, and this was finally allowed. He was replaced by his cousin, Şadr al-Dîn Ibn Abî al-(Izz.[90] He also remained only a couple of months; he was deposed and returned to Damascus.[91] Finally Sharaf al-Dîn Ibn Manşûr, the man who had first been nominated by Burhân al-Dîn Ibn Jamâ(a, was chosen as chief judge.[92] He lasted almost a year, until, in the middle of 778, he resigned.[93]

The chief judgeship then fell to a local Ḥanafî, Jalâl al-Dîn Jâr Allâh. He had held several teaching posts prior to this and had served as *nâ'ib* to his father-in-law, Sirâj al-Dîn al-Hindî. However, the most important factor in his appointment was probably the fact that he was the personal physician of the Sultan al-Ashraf Sha'bân, and had successfully treated him during an illness.[94] When Jâr Allâh died in 782, the *amîr* and future sultan Barqûq tried to offer the judgeship to Rasûlân al-Tabbânî, but he refused again, as he had done earlier in 776.[95] The Shâfi'î *qâḍî al-quḍât* suggested Ṣadr al-Dîn Ibn Manṣûr, the older brother of Sharaf al-Dîn Ibn Manṣûr, who had resigned in 778. The new candidate was summoned from Damascus, and duly appointed.[96] His tenure extended into the Burjî period.[97]

The one overriding characteristic of the appointments of the Ḥanafî chief judges is that so many of them were summoned from Damascus to fill the vacancies in that office rather than drawing on native Egyptians. Such activity reached almost absurd proportions following the death of Ṣadr al-Dîn Ibn al-Turkumânî in 776, when three Ḥanafî *'ulamâ'* were summoned to Egypt to become *qâḍî al-quḍât*, but each returned home after very brief terms. To these can be added the names of Ṣadr al-Dîn al-Adhra'î, Shams al-Dîn Ibn al-Ḥarîrî, Burhân al-Dîn Ibn 'Abd al-Ḥaqq, and Ṣadr al-Dîn Ibn Manṣûr, all of whom had longer terms of office in Egypt but were originally Damascenes. This phenomenon is difficult to explain, unless there were an insufficient number of Ḥanafîs in Egypt to choose from, or enough who were willing to accept the office. In several cases the Shâfi'î chief judge had to suggest a candidate, and at other times *umarâ'* and people at the Mamlûk court made suggestions, but even then it was sometimes difficult to find someone to accept the job. All this reminds us of al-Maqrîzî's assertion that Ḥanafîs (and Ḥanbalîs) started to come to Egypt only in the late Ayyûbid period, and that they had emigrated from Syria and further East. Jalâl al-Dîn Rasûlân, who was probably a Persian himself, refused the chief judgeship twice, saying that he was a foreigner unfamiliar with Egyptian customs. Sirâj al-Dîn al-Hindî was definitely from India, while we have already seen how many of the candidates for the Ḥanafî chief judgeship had to be called from Damascus. All this points to a scarcity of Egyptian Ḥanafîs; at least ones qualified for the chief judgeship. In opposition to this we have the conniving of Sirâj al-Dîn al-Râzî, who won half the chief judgeship of Egypt by agreeing to a legal decision pleasing to the sultan, as well as the relentless political maneuvering of al-Hindî himself. Finally there was the power of nepotism, as evidenced by the family of Ibn al-Turkumânî. The founder of this dynasty was apparently friendly with some Mamlûk *umarâʾ*. THe other members of this family were not able to succeed one another consecutively, but the family seems to have enjoyed a good reputation and was probably able to build up a network of friends and acquaintances because of their closeness to court and religious circles. Thus the reasons lying behind the appointments of the Ḥanafî chief judges were varied, often complex, and sometimes involved a considerable amount of political machinations.

Shâfi‘îs

Shâfi‘î Chief Judges

1.	Tâj al-Dîn Ibn Bint al-A‘azz		663-665
2.	Taqî al-Dîn Ibn Razîn	al-Qâhira only	665-676
3.	Muḥyî al-Dîn Ibn ‘Ayn al-Dawla	Fusṭâṭ only	665-676
	Taqî al-Dîn Ibn Razîn		676-678
4.	Ṣadr al-Dîn Ibn Bint al-A‘azz		678-679
	Taqî al-Dîn Ibn Razîn		679-680
5.	Wajîh al-Dîn al-Bahnasî		680-681
	Wajîh al-Dîn al-Bahnasî	Fusṭâṭ only	681-685
6.	Shihâb al-Dîn Ibn al-Khuwayyî	al-Qâhira only	681-686
7.	Burhân al-Dîn al-Sinjârî	al-Qâhira only	686
8.	Taqî al-Dîn Ibn Bint al-A‘azz	Fusṭâṭ only	685-686
	Taqî al-Dîn Ibn Bint al-A‘azz		686-690
9.	Badr al-Dîn Ibn Jamâ‘a		690-693
	Taqî al-Dîn Ibn Bint al-A‘azz		693-695
10.	Taqî al-Dîn Ibn Daqîq al-‘Îd		695-702
	Badr al-Dîn Ibn Jamâ‘a		702-710
11.	Jamâl al-Dîn al-Zar‘î		710-711
	Badr al-Dîn Ibn Jamâ‘a		711-727
12.	Jalâl al-Dîn al-Qazwînî		727-738
13.	‘Izz al-Dîn Ibn Jamâ‘a		738-759
14.	Bahâ’ al-Dîn Ibn ‘Aqîl		759
	‘Izz al-Dîn Ibn Jamâ‘a		759-766
15.	Bahâ’ al-Dîn al-Subkî		766-773
16.	Burhân al-Dîn Ibn Jamâ‘a		773-779
17.	Badr al-Dîn al-Subkî		779-781

Burhân al-Dîn Ibn Jamâ'a 781-784

As we have seen earlier the Shâfi'î chief judge at the time of the establishment of the four judgeships was Tâj al-Dîn Ibn Bint al-A'azz. Since the present study begins in 663, it might seem at first that Tâj al-Dîn, whose term of office ended when he died in 665, was not a major figure. However, this was not the case. Firstly, he was the founder of a small, but significant clan of Shâfi'î judges who would figure prominently in the Baḩrî period, in part because of the first infusion of prestige which he gave to the family name. His role as the pivotal figure in the establishment of the four chief judgeships, though perhaps not its cause, has been the subject of an earlier chapter. Even more important is to look at the career of Tâj al-Dîn as a benchmark to which we can compare the careers of later judges, because few subsequent judges would hold as many important posts as he did. He held a total of fifteen posts during his lifetime, some of them simultaneously, including various teaching positions and bureaucratic offices, the most important of which was that of *wazîr*.[98] Of all the judges under study only three Shâfi'î judges ever held this office, and then only in the early years of the Baḩrî period.

At Tâj al-Dîn's death, the power of the Shâfi'î chief judge was dealt a severe blow, when its jurisdiction was placed in the hands of two judges, one with authority over al-Qâhira and Lower Egypt, and the other over Fusţâţ and Upper Egypt. This division of powers was by no means an innovation, and even Ibn Bint al-A'azz himself had held jurisdiction over only one half for a period of time.[99] However, it may be that this was an attempt to further limit the powers of the Shâfi'î chief judge, coming as it did only two years after its powers were first limited by the establishment of the four chief judgeships. From another angle, it may also have been a move by Sultan Baybars to insure that no other *'âlim* would try to take Tâj al-Dîn's place and exert the influence he personally had held.

In any case, the judgeship was now divided: Taqî al-Dîn Ibn Razîn took al-Qâhira and Muḥyî al-Dîn Ibn 'Ayn al-Dawla took Fusṭâṭ. This situation would continue for twelve years until Baybars' death in 676. Ibn Razîn was born in Ḥamâ, but his early career was in Damascus. He did not come to Egypt until the year 658, at the age of fifty-five, when he fled Syria because of the invasion of Ḥûlagû. As a young man he was a noteworthy student, and gave his first lecture at the age of eighteen. He had held a number of important teaching posts in Damascus. Therefore, it must have been a harsh blow for him when he arrived in Egypt to be able to secure a position only as a *mu'îd*. Yet the situation soon improved, and four years later he was appointed as first Shâfi'î teacher of *fiqh* at al-Ẓâhiriyya, and three years after that as chief judge.[100] His credentials as a scholar are obvious, but the reason for his selection as chief judge is not. If we could know why he was selected as the first Shâfi'î teacher at al-Ẓâhiriyya, which was built by Sultan Baybars himself, this later selection as chief judge might be more easily explained. It is possible that the teaching position was granted somewhat out of pity to a reputable and mature scholar recently driven from his home. Such a gesture might have made Ibn al-Razîn feel indebted to the sultan, and the appointment to the judgeship could have strengthened this feeling. His appointment can also be seen as an astute political move by the sultan: the appointment of a recently uprooted and older scholar who was apparently not well connected to any influential persons to be one of the successors to the influential Tâj al-Dîn Ibn Bint al-A'azz, and perhaps to balance the power of his cohort, Muḥyî al-Dîn Ibn 'Ayn al-Dawla.

This second judge who shared the jurisdiction with Ibn Razîn was older than his fellow judge; probably he was sixty-eight years old. Unlike Ibn Razîn, Ibn 'Ayn al-Dawla was quite well connected. Not only had his father been chief judge of al-Qâhira at a much earlier period, but he could regard the sometime *wazîr*, Bahâ' al-Dîn Ibn Ḥannâ, as his patron.[101] The allotment of only one-half the jurisdiction to Ibn Ḥannâ's protege may have been an attempt to limit the *wazîr's* influence. In any case, it is not possible to say which of these factors caused the division of the Shâfi'î judgeship and the appointment of these two men. It is not unreasonable to assume that all these factors played a part. When Ibn 'Ayn al-Dawla left office in 676 because of poor health, Ibn al-Razîn assumed jurisdiction over all Egypt.[102]

The year 678 brought Salâmish to the sultanate for a very brief period, during which time Ibn al-Razîn was replaced by Ṣadr al-Dîn Ibn Bint al-A'azz, one of Tâj al-Dîn's sons, and his father's replacement at al-Ṣâliḥiyya.[103] His term as judge lasted only about as long as the sultanate of Salâmish, and Ṣadr al-Dîn died shortly thereafter. As we have seen in our discussion of the other chief judges during that period, Ṣadr al-Dîn may well have been the only chief judge in power in that year. Soon after Qalâ'ûn became sultan, he was replaced by Ibn Razîn who served until his own death, less than a year later.[104]

Ibn Razîn was succeeded by Wajîh al-Dîn al-Bahnasî, who was probably a native Egyptian. He had been on good terms with Tâj al-Dîn Ibn Bint al-Aʿazz, who had relied on his advice, and had held several teaching posts. Although we do not know his date of birth, he was probably of an advanced age or feeble when he took office.[105] If Ibn Bint al-Aʿazz had relied on him for advice, he must have been at least his contemporary, if not older, and Ibn Bint al-Aʿazz had died fifteen years earlier at the age of fifty-five. Finally, al-Bahnasî, who had been given jurisdiction over all Egypt, asked to be relieved of the judgeship of al-Qâhira, because he found it too difficult to travel there for court sessions from his home in Fusţâţ.[106] His request was granted, and one year after his appointment, the judgeship of al-Qâhira went to Shihâb al-Dîn Ibn al-Khuwayyî.

The new judge of al-Qâhira was not a young man either, being approximately sixty years old when he became judge. He had a notable genealogy and a more varied experience as judge than any of his predecessors. His father had been chief judge of Damascus, but died when Shihâb al-Dîn was only eleven years old. The residence of the Shâfiʿî *qâḍî al-quḍât* of Damascus was the ʿÂdiliyya *madrasa,* and after his father's death he continued to live there, and probably pursue his education through the charity of that institution. While still a young man, he taught in *madâris* in Damascus, then held the post of judge in Jerusalem, al-Mahalla,[107] al-Bahnasa,[108] and Aleppo, before being appointed judge in al-Qâhira.[109]

It may well have been a practice to install people who would not be trouble makers or political connivers in the office of chief judge; and we must not forget that the Shâfiʿî judgeship was more powerful than the others. Wajîh al-Dîn al-Bahnasî was a well established scholar, but obviously quite feeble, and apparently without any special connection in court circles. Although he had been an intimate of Tâj al-Dîn Ibn Bint al-Aʿazz, there is no evidence that he used this connection for his own aggrandizement. Ibn al-Khuwayyî was a man of considerable judicidial experience, but, aside from his term in Aleppo, all his appointments had been in minor towns or cities.

However, this apparent trend of appointing politically weak or older men to the judgeship took an abrupt about-face when al-Bahnasî died in 685 and Taqî al-Dîn Ibn Bint al-Aʿazz, another of Tâj al-Dîn's sons, was appointed the new judge of Fusṭâṭ. Unlike his predecessors, who assumed office fairly late in life, Taqî al-Dîn was only forty-six years old when he became judge. He was also much more amibitious than his brother Ṣadr al-Dîn, and when he had become *qâḍî al-quḍât* some six years earlier, Taqî al-Dîn took over his post as *nâẓir* at al-Ṣâliḥiyya; at that time he was already *nâẓir al-khazâʾin*[110] and the holding of both posts at once was probably lucrative as well as a source of influence.[111]

Soon after Taqî al-Dîn assumed office, the news came to Egypt of the death of Ibn Zakî, the Shâfiʿî chief judge of Damascus. Taqî al-Dîn saw this as his opportunity to become sole judge of Egypt, and he worked for Ibn al-Khuwayyî's appointment as Ibn Zakî's replacement, which did in fact occur.[112] However, events did not turn out as Taqî al-Dîn had planned. Instead of being granted the other half of the judgeship, the jurisdiction remained split, and Burhân al-Dîn al-Sinjârî was named to replace Ibn al-Khuwayyî.

In several ways this was an astute political move by Sultan Qalâ᾽ûn. Al-Sinjârî had been involved in the political machinations of the Mamlûk empire for some time, but the influence of his opponents had usually been stronger than his own. He had been appointed *wazîr* in 677 at the time of the death of Ibn Ḥannâ, who had been his enemy, but was deposed a year later at the instigation of al-Shujâʿî,[113] at which time both he and his son were jailed and much of their wealth confiscated. Very soon after that, in 679, he was reinstalled as *wazîr*, but again deposed and imprisoned with his son in 680. Much earlier than all this, in 659, he had shared the Shâfiʿî chief judgeship with his brother. After his second release from prison, he was made teacher and *nâẓir* of the *madrasa* al-Shâfiʿiyya (in 682),[114] but was no longer politically active in the way he had been.[115] Probably Qalâ᾽ûn wanted to keep al-Sinjârî close at hand, and also felt that this old politician could keep Ibn Bint al-Aʿazz in check. The sultan even gave al-Sinjârî a seat above that of Taqî al-Dîn in the *dâr al-ʿadl*, a move which so infuriated Taqî al-Dîn that for a time he even refused to attend the sessions of the *dâr al-ʿadl*.[116] Qalâ᾽ûn's plan failed when al-Sinjârî died after only twenty-four days in office; some say that he was poisoned by al-Shujâʿî.[117] Whatever the truth of the matter, Ibn Bint al-Aʿazz finally had his wish, and he became the one and only Shâfiʿî *qâḍî al-quḍât* in Cairo. As we shall see in more detail in a later chapter, he would even become *wazîr* in addition to his judicial duties.

Taqî al-Dîn's high position in Qalâ᾽ûn's administration was terminated by the advent of the new sultan, al-Ashraf Khalîl. Although there is no indication of any enmity between the new sultan and Taqî al-Dîn, the chief judge and the new *wazîr*, Ibn Sal'ûs, were not at all on good terms, and Ibn Sal'ûs arranged for Taqî al-Dîn to be replaced by Badr al-Dîn Ibn Jamâ'a. This was, however, after the sultan had summoned the notables from among the Shâfi'î *fuqahâ'* of Cairo to nominate one of themselves for the post. They could not agree on anyone, so the sultan told Ibn Sal'ûs what had happened, and the *wazîr* selected Ibn Jamâ'a.[118]

This was the first of three terms of office as chief judge of Egypt for Ibn Jamâ'a. He is a most important figure in the history of the *'ulamâ'* of the Mamlûk empire, because he was really the founder of the Ibn Jamâ'a dynasty of Shâfi'î jurists. Not only would his son and grandson eventually follow him in the chief judgeship of Cairo, but branches of this family would figure prominently in the religious hierarchy of Ḥamâ, Jerusalem, and Cairo.[119] Badr al-Dîn himself was a man of some repute prior to his appointment to the chief judgeship, having been a teacher in Damascus, and judge as well as *khaṭîb* in Jerusalem; the latter post was held in his family until the Ottoman conquest.[120] However, these rather limited credentials counted for little compared to his earlier friendship with Ibn Sal'ûs. This friendship was the reason for his appointment.[121]

When al-Malik al-Nâṣir Muḥammad assumed the sultanate at al-Ashraf's death, he recalled Taqî al-Dîn Ibn Bint al-A'azz to the chief judgeship at the suggestion of some *umarâ'*.[122] He held the office until his death in 695.

Ibn Bint al-A'azz was followed by one of the most famous *'ulamâ'* of the period, Taqî al-Dîn Ibn Daqîq al-'Îd. He is a most interesting case for several reasons. His family was from

Qûş in Upper Egypt, and he was raised there, although he was actually born at sea near Yanbû‘ while his parents were making the pilgrimage. He was educated primarily in the Mâlikî *madhhab* of his father, taught at Qûş, and was Mâlikî judge there.[123] At some later date he became Shâfi‘î, not for reasons of political ambition, but rather because he claimed that his *ijtihâd* was consistent with that of al-Shâfi‘î in almost all questions.[124] It is said that he accepted the offer to become *qâḍî al-quḍât* at the urging of some people who claimed that if he did not accept it, it would fall to one of two other unsuitable candidates, who are not named.[125] In a slightly different version, we are told that the *umarâ’* and notables agreed upon him and recommended him to the sultan. He had refused the judgeship several times before, but this time he accepted.[126] He was seventy years old at the time, and his appointment seems to have been due mainly to his pious reputation. His biographies are unique among all those under study in that they are very long and mostly filled with tributes to his piety and good character.[127] Although he tried to resign from office several times, he was always persuaded to remain, and he died in office in 702.[128] His noble reputation plus his advanced age probably made him the sort of pious and distinguished, yet neutral, character which was needed during those times. His seven year term spanned the reign of three different sultans.

At his death, Badr al-Dîn Ibn Jamâ‘a returned to the chief judgeship, which office he would hold for the next twenty-five years, except for a period of one year (710-11). He was chief judge of Damascus, a post he had held (except for the years 696-99) since he had been deposed as chief judge of Egypt in

694.[129] During his tenure in Damascus, Ibn Jamâ‘a had achieved considerable status. Within a year after he became judge there, he managed to be appointed *khaṭîb* of the Umayyad mosque, the first time that the posts of *khaṭîb* and *qâḍî al-quḍât* were combined in one person. Although he was deposed from the judgeship in the sultanate of Lâjîn, he was reappointed when al-Malik al-Nâṣir returned to the throne.[130] Ibn Jamâ‘a was obviously a man who worked hard to maintain and improve his position. When he left Damascus to take up his post in Egypt for the second time, a number of important Mamlûks, including the governor and notables rode out to bid him farewell.[131]

Ibn Jamâ‘a was a political opportunist, but he miscalculated when Baybars II took the sultanate for a short period in 708-709 by being too quick to pledge allegiance to him. As a result he was replaced by his *nâ᾿ib,* Jamâl al-Dîn al-Zar‘î when al-Malik al-Nâṣir returned.[132] The sultan asked some people who was most suitable to replace Ibn Jamâ‘a, and they said al-Zar‘î.[133] He was not only *nâ᾿ib* to Ibn Jamâ‘a in Egypt, but he had been his deputy in Damascus as well. He was also *qâḍî al-‘askar* and continued to hold that post when he became *qâḍî al-quḍât*. Ibn Jamâ‘a was soon forgiven, however, and regained his old position after about a year, and al-Zar‘î became chief judge of Damascus about a year after that.[134]

When Ibn Jamâ‘a resigned because of poor health in 727, he was replaced by Jalâl al-Dîn al-Qazwînî, who, like his predecessor, was chief judge of Damascus at the time of his appointment. He had been *khaṭîb* of the Umayyad mosque,[135] and in 724 the governor of Syria recommended him for the chief judgeship of Damascus. He sent Jalâl al-Dîn to Cairo to meet with the sultan, and the sultan grew to like him, perhaps because al-Qazwînî could speak Arabic, Persian, and especially Turkish. The sultan then learned (or was informed by the governor of Syria in a letter) that al-Qazwînî was in debt bcause of his generosity to the *fuqahâʾ* and the poor. The sultan paid his debt, sent him back to Damascus as chief judge and *khaṭîb* of the Umayyad mosque, and appointed one of his sons to the chancery in Cairo.[136] When Ibn Jamâʿa left office, some people were mentioned to the sultan as possible successors, but he did not like any of them and summoned al-Qazwînî from Damascus instead.[137] The sultan finally became very angry at him because of the illegal activities of his sons, and he and his children were exiled to Damascus in 738, although the blow was softened by his appointment as chief judge there.[138]

The sultan now turned to one of his old favorites to fill the judgeship and clean up the corruption left by the family of al-Qazwînî. He chose ʿIzz al-Dîn Ibn Jamâʿa, the son of Badr al-Dîn. In fact, the sultan had called together a number of judges and *fuqahâʾ* to ask them who should succeed al-Qazwînî. They recommended Ibn ʿAdlân,[139] but the sultan demurred and mentioned Ibn Jamâʿa instead. At that point the assembled *ʿulamâʾ* fell into line, praising Ibn Jamâʿa, and he was appointed. The sultan said that he had been fond of him ever since the days of his father, and if he had not been too young at that time, he would have appointed him as his father's successor.[140] He ruled for twenty-eight years, except for an eighty day interval in 759. During that interval the chief judgeship was held by Bahâʾ al-Dîn Ibn ʿAqîl. He had been *nâʾib* to both Jalâl al-Dîn al-Qazwînî and ʿIzz al-Dîn Ibn Jamâʿa, but had been deposed by the latter because of the foul language he had used in an argument with the Ḥanbalî chief judge. Later, the *amîr* Ṣarghitmish became friendly with him, and helped him to become chief judge. His term as chief judge ended when this *amîr* was jailed, and Ibn Jamâʿa returned to office.[141]

When Ibn Jamâʿa resigned in 766, he nominated a member of another famous family of *ʿulamâʾ*, Bahâʾ al-Dîn Muḥammad al-Subkî, to succeed him.[142] Yet it was neither his lineage nor any scholarly reputation,[143] but rather his own ambition which enabled him to acquire many of the posts he held. At first, it must be admitted, it was nepotism which gave him his original entry into the judicial bureaucracy. In 739, at the age of thirty-two he served as deputy to the chief judge of Damascus, Taqî al-Dîn al-Subkî, one of his relatives. He remained quiet for the next twenty years, until he was appointed chief judge of Damascus, but this lasted only a month, and he was exiled to Tripoli.[144] The local governor looked after him, and he became a judge there. Then Tâj al-Dîn al-Subkî intervened on his behalf with the *amîr* Yalbughâ, and Bahâʾ al-Dîn was permitted to enter Cairo.[145] The year 765 was a prosperous one for al-Subkî; during the course of it he became *qâḍî al-ʿaskar* and *nâʾib* to the chief judge, ʿIzz al-Dîn Ibn Jamâʿa.[146] The next year he stepped up to the chief judgeship. Bahâʾ al-Dîn is described in the sources as being greedy for offices. He certainly became quite successful in attaining them, and his instrument was that of winning the influence of powerful *umarâʾ*, either directly or through his relatives.[147] In a later chapter we shall see how he continued to use this same device, both in and out of office.

In 773 Sultan al-Ashraf Shaʿbân deposed al-Subkî, and

summoned Burhân al-Dîn Ibn Jamâʿa from Jerusalem to replace him. He was, of course, one of the members of this famous family. He had succeeded his father as *khaṭîb* in Jerusalem, and, after a while, became teacher in al-Ṣâliḥiyya there as well.[148] He did not enjoy a high reputation as a scholar, and was often criticized because of his lack of expertise in *fiqh*. Ibn Ḥajar al-ʿAsqalânî alleges that his appointment as chief judge was due to the influence of some *umarâʾ*, but omits any names or further details.[149]

After the death of al-Ashraf Shaʿbân, Badr al-Dîn al-Subkî, Bahâʾ al-Dîn's son, was named to replace Burhân al-Dîn Ibn Jamâʿa. Early in his career he had been a teacher in Damascus as well as *khaṭîb* of the Umayyad mosque. When his father went to Egypt, he went with him and became his *nâʾib*. He returned to Damascus briefly in 778 to be deputy judge to his brother, but very soon afterward returned to Cairo, where he taught *ḥadîth*, and followed his father as a teacher of *fiqh* at al-Shâfiʿiyya.[150] His appointment to the chief judgeship in 779 was accomplished by bribery. This apparently earned him a bad reputation and seems to have been instrumental in his downfall and the subsequent return of Burhân al-Dîn Ibn Jamâʿa to office after less than two years.[151]

The Shâfiʿî *madhhab* was the favored one of the Mamlûk empire, and its chief judge enjoyed the most privilege, power, and probably income. It is either because of this superior status or because of the greater interest of the historians and biographers that we are supplied with so many details of the intrigues and general circumstances surrounding the appointments of the Shâfiʿî chief judges. The friendship between the candidates for the judgeship and the Mamlûk *umarâʾ* and even sultans is obvious. The role of nepotism, as evidenced by the families of Ibn Jamâʿa, Ibn Bint al-Aʿazz, and al-Subkî, is also present, but this manifested itself not so much in the appointment to one post or another of a son by his father, for example, as in the introduction of later generations to court circles and the inevitable establishment of friendhsips and contacts. The appointment of ʿIzz al-Dîn Ibn Jamâʿa, the son of a previous chief judge, for instance, was due to the fondness which the sultan felt for him and had grown over the many years when his father had been chief judge of Cairo. Although all these Shâfiʿî judges had some sort of qualifications as teachers, jurists, judges, or bureaucrats, it seems that the only one who was certainly appointed because of his excellent reputation was Ibn Daqîq al-ʿÎd. Otherwise, political maneuvering and favoritism, especially patronage by some member of the Mamlûk oligarchy, as well as nepotism, were the factors behind the appointment of the Shâfiʿî chief judge.

Having examined the appointments of the chief judges in some detail, it is important now to try to gain an overview of the reasons which contributed to their appointments. At this time we shall not be concerned with the appointments of 663, since they were a special case, nor with an individual's appointment to the chief judgeship in Cairo after the initial one, because, having held this office once before, or even more often than that, the judge would be considered in a different light than someone who had never held it previously. Although some factors are better represented in one *madhhab* than in another, no factor or theme is unique to any one school of law. We must remember that the chief judgeship was not an elected office in the modern sense. On the contrary, the *qâḍî al-quḍât* was chosen by the sultan, often at the suggestion of one or more persons whose opinion(s) he respected. It is the factors behind these nominations which interest us.

As mentioned earlier, there are four basic themes lying behind the nomination and subsequent appointment of a man to the chief judgeship: nepotism, merit, *nâ᾿ib* succession and patronage. In quite a few cases, especially among the Ḥanafîs, it has not been possible to find any special reason why a particular man was nominated. Nevertheless, the factors mentioned are certainly present, sometimes combined with one another, and they are important in helping us understand these appointments.

Several of the judges had served as deputies to their predecessors and then been promoted to the full chief judgeship. Each judge usually had more than one deputy (see below, chapter IV), and these deputies were undoubtedly the best informed about the judicial activities and administration. Therefore, it is not surprising to se them rising to the chief judgeship when an opening occurred. Thus Taqî al-Dîn al-Akhnâ᾿î (M-5),[152] Jamâl al-Dîn Ibn Khayr al-Anṣârî (M-11), Bahâ᾿ al-Dîn al-Subkî (Sh-15), Jamâl al-Dîn al-Zarʿî (Sh-11), and Muʿizz al-Dîn al-Khaṭîbî (Hf-2) had served as deputies to their predecessors. *Nâ᾿ib* succession was sometimes combined with nepotism. In such cases a chief judge would appoint a close relative as his deputy, and at the former's death the deputy would become chief judge. ʿIzz al-Dîn Ibn ʿAwaḍ (Hb-2) was the son-in-law and deputy of his predecessor, Shams al-Dîn Ibn al-ʿImâd (Hb-1), and Nâşir al-Dîn Naşr Allâh (Hb-7) had the same relationship to Muwaffaq al-Dîn al-Maqdisî (Hb-6). A slightly different relationship existed among the Mâlikîs. Tâj al-Dîn al-Akhnâʾî (M-6) was the nephew as well as deputy of Taqî al-Dîn al-Akhnâʾî (M-5). Tâj al-Dîn was followed by his brother Burhân al-Dîn (M-8). Jamâl al-Dîn Ibn al-Turkumânî (Hf-11) had probably been his father's *nâʾib* (Hf-10).

Nepotism took other forms as well. The last member of the al-Akhnâʾî family to hold the Mâlikî chief judgeship was Badr al-Dîn al-Akhnâʾî (M-9). He was the nephew of his predecessor, Burhân al-Dîn (M-8), but there is no evidence that he had served as his deputy. It may well be that his good family name helped him gain this post, or he had managed to become well known in court circles because of the other influential members of his family. We have noted earlier D. Sourdel's comments on "fils de vizirs" having been chosen as *wazîr* in preference to others. This observation holds some validity for the progeny and relatives of the chief judges of this era as well. The reasons for their appointments are not always clear, but certain family names do keep appearing, and bearing one of these names seems to have been a source of some influence. Such people were chosen even many years after the founder of the dynasty or other members of the family had left office. Taqî al-Dîn Ibn ʿAwaḍ (Hb-5) was the son of ʿIzz al-Dîn (Hb-2) and the maternal grandson of Ibn al-ʿImâd (Hb-1). Şadr al-Dîn Ibn al-Turkumânî (Hf-13) had been *nâʾib* to his father (Hf-11), but not to his own predecessor, Sirâj al-Dîn al-Hindî (Hf-12). Şadr al-Dîn (Sh-4) and Taqî al-Dîn (Sh-8) were the sons of Tâj al-Dîn Ibn Bint al-Aʿazz

(Sh-1), and Burhân al-Dîn Ibn Jamâʿa (Sh-16) was the grandson of one judge (Sh-9) and the nephew of another (Sh-13). Thus, even in a delayed form, nepotism was a significant factor.

Although every judge had to be nominated for office by someone, the sources often indicate a special relationship or friendship between the nominator and the nominee. In the case of ʿIzz al-Dîn Ibn Jamâʿa (Sh-13) it was the sultan himself who urged his nomination after a group of judges and *fuqahâʾ* had recommended someone else. He said he had been fond of ʿIzz al-Dîn since the days of his father, Badr al-Dîn (Sh-9). This is a good example of how nepotism in its broadest interpretation worked, and we can see how ʿIzz al-Dîn had won the friendship of the sultan because his father's post as chief judge had brought the son into court circles. This nomination is considered an example of patronage, because of the stated fondness of the sultan for this member of the Ibn Jamâʿa family, but there is an element of nepotism here as well. This same sultan, al-Malik al-Nâṣir Muḥammad, had chosen Jalâl al-Dîn al-Qazwînî (Sh-12) as chief judge because of an earlier friendship the sultan had established with him. In a different vein, we know that Muḥyî al-Dîn Ibn ʿAyn al-Dawla (Sh-3) had been the protégé of the *wazîr* Ibn Ḥannâʾ, and Badr al-Dîn Ibn Jamâʿa (Sh-9) owed his first appointment to the chief judgeship to his old friendship with the *wazîr* Ibn Salʿûs. Bahâʾ al-Dîn Ibn ʿAqîl (Sh-14) gained the office with the help of the *amîr* Ṣarghitmish, but his term ended when the *amîr* was jailed. Ḥusâm al-Dîn al-Rûmî (Hf-4) was a close friend of the Sultan Lâjîn, and he also lost his post when the sultan was assassinated. Jalâl al-Dîn Jâr Allâh (Hf-17) was the son-in-law of Sirâj al-Dîn al-Hindî (Sh-12), but his success as personal physician to the sultan won him the chief judgeship in 778. The Mâlikî ʿAlam al-Dîn al-Bisâṭî (M-10) had been the *nâʾib* of his two predecessors, but it was only after he had solicited the help of the *amîr* Qaraṭây that he became chief judge. Finally, Nûr al-Dîn al-Sakhâwî won his appointment with the help of the *amîr* Shaykhû.

There are a few miscellaneous cases which might be described as political or due to expediency. Sirâj al-Dîn al-Râzî (Hf-6) was appointed chief judge of Fusṭâṭ after he had agreed to the transfer of some *awqâf* lands which Shams al-Dîn Ibn Ḥarîrî (Hf-5) had refused to sanction, and Burhân al-Dîn al-Sinjârî (Sh-7) was put in office almost certainly as a counterweight to Taqî al-Dîn Ibn Bint al-Aʿazz (Sh-8). Finally, Badr al-Dîn al-Subkî (Sh-17) secured his appointment by bribery.

A few of the judges were appointed clearly because of their superior qualification. Ibn Daqîq al-ʿÎd (Sh-10) was one such popular choice. Zayn al-Dîn Ibn Makhlûf (M-4) was chosen by Sultan Qalâʾûn because of this judge's strict support for the law when he had refused to be intimidated by the then *amîr* Qalâʾûn. When he became sultan, Qalâʾûn remembered him, and eventually appointed Ibn Makhlûf chief judge. Finally, Muwaffaq al-Dîn al-Maqdisî (Hb-6) was chosen as the most qualified Ḥanbalî following the scandal of 738.

The remaining judges do not lend themselves easily to categorizing, and usually there is not even a hint as to why they were appointed. This is certainly true for the appointments of Saʿd al-Dîn al-Ḥârithî (Hb-4), Nafîs al-Dîn Ibn Shukr (M-2), Taqî al-Dîn Ibn Shâs (M-3), Wajîh al-Dîn al-Bahnasî (Sh-5), Shihâb al-Dîn Ibn al-Khuwayyî (Sh-6), and Zayn al-Dîn al-Bisṭâmî (Hf-9).

In other cases, there is some information, but nothing definite enough to be very helpful. Sharaf al-Dîn al-Ḩarrânî (Hb-3) was *nâẓir al-khizâna al-sulṭâniyya* and continued to hold that office when he was appointed chief judge. Holding the first office may have helped him gain the second, but the sources do not indicate this. Similarly, we know that Sirâj al-Dîn al-Hindî (Hf-12) was friendly with the *umarâʾ*, as was ʿAlâʾ al-Dîn Ibn al-Turkumânî (Hf-10), prior to their appointments, but there is no direct evidence that this finally propelled them into the chief judgeship, although the evidence does point to these associations as being helpful. Ḩusâm al-Dîn al-Ghûrî (Hf-8) was probably in the right place at the right time, and as a newcomer was an attractive choice after the scandal of 738. Taqî al-Dîn Ibn Razîn (Sh-2) may have been appointed to offset the influence of Ibn Ḩannâʾ's protégé, Ibn ʿAyn al-Dawla (Sh-3), but the sources give no definite reason for his appointment. Shams al-Dîn al-Sarûjî (Hf-3) and Ibn al-Ḩarîrî (Hf-5) had previous experience as chief judges of Damascus, and Ibn ʿAbd al-Ḩaqq (Hf-7) had recommended Ibn al-Ḩarîrî for the chief judgeship of Cairo. Perhaps Ibn al-Ḩarîrî also recommended Ibn ʿAbd al-Ḩaqq as his own successor in Cairo. Najm al-Dîn (Hf-14) and Şadr al-Dîn Ibn Abî al-ʿIzz (Hf-15) and Sharaf al-Dîn Ibn Manşûr (Hf-16) all served for short terms after the death of Şadr al-Dîn Ibn al-Turkumânî. Ibn Manşûr was originally nominated by Burhân al-Dîn Ibn Jamâʿa, but was not immediately appointed, and Najm al-Dîn Ibn Abî al-ʿIzz's name was raised in a discussion at the court, but these circumstances do not help very much in our attempt at classification. Finally, Şadr al-Dîn Ibn Manşûr (Hf-18) was the brother of Sharaf al-Dîn (Hf-16), but since the latter served a very short term some four years before the appointment of the former and then returned to Damascus, nepotism does not seem to have been a strong factor.

In conclusion, if we ignore those cases where the reason for nomination and appointment is unknown or uncertain, we find that patronage was the main reason for an appointment to the chief judgeship, with nepotism second (see chart I). The succession of a *nâʾib* to the full chief judgeship was also significant. *Nâʾib* succession on its own was about as important a factor as nepotism. In a number of cases these two factors were combined; for example when a son-in-law was deputy judge to his father-in-law and then followed him as chief judge. If we combine the two factors of "*nâʾib* succession" and "*nâʾib* succession plus nepotism", we can see that it was very helpful for a candidate for the chief judgeship to have been a deputy judge. The few miscellaneous cases, which include bribery and cooperation with the sultan's plans, do not count for much, and neither does merit on its own. The number of unknown or uncertain cases is considerable, but many of these might have lent themselves to categorization if just a little more information had been available, or, perhaps, a more liberal interpretation of the evidence had been adopted. In short, the best way to become chief judge was to be a deputy judge when a vacancy for the chief judgeship occurred, or become friends with some important Mamlûk or official, because these were the most important considerations in having one's name proposed for the chief judgeship.

Chart I

Reasons for Appointments

Nepotism	Nâʾib Succession Plus Nepotism	Nâʾib Succession	Patronage	Merit	Misc.	Unknown
Hb-5	Hb-2	M-5	M-7	Hb-6	Hf-6	Hb-4
M-9	Hb-7	M-11	M-10	M-4	Sh-7	Hb-3
Hf-13	M-6	Hf-2	Hf-4	Sh-10	Sh-17	M-2
Sh-4	M-8	Sh-15	Hf-17			M-3
Sh-8	Hf-11	Sh-11	Sh-3			Hf-3
Sh-16			Sh-9			Hf-5
			Sh-12			Hf-7
			Sh-14			Hf-8
			Sh-13			Hf-9
						Hf-10
						Hf-14
						Hf-15
						Hf-16
						Hf-18
						Hf-12
						Sh-2
						Sh-5
						Sh-6
Total						
6	5	5	9	3	3	18

ENDNOTES

[1]Laoust, "Hanbalisme," p. 52.

[2]Al-ʿAynî, BN 1543, fol. 225b; Ibn Kathîr, XIII, 277.

[3]Laoust, "Hanbalisme," p. 53

[4]Rafʿ MS, fol. 103b; Wâfî, II, 10; al-Yûnînî, III, 280. On Ibn Ḥannâ (Bahâʾ al-Dîn ʿAlî ibn Muḥammad; d. 677), see Shadharât, V, 358; Ibn al-Suqâʿî, no. 148.

[5]This was al-Ẓâhiriyya, located in al-Qâhira, Bayn al-Qaṣrayn, which was completed in 662. Shâfiʿî and Ḥanafî *fiqh*, as well as *ḥadîth* and Quranic recitation were taught there (Khiṭaṭ, II, 378-79).

[6]Sadeque, Baybars, p. 199; Ibn ʿAbd al-Ẓâhir, al-Rawḍ al-zâhir, p. 183; Sulûk, I, 503.

[7]Rafʿ MS, fol. 88b. We know that he was Ibn al-ʿImâd's son-in-law, because Ibn al-ʿImâd is described as Taqî al-Dîn ibn ʿIzz al-Dîn Ibn ʿAwaḍ's maternal grandfather (al-ʿAynî, Ahmet III 2912/4, fol. 295a).

[8]Rafʿ MS, fol. 88b. This source claims that Ibn ʿAwaḍ was replaced by his successor-to-be, Sharaf al-Dîn al-Ḥarrânî, in 678-79, then returned to office until his death in 696. This allegation occurs only in Ibn ʿAwaḍ's biography here, and nowhere else, not even in al-Ḥarrânî's biography in the same source (cf. Rafʿ, II, 365). It seems that Ibn Ḥajar has made a mistake here, and simply assumed that the Ḥanbalî chief judge was deposed, because the other three chief judges were deposed briefly at this time (cf. Sulûk, I, 657; al-ʿAynî, BN, fol. 231a; Ibn Kathîr, XIII, 288). Al-Yûnînî records his installation in 679 (IV, 52) noting that the Ḥanafî and Mâlikî judges were returned to office at that time, and the sultan established *(rattaba)* a Ḥanbalî chief judge, ʿIzz al-Dîn Ibn ʿAwaḍ, along with them. His avoidance of the word "returned" is significant.

[9]Al-Nuwayrî, Leiden Or. 20, fol. 42a. It is strange that this is the only source to mention the change of *madhhab;* not even Ibn Rajab in his Ḥanbalî *ṭabaqa* mentions this (II, 358).

[10]See chapter V, pp. 176ff.

[11]Ibn Rajab, II, 358; Raf⁽, II, 365; Wâfî, BN 2066, fol. 239b. See also Durar, II, 499 and al-ʿAynî, Ahmet III 2912/4, fol. 273b.

[12]Ibn Rajab, II, 358; Laoust, "Hanbalisme," pp. 21, 54. Ḥasan Q. Murad, "Mihan of Ibn Taymiyya: A Narrative Account Based on a Comparative Analysis of the Sources," (unpublished M.A. thesis, McGill University, 1968), p. 93.

[13]Aʿyân, fol. 589a; Durar, V, 116; Rafʿ MS, fol. 133a; Ibn Rajab, II, 364.

[14]Al-ʿAynî, Ahmet III 2912/4, fol. 296b; Sulûk, II, 113, 117.

[15]Ibn al-Bâbâ was a Mongol who had fled to the Mamlûk empire at the beginning of the century, and at that time he was given a number of *iqṭâʿât*. He enjoyed considerable prestige in Mamlûk circles, and his daughter was married to Ibrâhîm, the son of al-Malik al-Nâṣir Muḥammad (Durar, II, 76-77). He was also a supporter of Ibn Taymiyya, and himself a Ḥanbalî (al-ʿAynî, Ahmet III 2912/4, fol. 367b).
The circumstances surrounding the deposition of the three chief judges will be discussed in the appropriate chapter.

[16]Durar, II, 404; Rafʿ, II, 298; Sulûk, II, 443. Al-ʿAynî (Ahmet III, 2911/c34, fols. 65b-66a) indicates the support of the *umarâʾ*.

[17]Durar, II, 404.

[18]Inbâʾ al-ghumr, III, 190; Rafʿ MS, fol. 136a; Durar, V, 163; Shadharât, VI, 343.

[19]D. Sourdel, Le Vizirat ʿAbbâside (Damascus, 1959-60), II, 568.

[20]See especially al-ʿAynî, Ahmet III 2911/c34, fols. 65b-66a.

[21]Ibn Kathîr, XIII, 260; Ibn al-Ṣabûnî, Takmilat, 233-35; Rafʿ MS, fols. 88b-89a; al-Nuwayrî, BN 1578, fol. 46a; Wâfî, Ahmet III 2920/22, fols. 188b-189a; al-Yûnînî, II, 461.

[22]Raf(MS, fol. 130b.

[23]Sulûk, I, 657, 668; al-Yûnînî, IV, 7, 52; al-(Aynî, BN 1543, fol. 231a only notes his deposition.

[24]Here again our primary source is Raf(, and the matter is more confused than the story concerning the Ḥanbalî chief judges, Ibn (Awaḍ and al-Ḥarrânî (see above note 8). Raf((I, 205) says that Taqî al-Dîn Ibn Shâs was chief judge from Dhû al-Ḥijja, 668 to Ramaḍân, 669, was deposed, and did not return to office until 681. The years 668 and 669 should read 678 and 679 to make any sense at all, and thus refer to the short reign of Salâmish. Also, he was appointed in 680, not 681 (Sulûk, I, 704) when Ibn Shukr died (Raf(MS, fol. 130b). Here again Raf(is the only source that mentions this earlier term of office, and in view of the confusion over dates, this claim should be dealt with cautiously.

[25]Al-Nuwayrî, BN 1579, fols. 86b-87a; see also Durar, III, 202; Raf(, II, 405-406.

[26]Raf(MS, fol. 132a.

[27]Durar, IV, 27.

[28]Ibid., p. 28.

[29]Raf(MS, fol. 126a; A(yân, fol. 532b; Durar, V, 12.

[30]Raf(MS, fol. 126a.

[31]Ibn Ṭûlûn, Quḍât dimashq (Damascus, 1956), p. 93.

[32]See chapter V, pp. 179-80.

[33]Sulûk, III, 19, 21.

[34]This was Sayf al-Dîn Shaykhû al-Nâṣirî (d. 758; Durar, II, 293-94; see also Khiṭaṭ, II, 313-14).

[35]Durar, III, 150-51. This was actually a mosque and *khânqâh* complex. It was completed in 756, and the teaching of *fiqh* according to all four schools of law as well as *ḥadîth* and Quranic recitation were established there (Khiṭaṭ, II, 313, 421).

[36]Sulûk, III, 19. There is an error in K.S. Salibi, "Listes chronologiques des grands cadis de l'Egypte sous les Mamelouks," Revue des Etudes Islamiques, XXV (1957) at this point (p. 111). He thinks, although with some reservations, that a certain Taqî al-Dîn Muḥammad Ibn Shâs (Durar, III, 407-408) succeeded al-Sakhâwî. There is little doubt, however, that Tâj al-Dîn al-Akhnâ'î returned to office after al-Sakhâwî's death. In addition to the reference in Sulûk (III, 19), see also the biography of Burhân al-Dîn al-Akhnâ'î (Raf', I, 40), where he is described as having succeeded his brother, Tâj al-Dîn. Ibn Shâs had been a deputy judge only, and had died in 760 (Sulûk, III, 49). Even Ibn Ḥajar (Durar, III, 407) only says that he was a *qâḍî*, not a *qâḍî al-quḍât*. He is mentioned in the poem at the beginning of Raf' (I, 18, note 14), but this really refers to Taqî al-Dîn al-Husayn Ibn Shâs, who was the second Mâlikî chief judge in this study (in office 680-685).

[37]Manhal, I, 130.

[38]Sulûk, III, 19.

[39]Sulûk, III, 60, 73.

[40]Sulûk, III, 73. In Cairo this refers to the controllership of al-Manşûrî hospital (La Syrie, p. LXXX; Popper, Notes, I, 101).

[41]Inbâ' al-ghumr, I, 159.

[42]Raf', I, 41.

[43]Sulûk, III, 191.

[44]Raf', II, 284.

[45]Inbâ' al-ghumr, II, 114.

[46]Raf', II, 284-85; Sulûk, III, 285, 293; Manhal MS, fol. 478b.

[47]Inbâ' al-ghumr, II, 168; Raf', II, 249.

[48]Sulûk, III, 293; Manhal MS, fol. 33a; Inbâ' al-ghumr, I, 198; Raf', II, 249; Durar, II, 243.

[49] Sulûk, III, 443.

[50] Raf‘, II, 342.

[51] The *qâḍî al-‘askar* was responsible for handling judicial cases which arose while the army was on campaign. All but the Ḥanbalîs were allowed to have such a judge in Egypt, and when not travelling with the army, they would attend the sessions of the *dâr al-‘adl*, sitting a rank below the chief judges (La Syrie, p. LXXVII). There was no *qâḍî al-‘askar* in Alexandria (al-Qalqashandî, Ṣubḥ, IV, 63).
According to al-Maqrîzî, the first Ḥanafî to occupy this post in Egypt was ‘Alâ’ al-Dîn ‘Alî ibn al-Atrûsh, who was appointed in 749 (Sulûk, II, 772; for biographical details, see ibid., III, 38).
Concerning al-Adhra‘î, see especially Ibn al-Suqâ‘î, Ṭâlî, no. 115; Wâfî, BN 2065, fol. 67b; al-Lakhnawî, al-Fawâ’id, pp. 80-81. See also al-‘Aynî, BN 1543, fol. 227b; Ibn Ṭûlûn, Quḍât, p. 190; Ibn Kathîr, XIII, 281.

[52] Al-Nu‘aymî, Dâris fî târîkh al-madâris (Damascus, 1948), I, 474, 549.

[53] Al-‘Aynî, BN 1543, fol. 231a; Sulûk, I, 657, 668; al-Yûnînî, IV, 7, 52. See also Wâfî, British Museum MS Add. 23359, vol. 14, n.p.; Ibn Abî al-Wafâ, Jawâhir, II, 201.

[54] Raf‘, I, 50.

[55] Ibid., p. 51; Durar, I, 96-97.

[56] A‘yân, fols. 154b-155a; Raf‘, I, 183-85; Durar, II, 91; al-‘Aynî, Ahmet III 2912/4, fol. 203a; Ibn Ṭûlûn, Quḍât, p. 191.

[57] Durar, IV, 158.

[58] Durar, III, 270, IV, 159; Sulûk, II, 173-74; al-‘Aynî, Ahmet III 2912/4, fol. 317b.

[59] Raf‘, I, 36-7. See also Durar, I, 48; Manhal, I, 108; A‘yân, fols. 11a-b.

[60] Ibn Kathîr, XIV, 142.

[61] He was one of the three chief judges deposed in 738. For details see chapter VI.

[62]Raf(, I, 202; Durar, II, 127.

[63]Sulûk, II, 437; al-(Aynî, Ahmet III 2911/c34, fol. 48b.

[64]Durar, III, 245.

[65]Sulûk, II, 813; see also Raf(, II, 401.

[66]Khiṭaṭ, II, 392.

[67]Sulûk, II, 797; Manhal MS, fol. 422a. Al-Maqrîzî (Sulûk, II, 797) says he was less than thirty years old at the time, but Raf((II, 286) says he was born in 715, which would make him thirty-five years old then.

[68]Sulûk, II, 798; Raf(, II, 286.

[69]Ibn Ḥajar, (Raf(, II, 286) says that he was appointed independently after the death of his father, which implies that he had been a *nâ)ib* previously. Cf. the biography of Tâj al-Dîn al-Akhnâ)î, who is described as having been *nâ)ib* to his uncle (and predecessor), then judge independently (Raf(MS, fol. 126a).

[70]Inbâ) al-ghumr, I, 29.

[71]Ibid.

[72]Inbâ) al-ghumr, I, 30.

[73]Ibid.

[74]Ibid., Durar, III, 230; Raf(MS, fol. 87b. This was Quṭb al-Dîn Muḥammad ibn Abî al-Thanâ), known as al-Hirmâs (694-769; Durar, IV, 33).

[75]Sulûk, III, 44, 48; Inbâ) al-ghumr, I, 30.

[76]This is Shams al-Dîn Muḥammad ibn (Alî Ibn al-Naqqâsh (720-63); Durar, IV, 190-91).

[77]Sulûk, III, 48; Khiṭaṭ, II, 76.

[78]Durar, IV, 33.

[79]Durar, III, 230; Raf‘ MS, fol. 87b.

[80]Raf‘ MS, fols. 113b-114a.

[81]Manhal MS, fol. 659b.

[82]Sulûk, III, 238; Raf‘, I, 90. In Sulûk he is called Ibn Abî al-‘Izz, but Raf‘, quoting al-Maqrîzî, calls him Ibn Manṣûr. I shall call him Ibn Manṣûr; the problem of his genealogy will be discussed in the following chapter.

[83]Sulûk, III, 240.

[84]In Sulûk (ibid.) the *amîr* Nâṣir al-Dîn spoke for the nomination, but Raf‘ (I, 90) says that it was Ṭashtamur.

[85]This is Jalâl al-Dîn Rasûlân ibn Aḥmad ibn Yûsuf al-Tabânî al-Rûmî, a *mudarris* in Cairo. There is no entry for him in Durar, but he is listed in Shadharât (VI, 327-28) as Rislân; see also Sulûk, III, 756-57, and Inbâ’ al-ghumr, III, 187-88. He died in 793.

[86]Sulûk, III, 240; Inbâ’ al-ghumr, I, 93.

[87]This was almost certainly Majd al-Dîn al-Kinânî, who would be made *qâḍî al-‘askar* in 777 (Sulûk, III, 255) and eventually become chief judge in 792 (ibid., III, 723). See also Raf‘, I, 116-19.

[88]Sulûk, III, 240.

[89]Raf‘, I, 90.

[90]Sulûk, III, 253; Inbâ’ al-ghumr, I, 152.

[91]Inbâ’ al-ghumr, I, 153.

[92]Sulûk, III, 255; Raf‘, I, 89-90.

[93]Inbâ’ al-ghumr, I, 191.

[94]Ibid., and II, 38.

[95]Sulûk, III, 398.

[96]Ibid., III, 399.

[97]Raf' MS, fol. 119b.

[98]The office of *wazîr* went through great changes during the Baḥrî period. Theoretically this was the highest civilian post in the bureaucracy and had overall supervision of the finances of the empire. However, during the Baḥrî period it was held by a great assortment of people, including Mamlûks. The office itself was abolished by Sultan al-Malik al-Nâṣir during the first part of the 8th century A.H., and its functions divided among four lower officials. See H. Rabie, The Financial System of Egypt (London, 1972), pp. 138ff.; La Syrie, pp. LXVI-LXIX; Popper, Notes, I, 96.

For summaries of Tâj al-Dîn's career, see al-Nuwayrî, BN 1578, fols. 35b-36b; al-'Aynî, BN 1543, fol. 194a; Wâfî, Ahmet III 2920/19, fols. 141a-142a; Raf', II, 375-83.

[99]See the references to Tâj al-Dîn's life in the previous note.

[100]Wâfî, III, 18; Raf' MS, fol. 108a; al-Asnawî, I, 594; al-Subkî, V, 19.

[101]Raf', II, 301. Salibi ("Listes," p. 82), probably following al-Yûnînî (II, 362), assigns him the *ism* 'Abd al-Qâdir, but it should be 'Abd Allâh; see Raf', II, 301; Sulûk, I 562, 647, 674; al-Asnawî, I, 545; Wâfî, Ahmet III 2920/7, fol. 153a; al-Nuwayrî, BN 1578, fol. 36a.

[102]Wâfî, Ahmet III 2920/7, fol. 153a.

[103]Al-Yûnînî, II, 362; al-Nuwayrî, BN 1579, fol. 36a.

[104]Sulûk, I, 657; al-Yûnînî, IV, 7, 52; Ibn al-Furât, Târîkh, VII, 149. See also al-Nuwayrî, BN 1579, fol 29b; al-'Aynî, BN 1543, fol. 231a.

[105]Raf', II, 374.

[106]Ibid., p. 375; Sulûk, I, 706.

[107]EI-1, III, 110.

[108]EI-2, I, 926.

[109]Ibn Kathîr, XIII, 337; Wâfî, II, 137-39; al-Asnawî, I, 501-502; Raf' MS, pp. 97b-98a; al-Yûnînî, IV, 144-45.

[110]Perhaps this should read *nâẓir al-khizâna*, because in a later list of his offices this one is mentioned, but not that of *nâẓir al-khazâ'in* (Sulûk, I, 773; Raf', II, 327; al-Yûnînî, IV, 320-21). See also chapter V, pp. 178-83.

[111]See references in previous note.

[112]Ibn Ṭûlûn, Quḍât, pp. 78-79; al-Yûnînî, IV, 315; al-Nuwayrî, BN 1579, fol. 63a.

[113]'Alam al-Dîn Sinjâr al-Shujâ'î (Ibn al-Ṣuqâ'î, Tâlî, no. 132).

[114]This was known as al-Nâṣiriyya bi-al-Qarâfa (Khiṭaṭ, II, 400-401).

[115]Raf', I, 221-41; Ibn al-Ṣuqâ'î, Tâlî, no. 105; Manhal MS, fols. 299b-300a; al-Yûnînî, IV, 319-20.

[116]Al-Nuwayrî, BN 1579, fols. 63b-64a; see also Sulûk, I, 734.

[117]Ibn al-Ṣuqâ'î, Tâlî, no. 105.

[118]Sulûk, I, 771.

[119]EI-2, III, 748-49.

[120]Ibid.

[121]Sulûk, I, 771.

[122]Al-'Aynî, Ahmet III 2912/4, fol. 167a.

[123]Al-Asnawî, II, 227, 229.

[124]<u>Wâfî</u>, IV, 193-94.

[125]Al-Asnawî, II, 229.

[126]Al-ʿAynî, Ahmet III 2912/4, fol. 175a.

[127]E.g., <u>Wâfî</u>, IV, 193-209.

[128]<u>Ibid</u>., pp. 193-94.

[129]Ibn Ṭûlûn, <u>Quḍât</u>, p. 80.

[130]<u>Sulûk</u>, I, 809; <u>Durar</u>, III, 367-69.

[131]Ibn Ṭûlûn, <u>Quḍât</u>, p. 81.

[132]Al-Asnawî, I, 386; <u>Durar</u>, III, 367-69. Al-Asnawî and following him Ibn Taghrî Birdî (<u>Manhal</u> MS, fol. 630b) claim that all the judges, except the Mâlikî, were deposed at this time as well. <u>Rafʿ</u> (II, 250) says that all the judges were deposed and replaced by their *nuwwâb*, but this story is not confirmed by any other source and should be rejected.

[133]<u>Rafʿ</u> MS, fol. 105a.

[134]<u>Durar</u>, II, 256; <u>Rafʿ</u>, II, 251; <u>Aʿyân</u>, fol. 201b.

[135]<u>Sulûk</u>, II, 30; <u>Wâfî</u>, III, 242.

[136]Al-ʿAynî, Ahmet III 2912/4, fol. 352b; see also <u>Sulûk</u>, II, 254.

[137]Al-Nuwayrî, Leiden Or. 19b, fol. 120b.

[138]Ibn Kathîr, XIV, 185; al-Asnawî, II, 330; <u>Sulûk</u>, II, 439-42; al-ʿAynî, Ahmet III 2911/c34, fols. 61a ff.

[139]Shams al-Dîn Muḥammad ibn Aḥmad ibn ʿAdlân (<u>Durar</u>, III, 423-24).

[140]<u>Sulûk</u>, II, 442; al-ʿAynî, Ahmet III 2911/c34, fols. 64a-65a.

[141] Raf‘, II, 285; Durar, II, 372; see also al-Asnawî, II, 240.

[142] Sulûk, III, 99.

[143] Inbâ’ al-ghumr, I, 184.

[144] Durar, IV, 110.

[145] Inbâ’ al-ghumr, I, 185.

[146] Sulûk, III, 91-92.

[147] Inbâ’ al-ghumr, I, 185.

[148] Durar, I, 39; Raf‘, I, 29-31.

[149] Raf‘, I, 31.

[150] See chapter V, note 58.

[151] Inbâ’ al-ghumr, IV, 323-24; al-Sakhâwî, al-Ḍaw’ al-lâmi‘, (Cairo, 1934-36), IX, 88-89.

[152] These notations refer to the individual judge's entry on the list of judges by *madhhab* in this chapter. M is Mâlikî, Hb is Ḥanbalî, Hf is Ḥanafî, and Sh is Shâfi‘î. M-5, therefore, refers to the fifth name in the list of Mâlikî chief judges where the dates of the individual's term of office are also to be found.

CHAPTER III

Social and Geographic Origins of the Chief Judges

In the previous chapter we discussed the importance of nepotism as a factor in the appointments of the chief judges. The present chapter is a more detailed study of the family relationships of these judges, and is especially concerned with their social as well as geographic origins. Some attempt will also be made to discuss the judges' brothers, sons, sons-in-law, etc. in order to compose a more complete picture of their extended families. Hopefully, this will allow us to determine certain trends as regards the familial and geographic backgrounds of the chief judges of the Baḥrî period.

Ḥanbalîs

The first Ḥanbalî chief judge, Shams al-Dîn Ibn al-ʿImâd (in office 663-670), was born in Damascus, the son of the Ḥanbalî *ʿâlim*, ʿImâd al-Dîn Ibrâhîm ibn ʿAbd al-Wâḥid.[1] Shams al-Dîn studied both in Damascus and Baghdad, where he married.[2] We do not know exactly when he came to Egypt, but it was probably no later than the year 646, when he was about forty-three years old.[3] Shams al-Dîn came from distinguished Damascene Ḥanbalî stock, and this may have been some help to him in furthering his career. However, his father died in 614,[4] before Shams al-Dîn had gone to Cairo. His paternal uncle, al-Ḥâfiẓ ʿAbd al-Ghanî, had come to Egypt from Damascus late in life, and although he was quite a famous *faqîh,* he died in 600, three years before Shams al-Dîn was born.[5] Shams al-Dîn seems to have been the last of this family to have achieved any fame. His brother was an itinerant scholar who suffered poverty[6] and his son was only an *imâm* at a mosque and several *madâris.*[7]

Shams al-Dîn's successor, ʿIzz al-Dîn ʿUmar ibn ʿAwaḍ (in office 678-696), is not as well documented a figure. The fact that he carried the *nisba* al-Maqdisî does not necessarily mean that he himself was born in Jerusalem, as Salibi alleges.[8] We do know that both he and his brother studied *fiqh* with his predecessor, Ibn al-ʿImâd, and that ʿIzz al-Dîn eventually became his *nâʾib,* while his brother Muḥammad became a *muḥtasib* in Syria.[9] More important, however, is that ʿIzz al-Dîn married Ibn al-ʿImâd's daughter, and was thus his predecessor's son-in-law.[10] He was also the father of the future Ḥanbalî chief judge, Taqî al-Dîn Aḥmad Ibn ʿAwaḍ (in office 712-738).

The next judge, Sharaf al-Dîn al-Ḥarrânî (in office 696-709), was indeed born in Ḥarrân in northeastern Syria, where his great grandfather had been a *qâḍî.*[11] He studied in Damascus,[12] Ḥamâ, and finally Cairo.[13] His successor, Saʿd al-Dîn al-Ḥârithî (in office 709-11) is unique not only because his term of office was shorter than that of any other Ḥanbalî judge, but also because his father was a merchant.[14] Saʿd al-Dîn was born near Baghdad, and only later did he come to live in Cairo.[15]

Taqî al-Dîn Ibn ʿAwaḍ (in office 712-738), the son of ʿIzz

al-Dîn, who had been judge earlier, seems to be the first native born Egyptian of the Ḥanbalî judges. He was born in 662.[16] His father was carrying out the functions of the Ḥanbalî chief judge after Ibn al-ʿImâd was deposed in 670, and had studied with him and been his *nâʾib* prior to that,[17] perhaps since the establishment of the four judgeships in 663. This comes very close to placing the father in Egypt at the time of Taqî al-Dîn's birth; close enough to make it almost certain that he was born in Egypt. Taqî al-Dîn's son, Ṣadr al-Dîn Muḥammad,[18] was a disgrace, and Ibn Ḥajar blames Ṣadr al-Dîn's illegal manipulations of *awqâf*[19] and his devotion to the keeping of (race?) horses as the cause of his father's deposition from office.[20] Although al-ʿAynî does not blame the son for his father's deposition,[21] Ṣadr al-Dîn seems to have been an unsavoury character. Oddly enough, he also taught Ḥanbalî *fiqh* at a number of *madâris*.[22]

Although the birthplace of Muwaffaq al-Dîn al-Maqdisî (in office 738-769) is never explicitly stated, it may be that he was born outside Egypt. He travelled a great deal in the course of his studies, stopping in Damascus, Egypt, and Mecca, and only after he became famous did he move *(taḥawwala)* to Cairo.[23] I suspect that if he had been born in Egypt or Cairo then the sources would have spoken about his return, if in fact they did know where he was born. In any case, he is quite important for his relationship to those who came later. He was the father-in-law of his successor, Naṣr Allâh,[24] and the maternal grandfather of Naṣr Allâh's son, Aḥmad, who would also become a chief judge, but in the Burjî period.[25] His son-in-law, Naṣr Allâh (in office 769-795), was apparently born outside Egypt, but grew up *(nasha'a)* in Cairo.[26] In one source, he is assigned the *nisba* al-Ḫijâwî, or in a variant reading, al-Ḫijârî, and this is said to be his place of origin *(al-aşl)*.[27] Although there is an al-Ḫijârâ in Spain,[28] it is doubtful this is the place, since a Ḫanbalî presence was virtually unknown there. It is more likely that this should read al-Ḫijâzî, but it still remains an open question. The fact that the sources say that he grew up in Cairo is an almost certain indication that he was not born there. In any case, his son succeeded him as chief judge, and his son in turn followed him, but all this was in the Burjî period and cannot concern us here.[29]

The origins, geographic and social, of the Ḫanbalî judges are mixed and sometimes cloudy. Shams al-Dîn Ibn ʿAwad and Sharaf al-Dîn al-Ḫarrânî were definitely born outside Egypt, within Greater Syria, while Taqî al-Dîn Ibn ʿAwaḑ can almost certainly be described as having been born in Cairo, where his father was employed at the time of his birth. Saʿd al-Dîn al-Ḫârithî and Naşr Allâh were probably born outside Cairo, but grew up there. The birthplaces of the others are not known. When we look at fathers' occupations, the situation is not much better. Two were the sons of judges and one the son of a merchant; the rest are unknown. It is interesting that we can place or lean towards placing the origins of so many of these judges outside Egypt. On the one hand, Cairo was the capital of the empire, where an ambitious man could achieve the greatest success; but on the other hand, there were probably more Ḫanbalîs outside Egypt than inside it, and, as we have seen, the Ḫanbalîs enjoyed very long terms in office, a possible indication of the lack of competition for these posts. The failure to reappoint a

Ḫanbalî chief judge immediately after the deposition of Ibn al-ʿImâd is another indication that the Ḫanbalîs were a small group and not in any special need of a chief judge. Nepotism was a significant factor among the Ḫanbalîs of this period, and, as we have mentioned earlier, the Ḫanbalî chief judgeship was almost dominated by the families of Ibn al-ʿImâd--Ibn ʿAwaḍ and al-Maqdisî--Naṣr Allâh.

Table A

Ibn al-ʿImâd--Ibn ʿAwaḍ

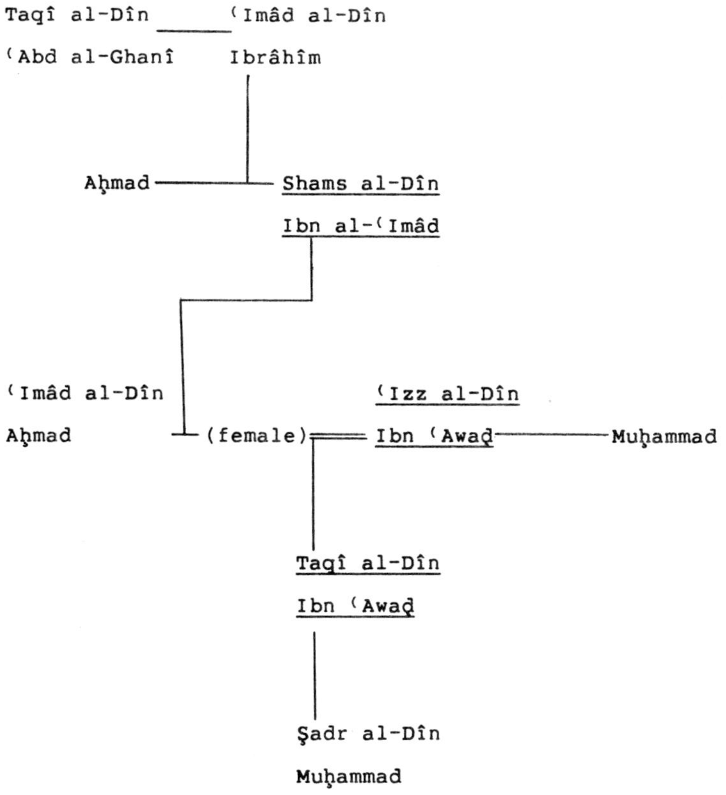

N.B. An underlined name indicates a chief judge.
A line between two names indicates a blood relationship.
Double parallel lines between two names indicate a marital relationship.

Table B

Al-Maqdisî--Naşr Allâh

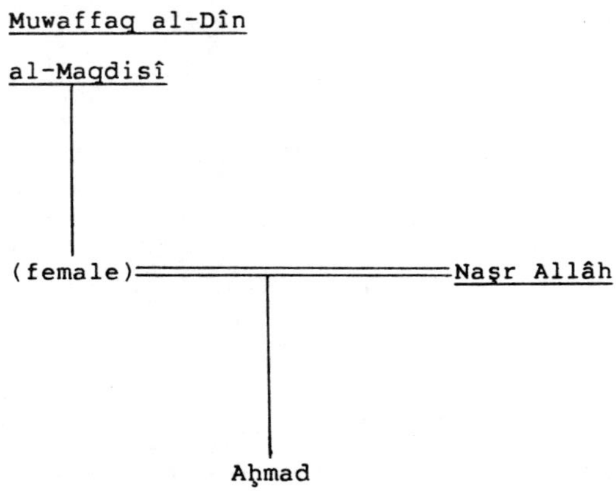

Mâlikîs

The Mâlikî chief judges of the Baḫrî period fall into two groups; those who were members of the al-Akhnâ'î family and those who were not. Neither group is very well documented as regards place of birth, although individuals of proven Egyptian origin are unusually well represented. Similarly, family backgrounds are too often lacking. This comparatively poor documentation is probably due both to the scarcity of Mâlikî biographical dictionaries, and their concern for the notables of the Maghrib at the expense of those of Egypt and Syria, as well as the general lack of interest in the Mâlikî chief judges among the historians and biographers in general. Al-Şafadî's biography of Ibn Makhlûf has been mentioned in chapter I. The fact that many of the Mâlikî judges whose birthplaces we do know came from small towns further complicates the problem of tracing their origins. The lack of interest in rural areas is a notorious feature of Arabic historiography.

Those Mâlikî judges who were not members of the al-Akhnâ'î family form the larger group. Of these, the origins and family backgrounds of Nafîs al-Dîn Ibn Shukr (in office 669-680), Taqî al-Dîn Ibn Shâs (in office 680-685), and Nûr al-Dîn al-Sakhâwî (in office for a short whle in 756) remain a mystery. The others in this group were all native Egyptians, but not Cairenes. Sharaf al-Dîn al-Subkî (in office 663-669) was born in a village called al-Şâliḫiyya in the district of al-Qalyûbiyya (Lower Egypt)[30] and Ibn Makhlûf (in office 685-718) was born in al-Nuwayra, one of the districts of al-Bahnasa in Upper Egypt.[31] We know that Ibn Makhlûf had a brother, Taqî al-Dîn Nâhid, who died in 732,[32] but nothing beyond these meagre facts. He also had a son, Muḥyî al-Dîn Muḥammad, who had been his father's *nâʾib* and was supposed to succeed him as chief judge, but the son died in 711, some seven years before his father.[33] ʿAlam al-Dîn al-Bisâṭî (in office 778-779, 779-783) was actually born in Bisâṭ, a village in the Gharbiyya of Lower Egypt. His father and uncle had settled there prior to ʿAlam al-Dîn's birth. His father died when he was still quite young, and he was raised by his uncle. Al-Bisâṭî's grandfather had a *zâwiya* there, which is probably why the two men came to that town.[34] Jamâl al-Dîn Ibn Khayr al-Anṣârî (in office 783-786) was born and raised in Alexandria. His father was probably a Mâlikî *ʿâlim* there, because we know that Jamâl al-Dîn studied *fiqh* with his father.[35]

The family of al-Akhnâʾî seems to have originated in Egypt as well. Although we do not know the birthplace of Taqî al-Dîn al-Akhnâʾî (in office 718-750), we do know that his brother ʿAlam al-Dîn Muḥammad, who was his junior by about four years, was born in Cairo. This Shâfiʿî brother, ʿAlam al-Dîn, went on to become judge of Alexandria and chief judge of Damascus.[36] More interestingly, it was ʿAlam al-Dîn's progeny which would keep the Mâlikî chief judgeship to itself in future years. Tâj al-Dîn al-Akhnâʾî (in office 750-763) was probably born in Egypt, since there is no evidence that his father, ʿAlam al-Dîn, left Egypt prior to his appointment as chief judge of Damascus. His brother Burhân al-Dîn (in office 763-777) was certainly born in Cairo.[37] The last of the three sons, Kamâl al-Dîn Aḥmad, did not become a chief judge, only a *qâḍî al-ʿaskar* and *nâẓir al-khizâna*,[38] but his son, Badr al-Dîn (in office 777-778;779), did manage to become a Mâlikî chief judge. Kamâl al-Dîn Aḥmad apparently remained a Shâfiʿî, and raised his son in this *madhhab,* although the son finally joined the rest of his family and became a Mâlikî as well.[39] He was probably Egyptian by birth also, since the family seems to have been well entrenched in Cairo by this time.

In short, the Mâlikî chief judges were generally native Egyptians, though not Cairenes, of apparently humble origins, with an important element being converts from the Shâfiʿî *madhhab.* The family of al-Akhnâʾî managed to keep the Mâlikî chief judgeship to themselves for many years, in spite of the fact that they were all originally Shâfiʿîs. What is also quite interesting about this family is that the judgeship was not passed from father to son, but rather from uncle to nephew or from brother to brother. Ibn Makhlûf's son was destined to follow his father as chief judge, and would have established another family of Mâlikî judges, had he not predeceased his father. Finally, the practice of passing on the judgeship to a son-in-law is entirely lacking in the history of the Mâlikî chief judges.

Table C

Al-Akhnâʾî

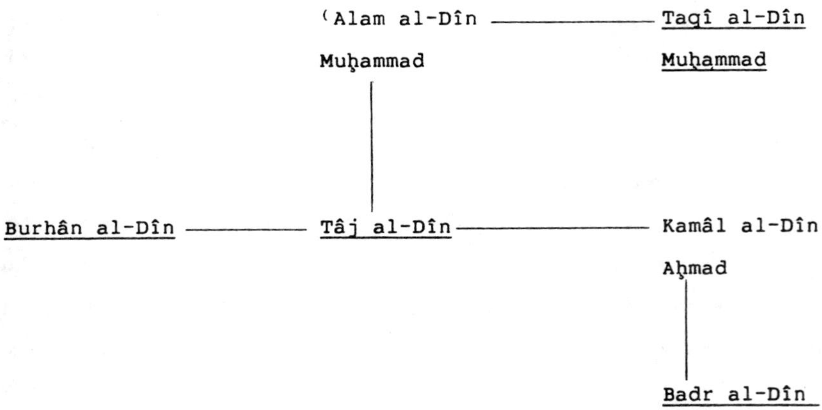

Ḥanafîs

The social and geographic origins of the Ḥanafî judges are rather uniform. Most of the Ḥanafî judges came to Egypt from Damascus, and they were in fact largely native Damascenes. The presence of important families contributing a number of candidates to fill the post of chief judge is quite apparent as well as the presence of sons-in-law eventually succeeding their fathers-in-law to the chief judgeship. On the other hand, some of the Ḥanafî chief judges came from an unknown or more "exotic" milieu and did not always leave the same sort of lasting impression. A possible example of this last facet is Mu'izz al-Dîn al-Khaṭîbî (in office 677-692), whose ancestry may go back to the town of Arzankan in Asia Minor, as the *nisba* which al-Maqrîzî assigns him would indicate, but this evidence is hardly decisive, and his origins must remain in doubt.[40] The fact that the leading Syrian biographers (al-Dhahabî in his Târîkh al-islâm, al-Nu'aymî, and Ibn Ṭûlûn) as well as Ibn Kathîr in the obituary section of his al-Bidâya exclude him would tend to indicate that he never held a post in Damascus and probably never lived there, but we cannot be more definite than this. A better documented example is that of Ḥusâm al-Dîn al-Ghûrî (in office 738-742), who came from Baghdad, and returned there after a term of only a few years as chief judge.[41] He had a short but stormy career in Egypt, but we know nothing of his ancestry or his progeny. A somewhat similar case is that of Sirâj al-Dîn al-Hindî (in office 769-773), a native of India, who left his home and made a very successful career for himself in Egypt.[42] Al-Hindî was the father-in-law of Jalâl al-Dîn Jâr Allâh (in office 778-782), who had originally come to Egypt during al-Hindî's term of office as chief judge, married his daughter, and became his *nâ᾿ib.* We cannot be sure of his exact place of birth, but Ibn Ḥajar does say that he came from the East, which probably means Iran or India.[43]

Another judge about whose background we are not very well informed is Shams al-Dîn al-Sarûjî (in office 692-696; 698-710). He was born in Thawnah, a small town in the area of Sarûj in northeastern Syria, where he also grew up.[44] He was originally a Ḥanbalî, and later became a Ḥanafî.[45] This conversion may explain why neither the Ḥanbalî nor Ḥanafî *ṭabaqât* supply any information about his family background, but, of course, the fact that he was from a small town in a remote area is probably a better explanation of this lack of documentation. On the other hand, like Sirâj al-Dîn al-Hindî, he was the father-in-law of a future judge, Sirâj al-Dîn al-Râzî, who became judge of Fusṭâṭ for only sixty-two days in 717 when Shams al-Dîn Ibn al-Ḥarîrî (in office 710-728) was temporarily deprived of its jurisdiction after a dispute with the sultan. Al-Râzî, in spite of his *nisba,* is one of the rare examples of a native born Egyptian who became a Ḥanafî chief judge. He was born in Fusṭâṭ, the son of Shihâb al-Dîn Maḥmûd, a *madrasa* professor.[46] Sirâj al-Dîn's son, Zayn al-Dîn Muḥammad, would establish a career for himself in Damascus as a *muftî.*[47] Shams al-Dîn al-Sarûjî married off another daughter to Kamâl al-Dîn ʿAbd al-Raḥman ibn Abî Bakr,[48] who, in turn, was the father of Zayn al-Dîn al-Bistâmî, the Ḥanafî chief judge of Cairo from 742 to 748. Zayn al-Dîn was probably a native Egyptian, since his father is described as a resident *(nazîl)* of al-Qâhira.[49]

Only one of the judges can definitely be placed as having originated in Rûm: Ḥusâm al-Dîn al-Rûmî (in office 696-698). He was born in Aq Sarâ,[50] and was judge of Malaṭya[51] for more than twenty years, before fleeing from there to Damascus out of fear of the Mongol invasion.[52] His father had also been a chief judge,[53] apparently in Rûm, and his own son Jalâl al-Dîn would become chief judge of Damascus after his father left for Egypt in 696, as well as later.[54]

Ṣadr al-Dîn al-Adhraʿî (in office 663-677) was, as his *nisba* indicates, from the town of Adhriʿât in present day Jordan; in Mamlûk times this town was part of the district of Damascus.[55] We do not have any information about his father, probably because Ṣadr al-Dîn was from such a remote area. Ṣadr al-Dîn himself achieved a considerable status in Damascus, and when he left to take up a judicial appointment in Egypt, he passed his teaching posts to his two sons, Taqî al-Dîn Aḥmad[56] and Shams al-Dîn Muḥammad.[57] The latter's son and grandson also became professors at *madâris* in Damascus.[58] Ṣadr al-Dîn was probably a distant ancestor of two other Ḥanafî chief judges of Cairo, since there are some similarities in the extended names. They would hold short terms about one hundred years after Ṣadr al-Dîn al-Adhraʿî had left office. The first of them, Najm al-Dîn Ibn Abî al-ʿIzz or Ibn al-Kishk (in office for a few months in 777) would also eventually attain the chief judgeship of Damascus.[59] His first cousin, Ṣadr al-Dîn Ibn Abî al-ʿIzz succeeded him, but also lasted only a few months before returning to Damascus.[60] Ṣadr al-Dîn grew up in Damascus, but we do not know if he was born there.[61]

Ṣadr al-Dîn Ibn Manṣûr (in office 782-786) was born in

Damascus.[62] He was the younger brother of Sharaf al-Dîn Ibn Manşûr (in office 777-778), but only by one year,[63] and although we cannot be certain of Sharaf al-Dîn's birthplace, it is reasonable to assume that he was also born in Damascus. They were the sons of ʿAlâʾ al-Dîn ʿAlî Ibn Manşûr, who had been a teacher at al-Tankiziyya in Jerusalem at some point.[64]

Burhân al-Dîn Ibn ʿAbd al-Ḩaqq (in office 728-738) was a member of a distinguished family of Syrian *ʿulamâʾ*. His father, Kamâl al-Dîn ʿAlî had been *qâḑî* of Ḩişn al-Akrâd in Syria.[65] Burhân al-Dîn may have been born there, but he grew up in Damascus.[66] His father had married the daughter of the Ḩanbalî *ʿâlim*, Ḑiyâʾ al-Dîn ʿAbd al-Ḩaqq ibn Khalaf al-Dimashqî, and this is the origin of the family name by which Burhân came to be known.[67] Burhân al-Dîn's paternal uncle, Najm al-Dîn Ismâʿîl, was a Ḩanafî professor in Damascus,[68] and Burhân al-Dîn studied with both his father and his uncle.[69] His younger brother, Shihâb al-Dîn Aḩmad, became chief judge of Damascus.[70] Burhân al-Dîn was deposed from the judgeship of Cairo and exiled to Syria in 738, but one of his children managed to become *muhtasib* of Damascus in 759.[71] Another judge, Shams al-Dîn Ibn al-Ḩarîrî (in office 710-728), was also a native Syrian, born in Damascus; he really was the son of a silk merchant.[72]

The family of Ibn al-Turkumânî was the most important dynasty of Egyptian Ḩanafî judges of the Baḩrî period. It drew its name from Fakhr al-Dîn ʿUthmân ibn Ibrâhîm al-Turkumânî[73] who was a famous Ḩanafî *faqîh* in Cairo, although he may not have been born there. Fakhr al-Dîn's son, ʿAlâʾ al-Dîn ʿAlî (in office 748-750) became the first of three chief judges of Egypt to be drawn from this family. His son, Jamâl al-Dîn (in office

750-769), and grandson, Ṣadr al-Dîn (in office 773-776), followed him into that office. ʿAlâʾ al-Dîn's brother, Tâj al-Dîn Aḥmad, was a deputy judge and professor in Cairo.[74] Tâj al-Dîn's son, Jalâl al-Dîn Muḥammad,[75] and another of ʿAlâʾ al-Dîn's sons, ʿIzz al-Dîn ʿAbd al-Wahhâb,[76] were both professors in Cairo as well. There is little doubt that all three chief judges of this family were born in Cairo.[77]

About half the Ḥanafî chief judges were born or raised in Greater Syria (including Rûm and Jordan), whereas slightly less than one-quarter of the total were born in Cairo. Most of this last group consists of the family of Ibn al-Turkumânî. The rest can be classified as miscellaneous or unknown. These characteristics are in sharp contrast to the Mâlikîs, among whom Egyptian origins and conversion into the *madhhab* from another figured so prominently. Our information on the occupations of these judges' fathers is not as good as we could have hoped for, but we can say that almost half of them were the sons of *quḍât* or *fuqahâʾ*.

Table D

Al-Sarûjî--al-Bistâmî--al-Râzî

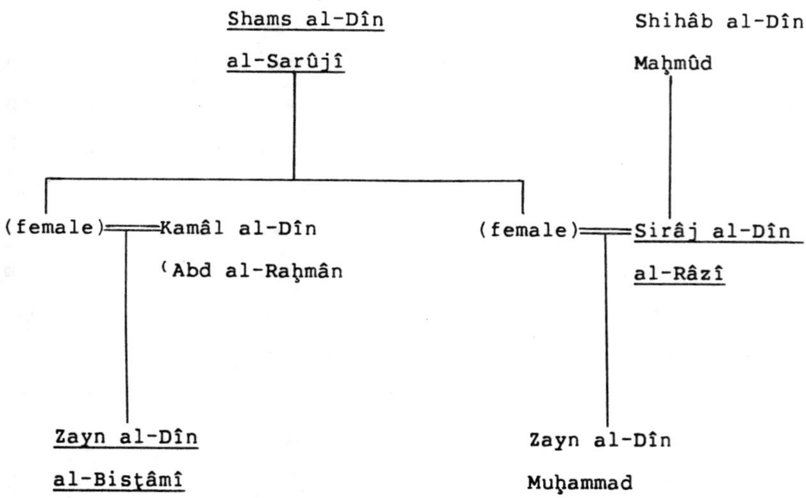

Table E

Ibn Abî al-ʿIzz (Ibn al-Kishk)

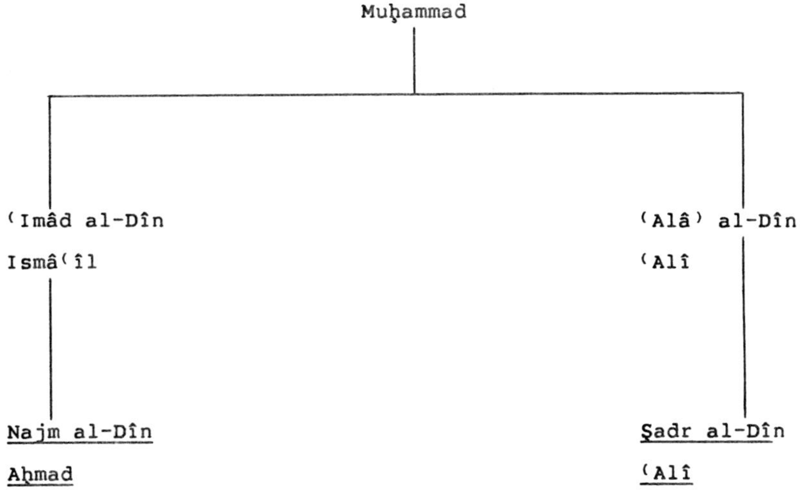

Table F

Ibn ʿAbd al-Ḥaqq

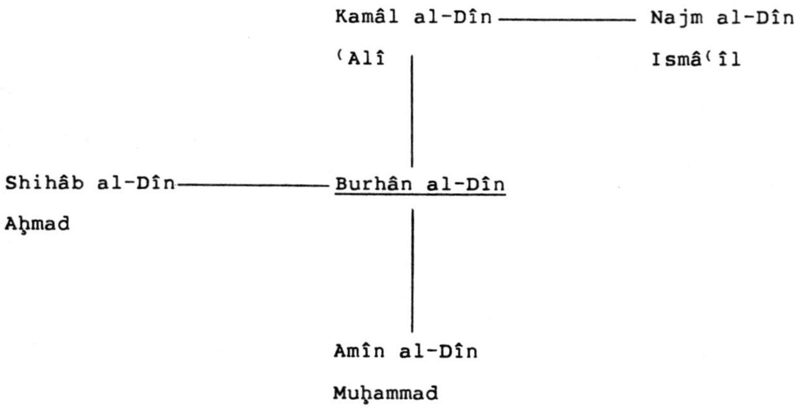

Table G

Ibn al-Turkumânî

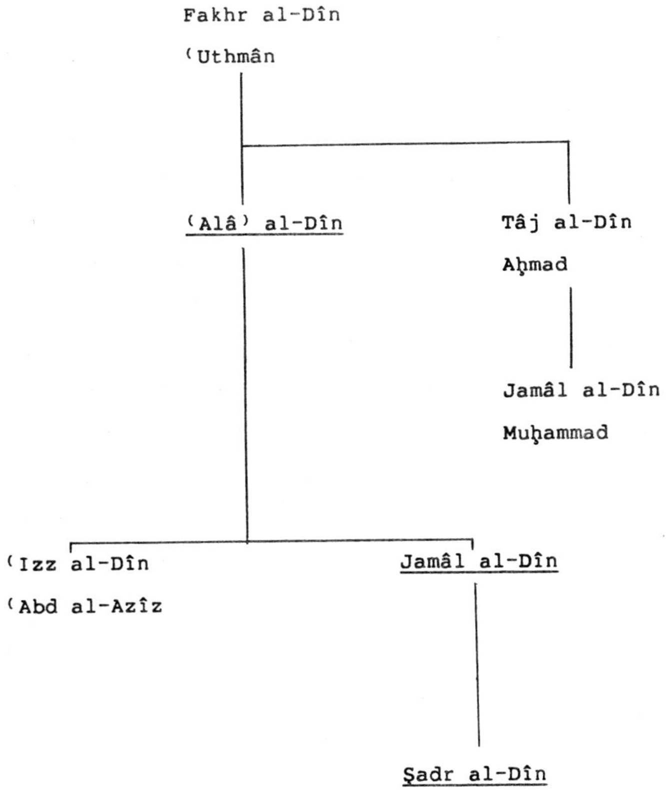

Shâfi^ʿîs

As might be expected, some of the leading families of *ʿulamâʾ* are represented among the Shâfiʿî chief judges of Mamlûk Egypt. Some of these families enjoyed success and prominence outside of Egypt, while others restricted their activities to the capital of the empire. Although overt nepotism as the cause of a judge's appointment is often difficult to prove, a good family name or acquaintances and friendships in court circles built up over many years undoubtedly played a part. Of course, marriage into a prominent family was also an important factor, and we see here again the phenomenon of a son-in-law succeeding his father-in-law after a term of apprenticeship as his *nâʾib*. On the other hand a number of the judges were unconnected to any important families, and we must not forget that even the most famous dynasties had to begin somewhere, usually with an ambitious man who established the base upon which future generations built. Finally, there was no guarantee that a son or close relative would automatically succeed to the judgeship, and there are many cases in which an individual with close ties to a *qâḍî al-quḍât* did not follow him into office, but rather went in some other direction, even if he had been his deputy. In short, personal ambition was a key factor behind an appointment to the chief judgeship.

The family of Ibn Bint al-Aʿazz was very prominent in the early Baḥrî period, supplying three of its number for the chief judgeship. The first member of this small dynasty, Tâj al-Dîn ʿAbd al-Wahhâb, was raised by his maternal grandparents when his father died in 612; the boy was only eight years old at the time. His maternal grandfather was al-A'azz ibn Shukr,[78] one of the *wuzarâ'* of Sultan al-Malik al-'Âdil Muḥammad ibn Ayyûb (ruled 512-615/1200-18), hence the family name, and he lived in the village of Damîra in the Gharbiyya.[79] Interestingly enough, al-A'azz's wife was not of Shâfi'î stock, but rather the daughter of a Mâlikî *'âlim,* Abû Manṣûr Ibn Ẓâfir.[80] Although Tâj al-Dîn was raised in a small town, his grandfather arranged for him to be educated in Cairo and Alexandria, where he was noticed by certain *'ulamâ'* and thus began his career.[81] Of Tâj al-Dîn's four sons, two became Shâfi'î chief judges of Cairo. Ṣadr al-Dîn (in office 678-679) took over his father's teaching post at al-Ṣâliḥiyya upon his father's death.[82] He was appointed chief judge during the brief sultanate of Salâmish. Perhaps his highly respected family name played a part in his selection, because he does not seem to have been very ambitious, having held neither before nor after his appointment any but teaching or controllership posts.[83] His brother, Taqî al-Dîn (judge of Fusṭâṭ, 685-686; chief judge of Cairo 686-690, 693-695), was, as we have seen, more ambitious, having held seventeen posts in his lifetime, and suffering imprisonment by his political enemies. There is no evidence that Taqî al-Dîn was helped by his family in his career, although he did take over some posts vacated by his brother.[84] It was clearly his own personal energy, conniving, and qualifications which counted. We have seen how he plotted to transfer the judge of al-Qâhira, Ibn al-Khuwayyî, to Damascus so that he himself could become chief judge of all Cairo. Although this was initially unsuccessful, he eventually became not only chief judge of both sections, but also *wazîr* at the same time.

Such responsibilities were reserved for a man of ability, not just one of good name. One of the other brothers, ʿAlâʾ al-Dîn Aḥmad, travelled in Yemen and Syria, received a teaching appointment in Damascus in 687,[85] and his son held several bureaucratic posts in Egypt.[86] The last brother remains a mystery; not even his name is known.[87]

The other two Shâfiʿî dynasties of the Baḥrî period have been discussed in some detail elsewhere.[88] They are different from the family of Ibn Bint al-Aʿazz because they divided their activities between Damascus and Cairo, and in the case of the Ibn Jamâʿa family, Jerusalem as well. Badr al-Dîn Ibn Jamâʿa was born in Hamâ in Syria, the son of a well known Shâfiʿî *ʿâlim,* but it was the ambitious Badr al-Dîn, twice chief judge of Damascus, three times chief judge of Cairo, who was the real founder of this dynasty.[89] His son, ʿIzz al-Dîn, was born in Damascus in 694, soon after his father was dismissed as chief judge of Cairo for the first time and made chief judge of Damascus.[90] However, he probably returned to Egypt at the age of eight when his father was reinstated as chief judge there. Burhân al-Dîn Ibn Jamâʿa (in office 773-779) was the nephew of ʿIzz al-Dîn; his own father had been *khaṭîb* of the al-Aqsâ mosque in Jerusalem, but he himself was born in Egypt.[91] Only two members of the al-Subkî family held the post of chief judge in Cairo during the Baḥrî period: Bahâʾ al-Dîn (in office 766-773) and his son Badr al-Dîn (in office 779-781). Bahâʾ al-Dîn was born in Cairo.[92] His father, Sadîd al-Dîn ʿAbd al-Barr ibn Yaḥyâ, does not appear in the biographical literature, but, judging from the rest of the family, he was probably some sort of *ʿâlim.* Badr al-Dîn was almost certainly born in Damascus.[93]

The nine remaining judges, comprising about one-half the total number of Shâfi'î judges under study, can be divided into three groups on the basis of place of origin. The first group were all born in Syria. Shihâb al-Dîn Ibn al-Khuwayyî (judge of al-Qâhira 681-686) was born in Damascus, the son of the Shâfi'î chief judge there, who died in office when Shihâb al-Dîn was only eleven years old.[94] Taqî al-Dîn Ibn Razîn (in office 665-680) was born in Ḥamâ, and enjoyed a considerable reputation in Damascus, until he fled to Egypt, probably with his brother Shams al-Dîn 'Abd al-Karîm, also a Shâfi'î *faqîh*, because of the Mongol invasion in 658.[95] Although we have no information on his father, Taqî al-Dîn's sons enjoyed some success. One of them, Badr al-Dîn 'Abd al-Laṭîf, held a number of teaching posts in Cairo, was *khaṭîb* at al-Azhar and assistant judge to his father[96] while another son, Ṣadr al-Dîn 'Abd Allâh, returned to Damascus to teach in a *madrasa* and died there in 695.[97] The last of this group is Bahâ' al-Dîn Ibn 'Aqîl (in office 759) who was born in Bâlis[98] in northern Syria, but spent most of his life in Egypt.[99] We know nothing of his ancestry or progeny, except that he married off a daughter to his *nâ'ib*, 'Umar ibn Raslân, better known as Sirâj al-Dîn al-Bulqînî, a professor and *muftî* in the *dâr al-'adl*, as well as a future chief judge of Damascus.[100]

The second group were all native Egyptians. Muḥyî al-Dîn Ibn 'Ayn al-Dawla was descended from a long line of judges, and his father had been judge of al-Qâhira before the establishment of the four chief judgeships.[101] We cannot be certain of Muḥyî al-Dîn's place of birth, but there is no evidence that his father ever lived outside Egypt. Taqî al-Dîn Ibn Daqîq al-'Îd was actually born on a boat in the Red Sea while his parents were making the pilgrimage to Mecca, but for our purposes it is more logical to call him an Egyptian, since his father's residence at the time was Qûṣ. His father was a Mâlikî *faqîh* there.[102] Taqî al-Dîn had ten children,[103] one of whom, Muḥib al-Dîn ʿAlî, was a professor and assistant judge to his father.[104] Although the exact birthplace of Wajîh al-Dîn al-Bahnasî is never given, it seems that he was a native Egyptian, but the evidence is admittedly more negative than positive. The Syrian historian Ibn Kathîr in the obituaries of his al-Bidâya and the biographer al-Dhahabî in his Târîkh al-islam ignore him; also, Rafʿ al-iṣr says that he studied in Egypt and then Damascus, which is certainly the wrong way around for a native Syrian. Finally, the only geographical *nisba* he carried, al-Bahnasî, refers to a place in Egypt.[105]

The last three judges are a mixed lot. The origins of Burhân al-Dîn al-Sinjârî (in office a few months in 686 as judge of al-Qâhira) remain a mystery. He and his brother, Badr al-Dîn Yûsuf, shared the chief judgeship of Cairo for a few years prior to 663,[106] but his brother returned to a teaching career, while Burhân al-Dîn tried to keep his hand in politics. Jamâl al-Dîn al-Zarʿî (in office 710-711) was born in Adhriʿat, but received his *nisba* because he was judge in Zarʿa.[107] His father, Mâjid al-Dîn ʿUmar, is called *al-khaṭîb,* but there are no biographies of him to be found for verificatin.[108] The last judge, Jalâl al-Dîn al-Qazwînî, was born in Mosul.[109] He and his brother, Imâm al-Dîn, fled in 690 because of the Mongol attacks and went to Damascus, where Imâm al-Dîn became chief judge and his brother his *nâʾib.*[110] His father was probably a professor and *faqîh,* because we know that Jalâl al-Dîn studied with him.[111] We also know that his paternal uncle, Badr al-Dîn Faḍl Allâh, was judge in Rûm and died in Damascus in 666 while visiting with his nephews on his way to Mecca for the pilgrimage.[112] When Jalâl al-Dîn was deposed from the chief judgeship of Cairo, he was made chief judge of Damascus, and three of his sons also managed to acquire teaching appointments there. Two of the three were also made their father's deputies, in addition to their teaching duties.[113]

The purpose of this chapter was to throw some light on the social and geographic origins of the chief judges of the Baḥrî period in the hope of detecting certain trends which would help us to characterize these judges more fully. As for family backgrounds, almost all the judges whose backgrounds we do know about came from *ʿulamâʾ* stock, and their children continued to hold jobs relating to the maintenance and propagation of the faith. However, very few directly followed their fathers into the chief judgeship. A number, of course, did gain that office later; such as, Ṣadr al-Dîn and Taqî al-Dîn Ibn Bint al-Aʿazz. However, these were only two of the four sons of Tâj al-Dîn Ibn Bint al-Aʿazz; the other two did not follow their father's lead, and even Ṣadr al-Dîn does not seem to have been very ambitious in this regard. What is especially interesting is the frequency of sons-in-law succeeding their fathers-in-law in the chief judgeship after having served as deputy judges. Of course, we do not know if these individuals were sons-in-law before they became *nuwwâb* or vice-versa. In any case, the point to be made here is that a blood or marital relationship to a chief judge could be helpful for someone desirous of the chief judgeship, but such relationships did not guarantee access to that office. On the contrary, the evidence points to personal initiative as a major factor in any attempt to further one's career, although the contacts with the relatives or children of judges made in court circles could prove to be advantageous later.

Geographic origins do not seem to have been a major factor in the appointment of a chief judge. There is no evidence that an individual was nominated for the chief judgeship simply because he was from a particular place. The fact that so many of the Mâlikî chief judges were born in Egyptian towns outside the capital points to the widespread presence of this *madhhab* throughout Egypt, and not just in a place like Alexandria where we would have expected some influence from the Maghrib. Quite a few of the judges were born and/or raised in Syria, and a few came from even farther afield, especially among the Ḥanafîs. This could indicate either a lack of qualified candidates in Cairo, or a preference for non-residents in general and Syrians in particular. However, when we see chief judges originating from areas as diverse as Syria, Iraq, Anatolia, Iran and India, and then, in some cases, returning to them, we cannot help but be struck by the mobility of these people. This willingness and ability to move from place to place in the hope of improving one's career seems to have been characteristic of the times. Nevertheless, the overwhelming majority of chief judges was born within the Mamlûk empire. The drift of so many Syrians to Cairo is best explained by the fact that the empire's capital and center of political power was in this city, and its chief judge undoubtedly enjoyed a special prestige.

Table H

Ibn Razîn

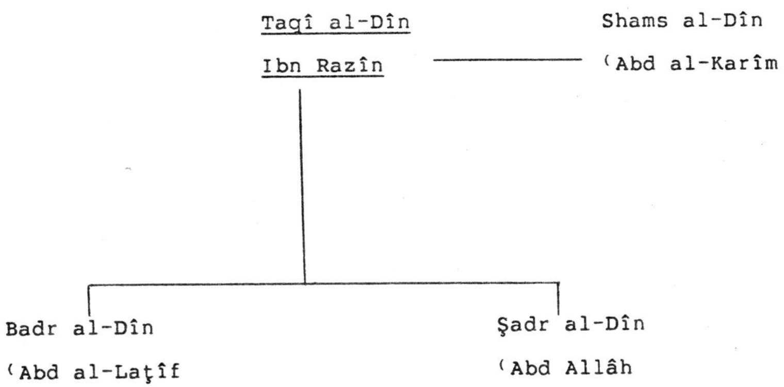

Table I

Al-Qazwînî

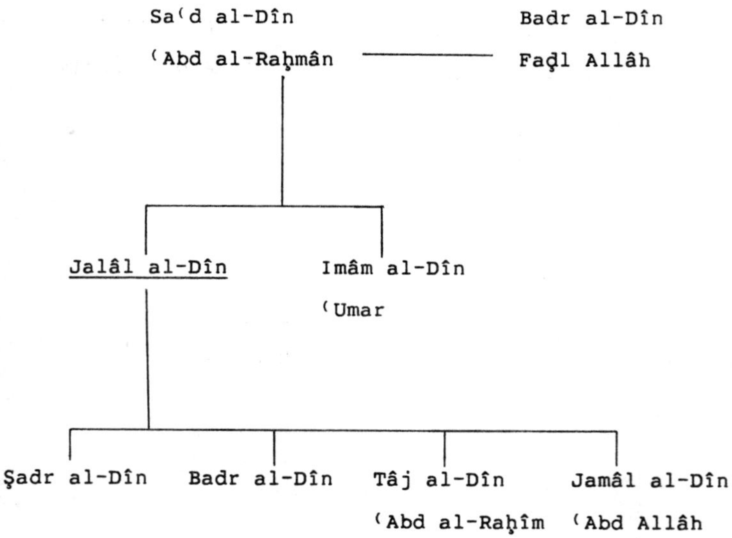

Chart II

Geographic Origins

	Syria	Egypt	Other	Unknown
Shâfiʿîs	8	7	1	1
Ḫanafîs	8	5	4	1
Mâlikîs	0	8	0	3
Ḫanbalîs	2	1	1	3
Total	18	21	6	8

N.B. These statistics refer to the individual's place of birth, or, if that information was not available, the place where he grew up.

ENDNOTES

[1]*Shadharât*, V, 57; *Wâfî*, VI, 49; Ibn Rajab, II, 93.

[2]Ibn Rajab, II, 295.

[3]Ibn al-Furât, *Târîkh*, MS, fol. 206b; "He resided in Egypt more than thirty years..."

[4]*Shadharât*, V, 57; *Wâfî*, VI, 49.

[5]*Shadharât*, IV, 345; Ibn Rajab, II, 9.

[6]*Wâfî*, VI, 218-19.

[7]*Ibid.*, VII, 319; *Durar*, I, 256.

[8]Salibi, "Listes," p. 120.

[9]*Rafʿ* MS, fol. 88b.

[10]See chapter II, note 7.

[11]*Rafʿ*, II, 365.

[12]*Manhal* MS, fol. 462b.

[13]*Durar*, II, 499.

[14]*Rafʿ* MS, fol. 133a.

[15]*Aʿyân*, fol. 589a; *Rafʿ* MS, fol. 133a; Ibn Rajab, II, 364.

[16]*Durar* (I, 240) says that he died in 738 at the age of seventy-six.

[17]Raf' MS, fol. 88b.

[18]Durar, III, 434.

[19]Raf', I, 92.

[20]Durar, III, 434.

[21]Al-'Aynî, Ahmet III, 2911/c34, fol. 65b.

[22]Durar, III, 434.

[23]Raf', II, 298.

[24]Salibi, "Listes," p. 121.

[25]Ibid., p. 88.

[26]Manhal MS, fol. 808b.

[27]Durar, V, 163.

[28]Yâqût, Mu'jam al-Buldân (Leipzig, 1886), II, 204.

[29]Salibi, "Listes," pp. 121-22, 124.

[30]Ibn al-Şâbûnî, Takmilat, p. 233; see also Popper, Notes, I, 13, and his map number 4.

[31]A'yân, fol. 347b; see also Popper, Notes, I, 13, and his map number 3.

[32]Sulûk, II, 252.

[33]Al-Nuwayrî, Leiden Or. 20, fol. 62b; see also Durar, IV, 209.

[34]Raf', II, 248. Unfortunately we do not have any information on the relationship of al-Bisâţî to Sufism.

[35]Manhal MS, fol. 442b; Raf‘, II,d 342.

[36]Ibn Ṭûlûn, Quḍât, p. 93.

[37]Raf‘, I, 40.

[38]Shadharât, VI, 113.

[39]Ibnâ’ al-ghumr, II, 113.

[40]Salibi, "Listes," p. 97; Sulûk, I, 785.

[41]Raf‘, I, 202-203.

[42]Raf‘ MS, fols. 87a-b; Inbâ’ al-ghumr, I, 29.

[43]Raf‘ MS, fol. 115b.

[44]Manhal, I, 188.

[45]Raf‘, I, 50.

[46]Ibn Abî al-Wafâ’, Jawâhir, I, 398-99, II, 164-65.

[47]al-Lakhnawî, al-Fawâ’id, p. 184.

[48]Durar, II, 434; he died in 728.

[49]Ibid.

[50]On Aq Sarâ, see EI-2, I, 312.

[51]On Malaṭya, see EI-I, III, 192-97.

[52]Raf‘, I, 183.

[53]In the listing of the extended *ism* his father is called *qâḍî al-quḍât;* Ibn Abî al-Wafâ’, Jawâhir, I, 187.

[54]Ibn Ṭûlûn, Quḍât, p. 192; Raf‘, I, 185.

[55]Shadharât, V, 357; on Adhri‘ât, see EI-2, I, 194, and Popper, Notes, I, 15.

[56]Nu‘aymî, Dâris, I, 475, 570, 595.

[57]Wâfî, III, 137.

[58]See Wiet, Manhal, nos. 2718, 1696.

[59]Manhal, I, 224; see also Raf‘, I, 55 and Ibn Ṭûlûn, Quḍât, p. 202. The names of al-Adhra‘î, and Ibn Abî al-‘Izz ibn Wahb or Ibn Wahb ibn Abî al-‘Izz appear in the complete forms of Najm al-Dîn's and Ṣadr al-Dîn al-Adhra‘î's names; cf. Shadharât, V, 357 and Raf‘, I, 55.

[60]Durar, III, 159; Ibn Ṭûlûn, Quḍât, p. 201.

[61]Manhal MS, fol. 512a. I have not been able to determine anything certain about the ancestry of either Najm al-Dîn or Ṣadr al-Dîn. Wiet provides a genealogy for this family, and claims that Najm al-Dîn's father, Ismâ‘îl, had been a Ḥanafî chief judge of Damascus (Wiet, Manhal, no. 446), but this is incorrect, because he never was chief judge of Damascus; see the list of Ḥanafî chief judges of Damascus: Ibn Ṭûlûn, Quḍât, p. 46. This genealogical chart is wrong from another point of view, since we have shown from Ibn Ṭûlûn (Quḍât, p. 201) that Ṣadr al-Dîn ‘Alî's father (Wiet, Manhal, no. 1607) was the brother, not the son, of Ismâ‘il (Wiet, Manhal, no. 446).

[62]Raf‘ MS, fol. 119b.

[63]Inbâ’ al-ghumr, II, 22.

[64]Durar, III, 209-210. Ibn Taghrî Birdî connects these brothers to the family of Ibn Abî al-‘Izz (as shown in the genealogical table, Wiet, Manhal, no. 446), but this table is wrong again, and must be ignored. Ibn Ḥajar (Durar, III, 209-210 and notes 62 and 63 above) clearly shows that these brothers are of a distinct and separate family.

[65]Durar, III, 87-88; on this city see EI-2, III, 502, 506.

[66]A‘yân, fol. 11a.

[67]Durar, I, 48; Raf', I, 36.

[68]Ibn Quṭlûbughâ, Tâj al-tarâjim fî ṭabaqât al-ḥanafiyya (Leipzig, 1862), no. 6.

[69]Raf', I, 36.

[70]Ibn Ṭûlûn, Quḍât, p. 193.

[71]Nu'aymî, Dâris, I, 624.

[72]Ibn Ṭûlûn, Quḍât, p. 193; Durar, IV, 158.

[73]Wiet, Manhal, no. 1570; Ibn Quṭlûbughâ, Ṭabaqât, no. 119; al-Lakhnawî, al-Fawâ'id, p. 110; Durar, III, 49.

[74]Durar, I, 210-211.

[75]Ibn Abî al-Wafâ', Jawâhir, II, 17.

[76]Wiet, Manhal, no. 1429.

[77]Ṣadr al-Dîn was certainly born in Cairo (Manhal MS, fol. 695b), and since the fathers of the other two enjoyed careers principally in that city, they were probably born there as well.

[78]'Abd Allâh ibn 'Alî; Shadharât, V, 100.

[79]EI-2, II, 107.

[80]Raf', II, 375.

[81]Ibid., 375-76.

[82]Al-Nuwayrî, BN 1578, fol. 36a.

[83]See, e.g., Sulûk, I, 687; al-Asnawî, I, 150.

[84]Sulûk, I, 687.

[85]Ibn al-Furât, _Târîkh_, VIII, 71.

[86]_Sulûk_, II, 421; _Durar_, III, 422-23.

[87]_Raf‘_ (II, 380) claims that there were four sons.

[88]K.S. Salibi, "The Banû Jamâ‘a..." _Studia Islamica_, IX (1958), 97-109; J. Schacht, "al-Subkî", EI-I, 494.

[89]_Manhal_ MS, fol. 548b; _Raf‘_, II, 355.

[90]Ibn Ṭûlûn, _Quḍât_, pp. 80-82.

[91]_Shadharât_, VI, 311.

[92]_Manhal_ MS, n.p. It is listed alphabetically; his full name was Muḥammad ibn ‘Abd al-Barr ibn Yaḥyâ.

[93]_Ibnâ‘ al-ghumr_, I, 185. His father went to Damascus in 739, and he was born in 741.

[94]_Shadharât_, V, 423; on the father see _Wâfî_, VI, 375-76.

[95]_Wâfî_, III, 18; his brother died in Cairo in 676 and he was buried in his brother's mausoleum (Ibn al-Furât, _Târîkh_, VII, 103).

[96]Al-Asnawî, I, 596.

[97]_Ibid._, pp. 595-96.

[98]Yâqût, _Mu‘jam_, I, 477.

[99]_Manhal_ MS, fol. 419b.

[100]Ibn Ṭûlûn, _Quḍât_, pp. 109-110; see also _Sulûk_, III, 41.

[101]_Wâfî_, III, 352-53.

[102]His father is mentioned in al-Adfuwî, _al-Ţâli‘ al-sa‘îd_ (Cairo, 1966), pp. 424ff.

[103]Wâfî, IV, 193-94.

[104]Al-Asnawî, II, 233.

[105]EI-2, I, 926.

[106]Ibn al-Şuqâ'î, Tâlî, no. 105; see also no. 278. Perhaps Badr al-Dîn really was born in Sinjâr, which is in upper Mesopotamia, west of Mosul in modern Iraq, because Shadharât (V, 313) mentions his return to that city.

[107]Ibn Kathîr, XIV, 167.

[108]Ibn Ţûlûn, Quḍât, p. 85.

[109]Sulûk, II, 470.

[110]Ibn Kathîr, XIV, 185; Wâfî, III, 242; al-Asnawî, II, 328-29.

[111]As-Asnawî, II, 330.

[112]Ibid.

[113]Ibn Kathîr, XIV, 181. Badr al-Dîn ibn Jalâl al-Dîn was a personal deputy, while the other son, Tâj al-Dîn 'Abd al-Raḥîm, held a separate jurisdiction at the *madrasa* al-Shâmiyya (al-Kubrâ) al-Barrâniyya. This *madrasa* is described in al-Nu'aymî, Dâris, I, 277-301.

CHAPTER IV

Judicial Activities

The principal duty of the *qâḍî al-quḍât* was to enforce the rules of Islamic law. The chief judges were aided in the execution of their duties by numerous assistants, both at the chief judge's court and elsewhere. In the market places the chief judges appointed both notaries *(shâhid;* pl. *shuhûd)* and magistrates to conclude marriage contracts *(ʿâqid;* pl. *ʿuqqâd)*. These notaries had been a well established feature of Islamic jurisprudence long before the Mamlûk era and sprang from a desire for personal testimony and a distrust of written evidence. A *shâhid* had to be well versed in law and was responsible for the proper execution of commercial transactions, bills of sale, etc.[1] *ʿÂqid* is short for *ʿâqid al-ankiḥa* which literally means a binder of marriages.[2] These magistrates were designated by the chief judges to perform marriages.[3] This post had existed prior to 663, and we know that the first Mâlikî chief judge, Sharaf al-Dîn al-Subkî had held it sometime prior to that year.[4] Many years later, the future Ḥanafî chief judge, Sirâj al-Dîn al-Hindî (in office 769-773), was assigned jurisdiction over *al-ʿuqûd wa-al-furûḍ* in a shop *(ḥânût)* at Bayn al-Qasrayn, opposite al-Ṣâliḥiyya *madrasa;* he was appointed by the then Ḥanafî chief judge, ʿAlâʾ al-Dîn Ibn al-Turkumânî (in office 748-750).[5] *Furûḍ* and *ʿuqûd* are synonyms, and the two words were probably used for a rhyming effect. This post must refer to the magistrate we have called *ʿâqid al-ankiḫa.* In the year 697, in al-ʿAynî's account, the Shâfʿî chief judge announced his resignation and sent word to the *aşḫâb al-ʿuqûd* to cease their activities.[6] Al-Maqrîzî relates the same incident, but refers to the *ʿuqqâd al-ankiḫa,*[7] which points to an identity of terms. We have mentioned in chapter I that in 661 a Ḫanbalî *ʿâqid* was (probably) appointed in Cairo as a subsidiary official to the Shâfiʿî chief judge, and here again it almost certainly refers to an *ʿâqid al-ankiḫa.*

Finally, there were deputy judges *(nâʾib;* pl. *nuwwâb).* All of the chief judges were empowered to appoint such deputies both in Cairo and in the provinces of Upper and Lower Egypt from 663 until 678, at which time the right to appoint deputies in the provinces was limited to the Shâfiʿî chief judge.[8] We have not studied these *nuwwâb* in any great detail, but there are a number of references to them in the literary sources.[9] For example, in the year 670 there was a Ḫanbalî *nâʾib* in the town of al-Maḫalla in the Gharbiyya district of Lower Eqgypt,[10] and his removal from that post led to trouble for the Ḫanbalî chief judge.[11] An example of a Shâfiʿî deputy chief judge outside the capital was Sirâj al-Dîn Yûnus al-Armanatî, who died in 726 while serving as judge in Qûş. But he had also served as deputy judge in Akhmîm and Bahnasa in Upper Egypt, and Bilbays and al-Sharqiyya in Lower Egypt.[12]

The deputy judges in the capital held court in various mosques and *madâris*. For example, prior to becoming Mâlikî chief judge of Damascus in 719, Sharaf al-Dîn Muḫammad ibn Abî Bakr Ibn Ẓâfir had been *nâʾib* to Taqî al-Dîn al-Akhnâʾî (in office

718-750) at *jâmiʿ* al-Ṣâliḥ (or al-Ṣâliḥî) outisde Bâb Zuwayla.[13] When he was transferred to Damascus, his post was filled by Fakhr al-Dîn ʿUmar ibn Yûsuf, who had been deputy judge at the mosque of Ibn Ṭûlûn.[14] Similarly, we know that the Mâlikî Shams al-Dîn Muḥammad ibn ʿAbd al-Qâsim (d. 713) was a *nâʾib* to Zayn al-Dîn Ibn Makhlûf (in office 685-718) in al-Ḥusayniyya.[15] The Shâfiʿî Shihâb al-Dîn Aḥmad ibn ʿAbd al-Kâfî (d. 706) was a deputy judge there as well as in al-Qarâfa.[16] Finally, after his appointment as Shâfiʿî chief judge in 690, Badr al-Dîn Ibn Jamâʿa appointed some deputies in al-Azhar.[17]

The total number of deputy judges varied during the Baḥrî period. Although there are no year-by-year statistics, in 731 there were fifty of them (probably just in Cairo), and they were all deposed.[18] This was evidently no final solution, because another decree was issued in 782 limiting the number to four per chief judge, with an additional Shâfiʿî *nâʾib* in Fusṭâṭ. At that time, the Ḥanbalî chief judge declined to accept any deputies,[19] and this may be an indication of the sparcity of the Ḥanbalîs in the capital.

The chief judge himself held court at al-Ṣâliḥiyya *madrasa*, where he also had a residence.[20] Although we do not have any detailed descriptions of this court or its ceremonial, we do know that there were *nuwwâb* and *shuhûd* here also,[21] and almost certainly scribes, chamberlains, and door keepers.[22]

The chronicles and biographical literature provide many examples of cases which came before the chief judges. Although the manuals of *fiqh* indicate an immense body of cases which fall under the jurisdiction of the *sharîʿa* and the authority of the *quḍât*, as well as the procedures to be followed in court, these manuals are certainly no substitute for the historical literature which desribes actual cases. This is not to say, however, that we are shown all the legal cases which the chief judge dealt with or a majority or even a representative sampling. On the contrary, it is safe to say that we learn about precious few of them, and as for their being representative of the whole, that is something we can never know for certain. The very fact that these cases were recorded might indicate that they were in some way out of the ordinary. However typical or atypical these cases may be, they are still useful for helping us to understand better the functions and activities of the chief judges.

The most severe punishment which a judge could impose was death, and such a sentence was usually carried out against a person found guilty of some sort of religious unorthodoxy. Several cases of this type are to be found in the historical literature, but one particular case, as related by al-Nuwayrî, is particularly important because of the many details of judicial procedure which it supplies. This is the case of Ismâ῾îl al-Zindîq, who was executed in 720.[23] This Ismâ῾îl was a well known scholar, who was knowledgeable not only in *fiqh*, grammar, etc., but also in the Torah and Gospels.[24] However, he also became famous for joking about religion and speaking about *kufr*, and this earned him the nickname Ismâ῾îl al-Kâfir, and then Ismâ῾îl al-Zindîq.[25] He was formally accused of *zandaqa* (here perhaps meaning atheism) at the court *(majlis)* of ῾Alâ᾿ al-Dîn al-Jawjarî,[26] who was one of the *nuwwâb* of the Mâlikî chief judge, Taqî al-Dîn al-Akhnâ᾿î.[27] A large number of people testified against Ismâ῾îl, and he was arrested while the deputy judge investigated the reliability of the witnesses. After he had decided to accept their testimony, the statement of charges *(maḥḍar)* was drawn up, and he asked the accused if there was anyone to refute these testimonies. The judge then waited three days, and when the period of time had expired, the chief judge al-Akhnâʾî, his deputy al-Jawjarî, other Mâlikî *nuwwâb,* a group of Mâlikî *fuqahâʾ* and others assembled at al-Nâṣiriyya *madrasa* in al-Qarâfa.[28] This was probably where al-Jawjarî held his court. When no one appeared to refute the charges, the chief judge al-Akhnâʾî approved the execution of Ismâʿîl in accordance with the guilty verdict which his deputy had decreed. However, the matter was still not finally settled, and at the next session of the *dâr al-ʿadl,* in the presence of the sultan, the decision to execute Ismâʿîl was read. The sultan inquired about the case and the reliability of the witnesses. All the (chief) judges assured him that there was no recourse but the accused's death. So the sultan ordered the governor *(mutawallî)* of al-Qâhira[29] to go with the judges and do as they ordered. All four chief judges, some of the *nuwwâb* and other *ʿulamâʾ* met in the Mâlikî portico of al-Ṣâliḥiyya *madrasa* and agreed on Ismâʿîl's death. They asked him to testify to the *shahâda.* He answered in a confused manner, and it was thought that he might be crazy; but the matter was doubtful, and the judges decided on his execution, which was carried out.

Another source claims that he was charged because of what he said against the Prophet Lûṭ (i.e. Lot),[30] and further that al-Akhnâʾî was hesitating to have Ismâʿîl executed until someone swore that he had seen the Prophets Lûṭ and Muḥammad in a dream, both of whom called for Ismâʿîl's execution.[31]

A similar case occurred in 701 and involved the Mâlikî chief judge Ibn Makhlûf. He charged that Fatḩ al-Dîn Aḩmad ibn Muḩammad al-Baqaqî[32] was a *kâfir*, and he wanted him executed. It was well known that Fatḩ al-Dîn did not fast during Ramaḑân, and he made fun of those who did. If he needed to get something from a high place, he would use the Quran as a footstool.[33] He used foul language, spoke disparagingly of the *quḑât*,[34] and mocked religion.[35] He had been jailed for the last mentioned offense in 686,[36] but it is not clear if he had spent all the intervening years in prison. These charges were raised against him once more in 701, but the true reason for the charges this time was that al-Baqaqî has started to write insulting remarks about the chief judge Ibn Makhlûf. When the judge heard about this, he developed a hatred towards Fatḩ al-Dîn and decided to bring him down. Many people, in order to gain Ibn Makhlûf's favour, began to make accusations against al-Baqaqî, charging him with *kufr*, and on this basis Ibn Makhlûf sentenced him to death.[37] Al-Baqaqî testified to the oneness of God and the prophethood of Muḩammad, but Ibn Makhlûf refused to accept his testimony.[38] However, the Shâfiʿî chief judge, Ibn Daqîq al-ʿÎd, did not agree to the execution of someone who pronounced the declaration of faith. At that point, some friends of al-Baqaqî worked to have his case transferred to the Shâfiʿî chief judge, and they claimed that Fatḩ al-Dîn was really insane. Ibn Daqîq al-ʿÎd said that he could not declare him insane, because he knew that he was rational.[39] The matter now came before the sultan, and Ibn Makhlûf, supported by the Ḩanafî chief judge, Shams al-Dîn al-Sarûjî, told the sultan that Fatḩ al-Dîn's *kufr* and *zandaqa* had been proved in the (Mâlikî's) court and death was prescribed.[40] The sultan agreed and a *majlis* was held at the Ṣâliḥiyya *madrasa* in the presence of the (four) judges and others.[41] Al-Baqaqî was led in and despite his insistence that he was a Muslim, his execution was ordered.[42] It was said that Ibn Daqîq al-ʿÎd finally agreed to it also.[43]

Not all the cases which came before the chief judges are described in as much detail as these two. In fact, the case of Ismâʿîl al-Zindîq is dismissed in a rather cursory manner by most of the sources. However, even at this point it is possible to make certain hypotheses about judicial procedure, at least in apostasy cases or in cases involving the death penalty during the Baḥrî period. First of all, a given chief judge did not enjoy a definite area of jurisdiction. Rather, it seems that convenience or hope for a favourable verdict led to the bringing of a given case before a certain judge. Obviously, Ibn Makhlûf was not the exclusive judge in al-Baqaqî's case, either by custom or law, because al-Baqaqî's friends brought his case before the Shâfiʿî chief judge in an attempt to have Fatḥ al-Dîn declared insane and avoid Ibn Makhlûf's harsh judgement. Even after one chief judge had decided on the death penalty, the matter had to come before the sultan in order to secure his agreement to the verdict and make the arrangements for the execution. All the judges were present at the *majlis* of the sultan and also at the subsequent *majlis* at al-Ṣâliḥiyya, where the chief judges usually held their courts. It was necessary for all the chief judges to agree on the verdict. At these *majâlis* there were many other people present, such as *nuwwâb* and *fuqahâʾ*. Their presence might be explained simply as ceremonial, but judging from the attempt to have the four chief judges agree on the verdict, it seems likely that the others were available in case their opinions were desired. By and large, there seems to have been an attempt to attain unanimity on a verdict; at least on a verdict which involved the death penalty.

The case of Ismâ'îl al-Zindîq provides a unique opportunity to see the relationship between the chief judge and his deputy, but since this is the only example of their working relationship that we have come across, it is difficult to know how typical this one case is. Obviously, if a chief judge could not have a man executed on his own authority, then a lower ranking deputy could not have it done either. The main question is, what were the limits of the deputy judge's authority? We have seen how deputy judges were stationed throughout the city (and even the empire), and most likely they were placed in order to make judges more accessible to the masses and facilitate the rendering of justice. Litigations would have been slowed if all the verdicts of the deputies had to be reviewed by the chief judges. Also, it is highly likely that the deputies in the provinces, who were far from the centers of power, had few checks on their authority. The rest of the cases we shall discuss will not usually involve the deputy judges, because there is little information on their judicial activities, and, aside from the incident just related, almost nothing on their relationships to the chief judges in Cairo. Few of the following cases are described in much detail by our sources, but considering the treatment of the incident of Ismâ'îl al-Zindîq by many of the sources aside from al-Nuwayrî, the historians usually did not bother with such details either because court proceedings were well known or because it was tedious and boring to dwell on unnecessary detail. Therefore, the generalizations mentioned above should be borne in mind, in spite of the frequent lack of detailed descriptions in the subsequent cases.[44]

Another incident which almost resulted in the death of the accused for *kufr* was that of Badr al-Dîn Aḩmad ibn Sâḩib[45] in the year 784. He had an argument with Sirâj al-Dîn al-Bulqînî over some scholarly matter, and al-Bulqînî called him a *kâfir.*[46] He was charged before the Mâlikî chief judge, Jamâl al-Dîn Ibn Khayr al-Ansârî,[47] but some other people worked to have the case transferred to the Shâfiʿî chief judge, in whose court Badr al-Dîn's life was spared.[48]

Another *ʿâlim* who almost lost his life in 737 was Shams al-Dîn Muḩammad ibn Aḩmad Ibn Labbân, who was a preacher *(wâʿiẓ)* in Cairo.[49] Although we know that he went to extremes in his sermons and was charged with some sort of religious heresy for that reason, there is some disagreement in the sources over exactly what he was preaching. According to al-Maqrîzî, he preached that the worshipping of idols was not forbidden *(ghayr muḩarram)* and that Shaykh Yâqût al-ʿArsh,[50] his own teacher, was superior to some of the Companions of the Prophet.[51] Al-ʿAynî tells a similar story, but has Shams al-Dîn say that the worship of idols is not reprehensible *(makrûh)*.[52] According to Ibn Ḩajar, he spoke according to the path of the Shâdhiliyya,[53] but he became carried away and began to speak like those who preached union with God, al-Ittiḩâdiyya.[54] Obviously, the man was a Sufi, and although Ibn Ḩajar seems to say that he spoke about Sufism according to the Shâdhiliyya order, al-ʿAynî says that he discussed *tafsîr.*[55] He certainly might have combined the two. In any case, a number of people testified against him, and he was summoned to the court of the Shâfi'î chief judge, Jalâl al-Dîn al-Qazwînî and charged.[56] Then all the (chief) judges gathered and informed the sultan, who said that if the charges were true, then death was prescribed.[57] When Ibn Labbân heard of this, he sought the intervention of some powerful people, including *umarâ'* such as Jankalî Ibn al-Bâbâ.[58] They persuaded the sultan to spare his life, but he was forbidden to speak in the mosques.[59]

A rather different case came before the Shâfi'î deputy judge Tâj al-Dîn al-Munâwî.[60] In 754 a Christian came from Tyre to Cairo and began slandering Islam. He was brought before al-Munâwî, whom he told there was no religion except Christianity, and he said this so that he might die a believer (i.e. a martyr). The judge had him beaten, but the Christian continued as before and he was finally executed.[61] A similar case had occurred in 725 when a Christian who had slandered Islam was brought before the Mâlikî chief judge, Taqî al-Dîn al-Akhnâ'î, who ruled that he should be executed. The case was brought before the sultan who approved, and the judge passed the final sentence in the Mâlikî portico of al-Şâliḫiyya. The Christian's head was cut off in the chief judge's presence.[62]

Not all the encounters between the chief judges and Christians (as well as Jews) resulted in such fatalities. On other occasions the chief judges were called upon to clarify the status of the *ahl al-dhimma*. For example, in the year 700 a *wazîr* from the Maghrib was visiting Cairo. He became angry at the way Christians and Jews were behaving, flaunting the Muslim sumptuary laws concerning the proper conduct of these minorities. He brought the matter to the *umarâ'* Sallâr and Baybars, and very soon thereafter the sultan ordered the *dhimmîyûn* to adhere to the laws regulating their behaviour. The chief judges then met at al-Şâliḫiyya and chose the Ḫanafî chief judge, Shams al-Dîn al-Sarûjî, as their spokesman to enforce the new regulations. The leaders of the Jews and the Christians were summoned and it was decreed that the Christians must wear blue turbans and the Jews yellow ones. Messages were sent throughout the empire announcing these regulations, which also forbade these minorities from holding posts in the *dîwân* of the sultan or of any *amîr*, and from riding horses or mules. The situation deteriorated further after Najm al-Dîn Aḫmad ibn Rif'a,[63] who may have been a deputy judge at the time,[64] issued a *fatwâ* authorizing the destruction of the churches of Cairo. However, the Shâfi'î chief judge, Ibn Daqîq al-'Îd, disagreed with this, and said that the only buildings which could be destroyed were those which had been erected since the beginning of Islam. There was general agreement on this.[65]

One of the judges, Shams al-Dîn Ibn al-Ḫarîrî al-Ḫanafî (in office 710-728), did not wait for such cases to come before him, but simply acted on the spot whenever he saw any Christians on the street. He was especially harsh towards the scribes who were Christians or recently converted to Islam (the *musâlima)*, and they complained to Karîm al-Dîn al-Kabîr, the *nâẓir al-khâşş* and himself a convert,[66] about the judges's actions. This may have been a factor in Ibn al-Ḫarîrî's loss of half the jurisdiction of Cairo in 717, but other factors were more probably to blame.[67]

Looking at some other problems regarding the religious side of life in Cairo, we must make some mention of Ibn Taymiyya and his disciples. One such disciple was Shihâb al-Dîn Aḫmad ibn Muḫammad Ibn Murrâ (or Ibn Mirâ).[68] He had come to Cairo with

Ibn Taymiyya, and remained there after Ibn Taymiyya had returned to Damascus.[69] He addressed the people in several mosques, including the mosque of the *amîr* Sharaf al-Dîn Ḥusayn Ibn Jandâr, where Badr al-Dîn Jankalî Ibn al-Bâbâ was the *nâẓir.*[70] He addressed himself to such questions as *istighâtha* (asking intercession from the Prophet), the agency of the Prophet *(al-wasîla)* and others; like Ibn Taymiyya, Shihâb al-Dîn was opposed to Sufism.[71] When Shams al-Dîn Ibn al-Jawzî came from Baghdad in 725, he was asked to speak about Sufism in the mosque of the *amîr* Ḥusayn. Shihâb al-Dîn attended that lecture, and denounced Ibn al-Jawzî, calling him a *zindîq.*[72] Ibn Murrâ's preaching against Sufism and his denunciation of Ibn al-Jawzî aroused the enmity of those who favored Sufism, and they tried to kill Ibn Murrâ, but he escaped.[73] Finally, these people brought charges against him in the court of the Mâlikî chief judge, Taqî al-Dîn al-Akhnâʾî, claiming that he was evil, a wine drinker, etc.[74] Al-Akhnâʾî kept him in jail while he presented the case to the other chief judges, *umarâʾ*, and sultan in the *dâr al-ʿadl*. Judging from other cases which we have discussed, al-Akhnâʾî may have wanted to impose the death penalty, but this is not stated in any source. When the matter came before the *dâr al-ʿadl*, arguments broke out. Ibn al-Bâbâ and the Shâfiʿî chief judge, Badr al-Dîn Ibn Jamâʿa, supported Ibn Murrâ, whereas the *amîr* Aydamur al-Khaṭîrî,[75] who was a supporter of the Sufis and an opponent of Ibn Taymiyya, opposed him.[76] The arguments became so intense that fighting almost occurred.[77] The sultan did not make a decision, but rather turned the matter over to his *nâʾib*, Arghûn, to do what was necessary according to the *sharîʿa*ʾ.[78] Arghûn eventually sent the matter back to the Mâlikî chief judge, who had Ibn Murrâ beaten and jailed. Finally, Ibn al-Bâbâ interceded, and Ibn Murrâ was released, but forced to leave Cairo.[79]

Here again we see the limits of the chief judge's authority. It is unfortunate that some details are lacking and we do not know if al-Akhnâ)î had declared the death sentence against Ibn Murrâ, although it is not unlikely. Whatever al-Akhnâ)î's verdict had been, even the sultan was intimidated by all the controversy and arguments, and as a result he gave the case to his *nâ)ib*. It is astonishing that he told his *nâ)ib*, at least in al-(Aynî's version, to act according to the *sharî(a*. Although we do know that Arghûn had studied some Ḥanafî *fiqh*,[80] this seems a poor substitute for the ruling of one or more chief judges, and this move seems to be a clear usurpation of the judges' authority. Strangely enough there is no indication that the chief judges expressed any opinion or opposition to the sultan's move, and it is probable that the sultan was looking for a political rather than a strictly judicial solution, i.e. a compromise that would satisfy everyone. If al-Akhnâ)î had in fact recommended the death penalty, his subsequent decision to have Ibn Murrâ beaten may have been the result of a compromise between the *nâ)ib* and the chief judge. As we shall see below, al-Akhnâ)î was an outspoken opponent of Ibn Taymiyya, and he certainly would not have had a charitable attitude towards one of Ibn Taymiyya's disciples. To make matters even more confusing, we are told that Arghûn was a supporter of Ibn Taymiyya when he was a *nâ)ib* in Egypt,[81] and if this is really true, he would not have turned over this disciple to one of Ibn Taymiyya's opponents unless some deal had been struck.

Ibn Taymiyya himself came into conflict with several of the chief judges of Cairo on more than one occasion.[82] The first time that Ibn Taymiyya faced the chief judges of Cairo was in the year 705. He had been accused before the Mâlikî chief judge Zayn al-Dîn Ibn Makhlûf concerning his beliefs that God is above the throne, that He speaks by letter and sound, etc. This accusation could have led to the death penalty, and it next came before the sultan's *majlis*, where all the judges, as well as *fuqahâ⁾*, *umarâ⁾*, and other notables were in attendance.[83] Ibn Taymiyya was not in Egypt at the time he was first charged in Ibn Makhlûf's court, but several inconclusive investigations of Ibn Taymiyya's belief had been carried out in Damascus just prior to this summons to Cairo, and Ibn Makhlûf, who had the support of the future sultan Baybars al-Jashnagîr in his opposition to Ibn Taymiyya,[84] wanted to find his own solution to the problem of this zealous fundamentalist. In contrast to the three councils in Damascus which had reached no definite conclusions, the session in Cairo was quick and to the point. When Ibn Taymiyya rose to defend himself before the sultan, Ibn Makhlûf cut him short, and told him they did not want to hear a *khuṭba*. When Ibn Taymiyya objected to Ibn Makhlûf as one of the judges because he was also one of his accusers, he was ignored and ordered imprisoned. Later, when Ibn Makhlûf learned that Ibn Taymiyya was receiving many visitors and gifts of food, he complained that if Ibn Taymiyya was not put to death for his religious views he should at least suffer some hardship; Ibn Taymiyya was then transferred to a stricter confinement.[85]

After Ibn Taymiyya had been in jail for about a year, Sallâr, the viceroy of Egypt, began a campaign to have Ibn

Taymiyya freed. He discussed the matter with various *fuqahâʾ* and *quḍât,* and a number of subsequent meetings and discussions took place, with the *ʿulamâʾ* urging some modifications in Ibn Taymiyya's creed. However, Ibn Taymiyya was angry at the way his trial had been carried out and he refused to leave prison until the *amîr* Ibn ʿÎsâ persuaded him to accept the offer of freedom. More councils of *ʿulamâʾ* were held, and finally one of these councils, with the chief judges absent (!), agreed on his final release. Al-Nuwayrî says that this was through the agreement of Ibn Makhlûf.[86] In other words, it took the chief judges of Egypt and the sultan to jail Ibn Taymiyya, but only a council of *ʿulamâʾ*, with the chief judges conspiciously absent, to free him. Obviously, an arrangement had been made with Ibn Taymiyya's chief antagonist, Ibn Makhlûf, and judicial procedure was set aside.

Ibn Taymiyya was soon back on the streets and in the mosques, lecturing and getting himself into trouble; this time by criticizing the Sufis. They brought charges against him in the court of the Shâfiʿî chief judge, Badr al-Dîn Ibn Jamâʿa, and although he was not convicted of anything, he was ordered to leave Cairo and return to Damascus. When Ibn Makhlûf, who had been ill, heard about this, he had one of his deputies lay charges against Ibn Taymiyya, and others followed suit, with the result that Ibn Taymiyya was imprisoned again.[87] In another version of the story, we are told that Ibn Taymiyya volunteered to be jailed in the interests of *maṣlaḥa;* i.e., to avoid further dissension in the community. He was soon after transferred to a prison in Alexandria.[88]

The same year (709) al-Malik al-Nâṣir Muḥammad returned to the throne for the third and final time. He summoned Ibn

Taymiyya from Alexandria and showed him great respect. The sultan wanted to have some of the (chief) judges executed because of their support for Baybars, whom al-Nâşir had just deposed from the sultanate, but Ibn Taymiyya opposed such an action. At this time also al-Nâşir reconciled Ibn Taymiyya with the chief judges, especially Ibn Makhlûf.[89]

Soon after this Ibn Taymiyya returned to Damascus, but even there he sometimes had to suffer the punishments of the Cairene judiciary. In the year 718 Ibn Taymiyya was jailed briefly in Damascus because of his views on the oath of repudiation *(ḩilf bi-al-ţalâq)*.[90] According to al-Maqrîzî this was accomplished through the efforts of the Ḩanafî chief judge, Shams al-Dîn Ibn al-Ḩarîrî, and his instigating the sultan against Ibn Taymiyya.[91] This represents a complete reversal of Ibn al-Ḩarîrî's attitude towards Ibn Taymiyya, because in the year 708 this same Ibn al-Ḩarîrî had been deposed as chief judge of Damascus at the instigation of Ibn Makhlûf, because of the former's expression of admiration for Ibn Taymiyya.[92] Ibn Taymiyya's imprisonment occurred after he had been ordered by the sultan not to give any *fatâwin* on this question and after three councils had been held in Damascus concerning Ibn Taymiyya's opinions on this point.[93]

In the year 726 Ibn Taymiyya was jailed again in Damascus, ostensibly because of his comments on *shifâʿa* or intercession of the Prophet. Once again this was due primarily to the Ḩanafî chief judge, Ibn al-Ḩarîrî.[94] The Mâlikî chief judge, Taqî al-Dîn al-Akhnâʾî, who was Ibn Makhlûf's successor, was also active in this opposition to Ibn Taymiyya and had even urged Ibn Taymiyya's death, but a meeting of the four chief judges had decided on the aforementioned imprisonment.[95] Al-Akhnâʾî had written rebuttals to Ibn Taymiyya's views, which Ibn Taymiyya, in turn, refuted. This led to al-Akhnâʾî's urging the sultan to deprive Ibn Taymiyya of his writing materials, which was ordered.[96] Ibn Taymiyya died soon after this in 728.

In this second group of cases we can also see the flexibility of the chief judge's jurisdiction. The case of Badr al-Dîn Aḥmad Ibn Ṣâḥib was moved from one chief judge to another in the hope, ultimately fulfilled, of a verdict more favourable to the defendant. The influence of powerful men in determining a verdict is also evident. The intercession of the *amîr* Ibn al-Bâbâ saved the life of Sham al-Dîn Ibn Labbân, and the enmity of the Mâlikî chief judges Ibn Makhlûf and al-Akhnâʾî was instrumental in the persecutions of Ibn Taymiyya. The formalities of legal procedure were followed even in such cases, but the influence of powerful individuals could not be ignored in a society where a consensus of the opinions of the most important people in the state was desired. As mentioned previously, the reason for holding a *majlis* in the presence of the sultan and then in al-Ṣâliḥiyya in the presence of various judges and *fuqahâʾ* was to insure a consensus of opinions before a man was executed. Thus if any member of any *majlis* would strongly express an opinion, attempts at reconciliation were made. This explains why Ibn Labbân was exiled and not executed, and similarly why Ibn Taymiyya suffered various degrees of imprisonment and not death.

Although cases involving life and death were the most dramatic ones with which the chief judges dealt, a great number of the cases which we learn about have to do with financial matters, such as *awqâf* and inheritances. One of these cases, which came before Tâj al-Dîn Ibn Bint al-A'azz has already been mentioned in connection with the establishment of the four chief judgeships. This happened in 663 during a session of the *dâr al-'adl* when the daughters of the Ayyûbid al-Malik al-Nâşir Şalâḥ al-Dîn complained that they had purchased a house from the *qâḍî al-quḍât* Burhân al-Dîn al-Sinjârî, but after the judge died his heirs claimed the house was part of a *waqf* and refused to release it. This angered the sultan, and the amîr Aydughdây, but Ibn Bint al-A'azz maintained the inviolability of the *waqf*, providing it had been properly established. He said that al-Sinjârî's heirs should return the purchase price of the house, but when asked the procedure if the judge's heirs did not have the money, he still said that the *waqf* must remain intact.[97]

This case was a dispute between civilians, but the other cases which we read about involve Mamlûks and the history of the Baḥrî period supplies many examples of attempts by Mamlûk sultans or *umarâ'* to modify or annul various *awqâf*. This culminated in an unsuccessful bid late in the Baḥrî period to annul all the *awqâf* in the empire. Certainly a great deal of wealth was tied up in *awqâf*, yet the Mamlûks preferred legal means to get at this wealth rather than outright confiscation. More often than not the judges cooperated with the Mamlûks in their endeavours, but still attempts were made to adhere to a legal formalism. A good example of this cooperation occurred in 723 when the Sultan al-Malik al-Naşir Muḥammad ordered the chief judges to release whatever Karîm al-Dîn al-Kabîr, who had been the Sultan's *nâẓir al-khâşş*, had established as *awqâf*. The judges said that this was not possible because Karîm al-Dîn had set up these *awqâf* according to the strictest legal principles, and therefore there was no way to get at them. The sultan continued to press the point, and the judges finally agreed that if Karîm al-Dîn testified against himself, saying that everything he had made into *awqâf* came from the money of the sultan, and no funds came from himself or his family, then his *awqâf* could be annulled. Such testimony was produced, and the *awqâf* were cancelled.[98] Some of these properties were made into a *waqf* by the sultan.[99] This same sultan had earlier used Karîm al-Dîn in a plot of his own after his return to the sultanate in 709. At that time he had disposed of his opponents, Baybars and Sallâr, and summoned the chief judges to show them that the wealth and *awqâf* of these two had all come from the state treasury *(bayt al-mâl)*, and thus the *awqâf* were invalid. After this had been verified and the properties released, the sultan sent Karîm al-Dîn and an *amîr* to sell off Baybars' estate; half the money went to the sultan and the other half to Baybars' daughter. Then Karîm al-Dîn seized various treasures from her and Baybars' wife.[100]

Some thirty years later, in 754, the *amîr* Ṣarghitmish[101] wanted to seize and sell the *awqâf* of Ibn Zanbûr.[102] He remembered the case of Karîm al-Dîn al-Kabîr and how his *awqâf* had been annulled without any objection from the Shâfi'î chief judge, Badr al-Dîn Ibn Jamâ'a; he was further encouraged in this plan by several *umarâ'* and notables at the court.[103] The fact that Badr al-Dîn's son, 'Izz al-Dîn, was now chief judge probably encouraged him in this plot. However, there was considerable opposition to this move, especially by the Ḥanbali chief judge, Muwaffaq al-Dîn al-Maqdisî. 'Izz al-Dîn Ibn Jamâ'a agreed with him, and when reminded of the actions of his father in the case of Karîm al-Dîn, he pointed out that the cases were different. Whereas Karîm al-Dîn had had absolute control over the funds of the sultan, Ibn Zanbûr, even though he had been *wazîr,* had derived his wealth from private business and trade. Therefore there was no justification for taking any of his wealth or *awqâf.* The *majlis* broke up, having supported Ibn Jamâʿa's argument.[104] In this case the judges did not cooperate with the plans of an *amîr,* and were able to successfully establish their point of view.

However, the chief judges were all too often ready to help the Mamlûks alter or abolish a *waqf.* In the year 730 the *amîr* Qawṣûn,[105] who had built a mosque with the help of the sultan near the Birkat al-Fîl, wanted to purchase a bath *(ḫammâm)* next to the mosque, but the *ḫammâm* was part of a *waqf.* The *amîr* then asked the chief judges, who turned the matter over to the Ḫanbalî chief judge, Taqî al-Dîn Ibn ʿAwaḍ. Meanwhile, a side of the bath was knocked down, undoubtedly at the direction of the *amîr.* At that point the Ḫanbalî chief judge decreed that the *waqf* was void, because the *ḫammâm* was in a state of ruin, and it was best that it be sold. The notaries were summoned to corroborate the ruined state of the building, but one of them refused to attest to this, saying that the building had been sound only the morning before. The objection was overcome by the dismissal of the recalcitrant *shâhid* and his replacement by another. The judge then confirmed the now unanimous opinion, and the *amîr* purchased the building.[106] A few years later, in 723, this same *amîr* purchased a house in al-Qâhira, which had been a *waqf.* Once again, it was with the help of a Ḫanbalî chief judge, although, according to al-Maqrîzî, the *waqf* deed had been drawn up under the careful supervision of several future chief judges.[107] The implication is that the *waqf* had been established with scrupulous attention paid to legal details, but in the long run even this did not matter when faced with the greed of an *amîr* and the complicity of a chief judge.

An even more unsavory episode occurred in the year 686. At that time Nâşir al-Dîn Ibn al-Maqdisî[108] came to Cairo from Damscus and spoke with the *wazîr* al-Shujâ'î.[109] This Ibn al-Maqdisî said that he could prove that Khâtûn, the daughter of the Ayyûbid al-Malik al-Ashraf,[110] had been legally incompetent at the time she had sold certain properties, and therefore the sales were invalid. The properties she had sold were extensive and valuable, and the annulment of these sales could result in considerable profit for the government of these two conspirators. Although the sultan was not in Cairo at the time, al-Shujâ'î was his deputy and proceeded on his own.[111] They presented their case to all the chief judges of Cairo, but the only one who agreed that they were right was the Mâlikî chief judge, Ibn Makhlûf.[112] An assembly was held, and one of the purchasers of land, al-Sâmarrî,[113] was summoned from Damascus, and shown that because of Bint al-Ashraf's incompetence his purchase was invalid. Ibn Makhlûf invalidated the sale from the very beginning, even though al-Sâmarrî had made the property into a *waqf*. Al-Sâmarrî had to pay back not only the purchase price, but also the revenues he had drawn from it over a period of thirty years. He had difficulty raising the money, and Ibn al-Maqdisî helped him by purchasing some shares of another village which al-Sâmarrî owned.[114] The result was that al-Sâmarrî was left a poor man, but he was only one of many Damascenes who suffered the same fate.[115] It was not long before Ibn al-Maqdisî established that Bint al-Ashraf really was legally competent, and he and al-Shujâ'î forced her to sell these properties to them at a very reasonable price.[116] We do not know if Ibn Makhlûf was involved in the subsequent establishment of her legal competence.

This is not to say that the chief judges always cooperated. We have seen above that in 754 two of them managed to preserve the *awqâf* of Ibn Zanbûr, and even Ibn al-Maqdisî and al-Shujâ'î had to shop around before they found a judge favourable to their plans. In these cases the uncooperative judges did not suffer, but the Ḥanafî chief judge, Ibn al-Ḥarîrî, was less fortunate when he did not cooperate with the plans of Sultan al-Malik al-Nâşir Muḥammad to exchange some *awqâf* lands for non- *awqâf* lands. The sultan had approached the judge to authorize this transfer, because he had been told that the Ḥanafîs approved of such exchanges. However, Ibn al-Ḥarîrî said that he himself did not agree to the interpretation of the law which allowed this, and he refused to sanction the exchange. Sirâj al-Dîn al-Râzî heard of this, and he approached Karîm al-Dîn al-Kabîr promising a favorable verdict if he was given the chief judgeship. As a result, al-Râzî was made chief judge of Fusţâţ, and Ibn al-Ḥarîrî was left with al-Qâhira. This arrangement continued for a few months until al-Râzî's death the same year (717), when Ibn al-Ḥarîrî was given back his full powers.[117]

Finally, in the year 780, there occurred what was the most dramatic confrontation between *'ulamâ'* and Mamlûks concerning *awqâf*. The future sultan Barqûq summoned the judges and *fuqahâ'* to an assembly in order to discuss the abolition of apparently all the *awqâf* of Egypt and (Greater) Syria, because these *awqâf* weakened the armies of the Muslims. Sirâj al-Dîn al-Bulqînî spoke up saying that the *awqâf* of the mosques, *madâris* and the like did not weaken the Muslims and could not be touched. Other *awqâf*, however, which had been purchased from the *bayt al-mâl* by trickery could be revoked, if proper judicial procedure were followed to prove this charge. The Shâfiʿî chief judge, Badr al-Dîn al-Subkî, also known as Ibn Abî al-Baqâʾ, took the most politically advantageous line by saying that all the land belonged to the sultan, and he could do whatever he liked. The *qâḍî al-ʿaskar* disagreed, saying that the sultan was just like anyone in this regard. This judge then added that (in any case) the *umarâʾ* gave order to the judges, and if the judges did not comply, then they would be deposed. The meeting finally broke up with the original aim of total abolishment of *awqâf* unfulfilled, but a number of *awqâf* were annulled and made into *iqṭaʿât*.[118]

The record of complicity between the chief judges and the Mamlûks in order to modify or annul *awqâf* is unmistakeable. In spite of all this, however, most of the *awqâf* in the Mamlûk empire continued to exist and function throughout the Baḥrî period, and they must have produced considerable income; otherwise the *umarâʾ* would not have been so interested in seizing them in 780. The fact that the Mamlûks so often made an effort to adhere to proper legal procedure of some sort is significant. Although the judges usually seemed eager to cooperate with the plans of the Mamlûks, occasionally there was successful opposition to these designs. Finally, we must remember that if there were no *awqâf*, there would be no religious life. These pious endowments supported teaching posts, students, mosque officials, hospitals, and many other offices and institutions connected to the maintenance and propagation of the religious life. To abolish all the *awqâf* would have led not only to massive unemployment, but also it would have undermined the status of Islam. It is doubtful that the Mamlûk *umarâʾ* had seriously considered the ramifications of their proposal in 780, and either they were simply interested in establishing as many *iqṭaʿât* as possible, or, having made such an outrageous proposal, they were willing to settle for a good deal less than they had originally demanded.

There were other ways in which the Mamlûks could acquire revenue with the help of the judiciary, but in the following cases the judges resisted attempts to take actions of which they did not approve. One example of this occurred in the year 697, during the sultanate of Lâjîn. The amîr Mankûtimur,[119] the sultan's *nâʾib,* sent a message to the Shâfiʿî chief judge, Taqî al-Dîn Ibn Daqîq al-ʿÎd, informing him that a merchant had died and had left a brother as his only heir. Mankûtimur wanted his own word to suffice as evidence of the truth of the man's claim to be the merchant's brother and heir, but the chief judge would not approve this claim only with the *amîr's* testimony. When this initial contact failed, the *amîr* started sending messengers to the judge, and when even this proved fruitless, he sent the *amîr* Kurt, the *ḥâjib,*[120] to him. He tried to persuade the judge to rely on Mankûtimur's testimony, but he was unsuccessful as well, and became exasperated, saying, "By God, this is Islam!" He returned to Mankûtimur and told him that he would have to work out this matter in the *dâr al-ʿadl.*

When it was the day for holding a session there, Ibn Daqîq

al-ʿÎd was on his way to the citadel for it, and Mankûtimur saw him coming. The *amîr* started sending messengers to him, one after the other, in order to arrange a meeting with him. This bothered the judge greatly, and he announced to the other judges that he was resigning from office. He returned to his home and sent word to his deputies and the binders of marriages to cease performing their duties until a new judge was appointed. When the sultan heard of this resignation, he became angry at Mankûtimur, and told him to stop interfering in the affairs of the judges. He then sent word to Ibn Daqîq al-ʿÎd, and finally persuaded him to come to the citadel, where the sultan cajoled him into resuming his duties.[121]

However, the sultans were not always that cooperative, nor were the judges always that successful in standing up against the Mamlûk state, especially when the infamous al-Nashw[122] was involved. The Mâlikî chief judge Taqî al-Dîn al-Akhnâʾî was in charge of the money (i.e. legacy) of the children of the *amîr* Arghûn, the *nâʾib*.[123] Al-Nashw came to this judge in the year 736 demanding some of this money. The judge refused, saying the sultan had no right to take the money of the orphans. Al-Nashw said that the sultan only wanted back the money which this judge's brother had stolen when he was *nâẓir khizânat al-khâṣṣ*, but the judge remained adamant. Al-Nashw was enraged and complained to the sultan who, in turn, summoned the judge and ordered him to bring the money which his brother had stolen. When he appeared, the sultan rebuked the judge for his opposition. In the end the judge was forced to capitulate and allow al-Nashw to take the money.[124]

Three years later, in 739, al-Nashw confronted the Shâfiʿî

chief judge, ʿIzz al-Dîn Ibn Jamâʿa. The incident began when the *amîn al-ḫukm* purchased property *(milk)* for some orphans from *mawdaʿ al-ḫukm.*[125] A tax official, who was in charge of collecting a royal tax called al-Qarârîtî,[126] demanded this tax from the *amîn,* because of the purchase he had just made. This led to an argument in ʿIzz al-Dîn's court between the *amîn al-ḫukm* and the tax collector which resulted in the judge reprimanding the latter. This tax official became very angry and complained to al-Nashw, who, in turn, brought the matter before the sultan. However, when al-Nashw told the story to the sultan, he embellished it, and claimed that the tax official had shown the edict *(marsûm)* to the *amîn al-ḫukm.* The sultan's name was on the edict, but, according to al-Nashw, this did not impress the *amîn,* who took the document and threw it on the ground. The sultan became very angry at this, summoned the *amîn al-ḫukm,* and had him beaten in the presence of al-Nashw. Then he made him pay the tax. Al-Nashw then turned on ʿIzz al-Dîn Ibn Jamâʿa, and told the sultan that this judge had inherited 80,000 dinars from his father, and a tax was due on this as well. The sultan would not agree to this, telling al-Nashw that he had reached as far as the chief judge, and that was far enough.[127] We have mentioned earlier this sultan's special fondness for ʿIzz al-Dîn, and this may be the real reason why he stopped al-Nashw. Judging from his remarks to Taqî al-Dîn al-Akhnâʾî, the sultan did not have a great respect for chief judges per se.

A year earlier (738) the sultan had forbade the chief judges from approving any wills. At that time one of al-Nashw's henchmen was seizing the estates of deceased individuals and turning the funds over to al-Nashw. Although the practice became severe and the sultan even reprimanded al-Nashw for it, al-Nashw was able to give excuses for these activities. It was at this point that the sultan (al-Malik al-Nâṣir Muḥammad) began to aid al-Nashw's schemes, and the sultan forbade the endorsement of any wills except by his own decree. This left the way open for al-Nashw's agent, al-Ṭayyibî, to increase his efforts to seize the funds from such legacies.[128] We do not know how long this edict lasted, but it was certainly no longer a problem in 759, when the Shâfiʿî chief judge, Bahâʾ al-Dîn Ibn ʿAqîl, changed the mechanism for writing wills. Previously, notaries had been able to draw up wills only be permission of the (Shâfiʿî chief?) judge. Ibn ʿAqîl removed that restriction, saying that a man could die before such permission was obtained.[129] It is doubtful that there would have been such concern for the drawing up of wills if the earlier confiscations were still widespread.

In many of the cases above we have seen the chief judges as the willing tools of the Mamlûks or registering unsuccessful protests against the actions of some *amîr*, court official, or sultan. This might lead us to believe that the chief judges were, for the most part, simply figureheads with no real power and whose principal role was to lend an air of legitimacy to such ceremonies as royal marriages,[130] the installation of sultans and caliphs,[131] state funerals,[132] and the like. Certainly, the presence of the chief judges at official ceremonies is to be expected, but the incidents we have discussed in some detail may, in fact, be misleading. It was almost impossible for anyone to oppose the sultan or important Mamlûk or official once they had decided on a course of action, because such people were clearly the most powerful men in the empire. On the other hand, the real function of the chief judges and their assistants was to rule on litigations which arose among the masses of the people and to help these people with other legal problems. Why else were deputy judges placed in mosques and *madâris* throughout Cairo and the provinces? And why else were notaries and marriage registrars stationed in shops in the market places?

Unfortunately, one of the weaknesses of Arabic historical writings is the lack of attention it pays to the common people. Only rarely do we hear of judges involved in cases brought by ordinary citizens, and then only because the often bizarre circumstances surrounding these cases attracted the historian's attention. For example, in the year 742 a husband and wife, along with the wife's father, came before the Ḥanafî chief judge, Ḥusâm al-Dîn al-Ghûrî. The wife complained that her husband was not living up to the marriage agreement as regards dowry and clothing. The dower was to be paid at the rate of one dinar per year. The judge told the woman to lower her veil, and after she had done so, the judge screamed at the father, calling him an idiot for letting his daughter marry for so little money. Then he called the husband a fool, because his wife was worth one hundred dirhems a night, not one dinar a year. Al-Maqrîzî says that al-Ghûrî usually sided with a woman against her husband, and was criticized for this attitude.[133] All this indicates that al-Ghûrî was not only different from other judges in his attitude towards such cases, but more importantly these cases were typical of the litigations over which he presided. This same *qâḍî*, again in 742, even judged a case in which workers from the sultan's kitchens were litigants. Unfortunately for the judge, they were not satisfied with his verdict, and as a consequence they wrecked his house at al-Ṣâliḥiyya and nearly killed him.[134] Not all of al-Ghûrî's dissatisfied litigants resorted to violence. In 740 Ṣalâḥ al-Dîn Yûsuf al-Maghribî brought a suit in al-Ghûrî's court demanding the sum of 10,000 dirhems from the *awlâd al-mulûk*.[135] He had sold them some land, but he had never received payment, because al-Nashw had seized the money from the *awlâd al-mulûk*. However, the money was still due to Ibn al-Maghribî, and this was the cause of his legal action. Al-Ghûrî would not agree with Ibn al-Maghribî, and an argument between the two of them developed. Both of them went separately to the sultan to complain about the other, but al-Ghûrî walked to the citadel, while Ibn al-Maghribî rode and thus arrived first. He told the sultan his story, and, in the end, the sultan rebuked the judge, had Ibn al-Maghribî's case brought before the *dâr al-ʿadl*, and forced the *awlâd al-mulûk* to pay the money.[136]

On another occasion, in 753, some Persian merchants appealed to the *ḥâjib*, who was probably substituting for the sultan, in the *dâr al-ʿadl*, because the Ḥanafî judge (perhaps the chief judge Jamâl al-Dîn Ibn al-Turkumânî) had not satisfied them in their complaint against a group of Cairene merchants who owed them money. The *ḥâjib* took over the case and satisfied their demands.[137] Although the chief judges could be overruled by the sultan or someone sitting in his place in the *dâr al-ʿadl*, this was but a single court of appeal. On the other hand, the chief judges and their deputies had courts throughout the city of Cairo, and it was before such courts that almost all litigations must have been presented.

Finally, the chief judges did enjoy some real moral and

legal power within the state. When taxes were levied on the *shuhûd* and *ʿuqqâd* in the year 700 to support the Mamlûk campaigns against the Mongols in Syria, the Mâlikî chief judge, Ibn Makhlûf, worked on behalf of these judicial subordinates and was able to have the tax removed.[138] At another time, in 699, the Shâfiʿî chief judge, Ibn Daqîq al-ʿÎd, opposed a plan to levy a tax on the populace in order to distribute moneys *(nafaqa)* to the armies. Such a *fatwâ* had been issued by the *fuqahâʾ* during the time of Quṭuz (ruled 657-658), but Ibn Daqîq al-ʿÎd refused to re-endorse it, saying that now the *umarâʾ* had plenty of money and could make the payments without any help from the masses; whereas this earlier *fatwâ* had been issued only after the *umarâʾ* had exhausted all their own funds. The masses were spared this tax, but, instead, the money was extorted from the wealthy and merchants.[139] Finally, the Ḥanbalî Muwaffaq al-Dîn al-Maqdisî headed an investigation into the forgeries of bills of debt *(masâtir)*[140] and the like. He had solicited the help of the *amîr* Shaykhû in this. Many houses were raided and such forged documents were found in great numbers.[141]

In conclusion, it is usually not possible to say why a given case came before a particular judge, but it seems that proximity to a certain judge's court or hope for a favorable verdict were important considerations. Of course, if both litigants were members of the same *madhhab,* they would probably seek a judge trained in that *madhhab.* On the other hand, we have seen Cairene judges becoming involved in cases which, it seems, should have been handled by a Damascene or Syrian; for example, the cases of Ibn Taymiyya and Bint al-Ashraf. However, these examples should not be exaggerated. Bint al-Ashraf's case was heard in Cairo because the conspirators in this swindle were in Cairo when they were hatching their plan. Ibn Taymiyya was charged in the Mâlikî chief judge's court in Cairo, and summoned before the sultan in that city, because his enemies knew they could win a verdict against him in Cairo. However, Ibn Taymiyya was a special case since he was a public figure, whose teachings aroused considerable emotion throughout the empire.

The numerous occasions when the Mamlûks were able to twist the provisions of the *sharî'a* to their own ends, usually with, but sometimes without, the cooperation of the chief judges are undeniable. However, the Mamlûks seem to have been generally concerned with adhering to the law in some form and consulting the *'ulamâ'*, including the chief judges, when making decisions. Most rulers or ruling elites want the support, or at least acquiescence, of their subjects in any action which these rulers take. Although the Mamlûk ruling elite was almost always eager to increase its wealth, it had to temper its greed by remembering that it was ruling a professedly Islamic state, where the religious law pervaded all areas of society and politics. The chief judges, who were the interpreters of this religious law, could not stand up against the ruling elite when this oligarchy was determined to have its way, but it could attempt to enforce some adherence to the *sharî'a*. The judges could also play on the insecurities of the Mamlûks. On one occasion an *amîr* who was in charge of some *awqâf* was being miserly in distributing their revenue to the *fuqahâ'*. The Ḥanafî chief judge, Sirâj al-Dîn al-Hindî, rebuked him for this, saying that the *umarâ'* had earned vast amounts of money from their *iqṭâ'ât*, while the *fuqahâ)* had little. The *amîr* answered that he had earned his *iqṭâ(* by *jihâd,* protecting the lands of the Muslims. The judge retorted, "And who taught you about *jihâd,* except the *fuqahâ)?*" This humbled the *amîr.*[142] Finally, the Mamlûks needed the chief judges to satisfy the legal needs of the populace; a task which the Mamlûks did not have the time, inclination, nor ability to perform in any great detail. Thus the four chief judges were the symbols of this Islamic state and necessary for its functioning; as such they were able to demand some adherence to the provisions of the *sharî(a.* They were also able to exert some moral influence on the ruling elite, although their record in this area was usually less than noteworthy. Nevertheless, as the principal interpreters of the Islamic law the chief judges filled important and necessary roles in the Mamlûk empire.

ENDNOTES

[1]See the monograph by E. Tyan, Le Notariat et les regime de la preuve par écrit dans la pratique du droit musulman (Beirut, 1954); also, M. Quatremère, Histoire des sultans mamlouks de l'Egypte (Paris, 1845), II, b, 111-13.

[2]Sadeque, Baybars, p. 197.

[3]Tyan, Histoire, p. 561, note 1. His reference to Quatremère is incorrect, and I have been unable to find the correct one.

[4]Ibn al-Şâbûnî, Takmilat, p. 234.

[5]Inbâʾ al-ghumr, I, 29.

[6]Al-ʿAynî, Ahmet III 2912/4, fol. 181b.

[7]Sulûk, I, 849.

[8]See above, chapter I.

[9]Since there are no lists of deputy judges, as there are for chief judges, it would be necessary to read all the biographical literature and chronicles in order to conduct a proper analysis. This is beyond the scope of the present study. Also, details of their terms of office (e.g. how long they served in any one place) are usually lacking, as evidence by what we know of one of the Shâfiʿî *nuwwâb* (see below note 12).

[10]See Popper, Notes, I, 14, and EI-1, III, 110.

[11]Sulûk, I, 602-603; al-Nuwayrî, Bibliotheque Nationale 1578, fols. 48a-b. This will be discussed in more detail in chapter V.

[12]For the place names, see Popper, Notes, I, 13-14. For biographical details of the judge, see Shadharât, VI, 70; Durar, V, 261-62; al-Adfuwî, Ṭâliʿ, pp. 729-33.

[13]Al-Nuwayrî, Leiden Or. 20, fols. 106a-b. For his biography, see Durar, IV, 24; Ibn Ṭûlûn, Quḍât, p. 247; Wâfî, II, 270. This mosque is described in ʿAli Mubârak, al-Khiṭaṭ al-jadîda, (Bûlâq, 1305/1887), V, 37-38.

[14]Al-Nuwayrî, Leiden Or. 20, fols. 106a-b; concerning this mosque, see Khiṭaṭ, II, 365.

[15]Al-Nuwayrî, Leiden Or. 20, fol. 77b. This probably refers to the Ḥusayniyya quarter of Cairo; see Popper, Notes, I, 33.

[16]Al-Adfuwî, Ṭâliʿ, p. 93. Here again this is probably not a mosque or college, but rather the district; see Popper, Notes, I, 36.

[17]Al-ʿAynî, Ahmet III 2912/4. fol. 148b.

[18]Sulûk, II, 333.

[19]Ibid., III, 400-401.

[20]The relationship of the chief judges to this *madrasa* will be discussed in more detail in the next chapter.

[21]See, e.g., Rafʿ MS, fol. 105a.

[22]Al-Maqrîzî provides a description of the chief judge's court during the Fâṭimid period (Khiṭaṭ, I, 404). A description of the chief judge's court and general judicial procedure, but from a much later period, is to be found in E.W. Lane, The Manners and Customs of the Modern Egyptians (London, 1954), pp. 116 ff.

[23]His full name was Ismâʿîl ibn Saʿîd al-Kurdî (Durar, I, 391-92; Sulûk, II, 212-213). Although this incident is related in several sources, the best account is al-Nuwayrî, Leiden Or. 20, fols. 117a-118b, and it is the one I have relied on here. A more meagre account is to be found in al-ʿAynî, Ahmet III, 2912/4, fol. 331a.

[24]Sulûk, II, 212; Durar, I, 391.

[25]Al-ʿAynî, Ahmet III 2912/4, fol. 331a; Durar, I, 391.

[26]This is Muḥammad ibn Naṣr Allâh, who died in 736 (Durar,

V, 44).

[27]Al-Nuwayrî, Leiden Or. 20, fol. 117a.

[28]Ibid., fol. 117b. See also Khiṭaṭ, II, 382 concerning this *madrasa*.

[29]This is the same as *wâlî* al-Qâhira, the governor and chief of police of al-Qâhira; Popper, Notes, I, 93.

[30]Al-ʿAynî, Ahmet III 2912/4, fol. 331a; EI-1, III, 53-54.

[31]Al-ʿAynî, Ahmet III 2912/4, fol. 331a; see also al-Nuwayrî, Leiden Or. 20, fol. 117b.

[32]Durar, I, 329-33; Wâfî, VIII, 158-59.

[33]Sulûk, I, 925; Quatremère, Histoire, II, b, 192. The Arabic text does not use the word Quran, but rather *al-rabʿa*, which R. Dozy in his Supplement aux dictionnaires arabes (Leiden, 1967; I, 503) translates as "exemplaire du Coran," but which E. W. Lane in An Arabic-English Lexicon (London, 1867; I/3, 103) says is a chest in which volumes of the Quran were kept.

[34]Sulûk, I, 925.

[35]Durar, I, 329.

[36]Ibid.; Ibn al-Dawâdârî, Kanz al-durar (Cairo, 1960), IX, 77.

[37]Sulûk, I, 925.

[38]Ibn al-Dawâdârî, Kanz al-durar, IX, 77; Durar, I, 329-30; Sulûk, I, 925; al-ʿAynî, Ahmet III 2912/4, fol. 212a.

[39]Durar, I, 332; al-ʿAynî, Ahmet III 2912/4, fol. 212b.

[40]Durar, I, 332-33; al-ʿAynî, Ahmet III 2912/4, fol. 213a; Sulûk, I, 926.

[41]Sulûk, I, 926; al-ʿAynî, Ahmet III 2912/4, fol. 213a.

[42]Sulûk, I, 926; al-ʿAynî, Ahmet III 2912/4, fol. 213a.

[43]Durar, I, 333.

[44]E. Strauss, in his article "L'Inquisition dans l'état mamlouk" (Rivista degli Studi Orientali, XXV (1950), 11-26), has surveyed the prosecution of many cases of religious unorthodoxy and heresy throughout the Mamlûk era and in all parts of the Mamlûk empire. He claims (ibid., p. 24) that ordinarily the Mâlikî chief judges in the principal cities (in Egypt this would be Cairo and Alexandria) passed judgement on cases of apostasy, although deputy judges could be authorized to deal with them. When such cases occurred in the provincial cities, the preliminaries were handled by the local (deputy) judge, but the accused was sent to the capital for final judgement.

Although the Mâlikî chief judge is present in many of the cases we have met (see more below), it is apparent that he did not have exclusive jurisdiction. The opinions of the other chief judges were solicited, and the cases often came before other chief judges. As for the relationship between the chief judges and the *nuwwâb*, there is not enough evidence from the present study of the Cairene chief judges to either confirm or deny his assertions. The examples which Strauss gives (and which I have been able to check) refer to Syria not Egypt.

Strauss also says (ibid., p. 25) that the sultan sometimes had all the chief judges assemble to decide on cases on apostasy, but at other times the sultan would direct a deputy judge or a chief judge whose opinion was pleasing to the ruler to decide on the case. On occasion the sultan would even pronounce judgement himself. The cases which I have studied do not show the sultan taking such a prominent role; rather, these legal cases were handled by the judicial bureaucracy.

[45]Inbâʾ al-ghumr, II, 229-30.

[46]Sulûk, III, 481. Ibn Ḥajar (Inbâʾ al-ghumr, II, 102) says the argument was concerning al-Khashâbiyya, which could refer to several different Muslim sects; see EI-1, II, 917-18.

[47]Sulûk, III, 481.

[48]Inbâʾ al-ghumr, II, 102.

[49]Durar, III, 420-21.

[50]This is Yâqût ibn ʿAbd Allâh, who died in 732 (Durar, V, 183; Ibn Kathîr, XIV, 159).

[51]Sulûk, II, 408.

[52]Al-ʿAynî, Ahmet III 2911/c34, fol. 28a.

[53]See J.S. Trimingham, The Sufi Orders in Islam (London, 1971), especially pp. 84-90.

[54]See R. Nicholson and G.C. Anawati, "Ittiḥâd," EI-2, IV, 282-83; Durar, III, 420-21.

[55]Al-ʿAynî, Ahmet III 2911/c34, fol. 28a.

[56]Ibid.; Durar, III, 421.

[57]Al-ʿAynî, Ahmet III 2911/c34, fols. 28a-b.

[58]Ibid., fol. 28a; Sulûk, II, 408.

[59]Sulûk, II, 408; al-ʿAynî, Ahmet III 2911/c34, fol. 28a.

[60]Muḥammad ibn Ishâq (Durar, III, 470); he was ʿIzz al-Dîn Ibn Jamâʿa's chief deputy as well as his son-in-law. In fact, al-Munâwî was the one who really handled the legal business, while ʿIzz al-Dîn performed the ceremonial duties and some teaching (Durar, II, 491).

[61]Sulûk, II, 894.

[62]Al-Nuwayrî, Leiden Or. 19b, fol. 101a.

[63]Wâfî, VII, 395; Durar, I, 303-306.

[64]Durar, I, 306.

[65]Sulûk, I, 909-12. See also D. P. Little, "Coptic Conversion to Islam under the Baḥrî Mamlûks, 692-755/1293-1354," Bulletin of the School of Oriental and African Studies, XXXIX/3 (1976); this incident is described on pp. 554-57.

[66]Wiet, Manhal, no. 1463; Durar, III, 15-18.

[67]Sulûk, II, 173. Al-Maqrîzî claims that this was the reason for his deposition from the judgeship of al-Qâhira, but this seems unlikely, because it is clear that the real reason for his deposition was his refusal to authorize the exchange of some

awqâf lands for other lands; a transfer which the sultan wanted, and which another *ʿâlim* offered to approve in exchange for the chief judgeship (ibid., II, 173-74). This other *ʿâlim*, Sirâj al-Dîn al-Râzî, approached Karîm al-Dîn al-Kabîr with his proposition. The presence of this Coptic convert to Islam in both incidents probably explains why al-Maqrîzî linked the two events. However, it was Ibn al-Ḥarîrî's refusal to approve the transfer of lands which led to the loss of half his jurisdiction, not Karîm al-Dîn's opposition, which could not have been very great anyway, since Ibn al-Ḥarîrî regained his old power shortly thereafter when al-Râzî died.

68 Durar, I, 323-24. Al-Ṣafadî (Aʿyân, fol. 60b) calls him Ibn Mirâ.

69 Al-ʿAynî, Ahmet III 2912/4, fol. 367a.

70 Aʿyân, fol. 60b; concerning this mosque, see Khiṭaṭ, II, 306.

71 Aʿyân, fol. 60b; Durar, I, 323. G. Makdisi has shown that Ibn Taymiyya was not opposed to Sufism per se, but rather its excesses. I assume his disciple shared his views. See G. Makdisi, "Ibn Taimiyya: A Ṣûfi of the Qâdiriya Order," The American Journal of Arabic Studies, I, (1973), 118-29.

72 Al-ʿAynî, Ahmet III 2912/4, fol. 367b.

73 Ibid., see also Durar, I, 323.

74 Al-ʿAynî, Ahmet III 2912/4, fol. 367b.

75 Ibid.

76 Durar, I, 324.

77 Ibid.; Sulûk, II, 263.

78 Al-ʿAynî, Ahmet III 2912/4, fol. 367b.

79 Ibid.; Ibn Ḥajar (Durar, I, 324) says that after his beating he was released from jail, started preaching again, and was jailed again. Only then did someone intercede for him, and he was forced to leave Cairo.

[80]*Durar*, I, 374.

[81]Ibn Kathîr, XIV, 155.

[82]Ibn Taymiyya's career, and especially his relationship with the Mamlûk state, have been discussed in great detail elsewhere. See H.Q. Murâd, "The *Miḥan* of Ibn Taymiyya," (unpublished M.A. thesis, McGill University, 1968); hereafter cited as Murâd. See also D.P. Little, "The Historical and Historiographical Significance of the Detention of Ibn Taymiyya," *International Journal of Middle Eastern Studies*, IV (1973), 311-27; and the works of H. Laoust, especially his *Essai sur les doctrines sociales et politiques de Takî-d-Dîn Aḥmad ibn Taimîya* (Cairo, 1939), and "Le Ḥanbalisme sous les mamlouks bahrides," *Revue des Etudes Islamiques*, XXVIII (1960), 1-71.

[83]Murâd, p. 92; al-Nuwayrî, Leiden Or. 20, fol. 27b; Ibn Kathîr, XIV, 38.

[84]Murâd, p. 83.

[85]*Ibid*., p. 82.

[86]Al-Nuwayrî, Leiden Or. 20, fol. 29b. See also Murâd, pp. 94-96.

[87]Al-Nuwayrî, Leiden Or. 20, fol. 30a.

[88]Murâd, pp. 98-99.

[89]Ibn Kathîr, XIV, 54; al-ʿAynî, Ahmet III 2912/4, fol. 272b; Murâd, pp. 101-102.

[90]Al-Nuwayrî, Leiden Or. 20, fol. 30b. The Ḥanafî chief judge of those years, Shams al-Dîn al-Sarûjî, was also an opponent of Ibn Taymiyya, and even wrote tracts rebutting Ibn Taymiyya's views; see *Sulûk*, II, 94, and Laoust, "Hanbalisme," p. 21.

[91]Sulûk, II, 185.

[92]Al-Nuwayrî, Leiden Or. 20, fol. 29a.

[93]Murâd, pp. 106-107.

[94]Sulûk, II, 273.

[95]Murâd, p. 108.

[96]Ibid., p. 111.

[97]See above, chapter I, pp. 20-21.

[98]Al-ʿAynî, Ahmet III 2912/4, fol. 346b.

[99]Sulûk, II, 888.

[100]Ibid., p. 82.

[101]Durar, II, 305-306.

[102]This is ʿAlam al-Dîn ʿAbd Allâh Ibn Zanbûr (ibid., p. 345).

[103]Sulûk, II, 888.

[104]Ibid., p. 889; Rafʿ, II, 299-300.

[105]Durar, III, 342-44.

[106]Al-ʿAynî, Ahmet III 2912/4, fol. 389b; Sulûk, II, 320-21.

[107]Sulûk, II, 362. Al-Maqrîzî says that the Ḥanbalî judge was Sharaf al-Dîn al-Ḥarrânî, which is impossible since al-Ḥarrânî died at the end of his term as chief judge in 709. Perhaps this refers to some deputy judge, or al-Maqrîzî is simply in error.

[108]See J. Sublet, "La Folie de la Princesse Bint al-Ashraf," Bulletin d'Etudes Orientales, XXVII (1974), p. 47, note 7.

[109]See ibid., p. 48, note 1.

[110]See ibid., p. 45, note 1.

[111]Ibid., p. 48.

[112]Haarmann, Quellenstudien (Arabic text) pp. 90-91.

[113]Sublet, "Folie," p. 48, note 2.

[114]Ibid., p. 48.

[115]Al-Nu⁽aymî, Dâris, I, 73.

[116]Sublet, "Folie," p. 49.

[117]Durar, IV, 159; Sulûk, II, 173-74; al-ʿAynî, Ahmet III 2912/4, fols. 316b-317a.

[118]Sulûk, III, 345-47; Inbâʾ al-ghumr, I, 273-74.

[119]Wiet, Manhal, no. 2544.

[120]Ibid., no. 1898.

[121]Al-ʿAynî, Ahmet III 2912/4, fols. 181b-182a; Sulûk, I, 848-49.

[122]ʿAbd al-Wahhâb ibn Fadl Allâh (Durar, III, 42-44).

[123]Durar, I, 374.

[124]Sulûk, II, 393-94.

[125]Sulûk, II, 458; al-ʿAynî, Ahmet III 2911/c34, fol. 116b.

[126]See Sulûk, II, 458, note 2.

[127]Al-ʿAynî, Ahmet III 2911/c34, fols. 116b-117b; Sulûk, II, 458-59.

[128]Sulûk, II, 435-36.

[129]Sulûk, III, 41.

[130]For example, the Ḥanafî chief judge, Shams al-Dîn Ibn

al-Ḥarîrî, concluded the marriage contract between an *amîr* and one of the daughters of the Sultan al-Malik al-Nâṣir Muḥammad in the presence of all the chief judges (al-Nuwayrî, Leiden Or. 19b, fol. 119b); see also Sulûk, II, 237 for another such marriage. Another occasion is described in Sulûk, (II, 612) where all four chief judges went to an *amîr's* house to conclude the marriage of the son of the *amîr*.

[131]E.g., Sulûk, II, 502-503; ibid., p. 843; ibid., p. 603.

[132]E.g., ibid., I, 744.

[133]Ibid., II, 611.

[134]Raf‘, I, 203, Durar, II, 128.

[135]According to the editor of Sulûk, this term could refer either to the children of deceased sultans or the children of the Ayyûbid rulers (Sulûk, II, 474, note 3).

[136]Al-‘Aynî, Ahmet III 2912/4, fols. 177b-178a; Sulûk, II, 490-91.

[137]Sulûk, II, 863-64. This is the case upon which later writers based their belief that the Mongol Yâsâ had become part of the legal system of the Mamlûk empire, and that this legal code was administered by the *ḥâjib*. Ayalon has shown that the Yâsâ was not at all a part of the Mamlûk legal system in his series of articles, "The Great Yâsa of Chingiz Khân. A Reexamination," Studia Islamica, XXXIII (1971), 97-140; XXXIV (1972), 151-80; XXXVI (1972), 113-58; XXXVIII (1973), 107-56. Concerning this particular incident, see ibid., XXXVIII (1973), p. 123.

[138]Sulûk, I, 907.

[139]Al-‘Aynî, Ahmet III 2912/4, fols. 201a-b; Sulûk, I, 897-98.

[140]Sulûk, II, 902, note 2.

[141]Ibid., p. 902.

[142]Inbâ᾽ al-ghumr, I, 30-31.

CHAPTER V

Other Posts

A. Non-Teaching

In addition to holding the office of *qâḍî al-quḍât,* all the chief judges held other posts as well during their careers. They were all employed in one or more positions at the time they were raised to the rank of chief judge. Sometimes, they were allowed to keep their previous posts, sometimes they were forced to give up all or some of them, and at other times they were given a whole new batch of posts to replace the ones they had lost. In any case, it is impossible to make generalizations about the timing of additional appointments; it depended entirely on the individuals involved. Only two generalizations are valid. All the judges held teaching posts before and after they were appointed; and, of the four *madhâhib,* the Shâfiʿîs were the most successful in acquiring posts, the Ḥanafîs second (but not nearly so successful), the Mâlikîs third, and the Ḥanbalîs were far behind everyone else.

Before continuing, however, we must remember one important point; namely, we can never know all the posts which all the judges held during their careers. The really famous judges, such as Tâj al-Dîn Ibn Bint al-Aʿazz or Badr al-Dîn Ibn Jamâʿa, received considerable attention in the sources, and their careers are described in considerable detail. On the other hand, less famous judges, especially among the Ḥanbalîs and Mâlikîs, received much less attention and we usually have much less information on their careers. This may be the reason why it seems they held less posts, but this is still an open question. It seems that the biographers and chroniclers were interested in the most important and dramatic personalities of their times. If a person really did hold a large number of posts it would certainly get reported. On the other hand, the biographers often have a tendency to generalize. Thus, if someone held, for example, ten different teaching posts in his lifetime, it would be unusual if we were to learn about all of them. Rather, it was customary to list a few teaching posts, usually the more prominent ones, as examples of the fact that the individual was a teacher of some prominence. The biographers had little patience to recite long lists of *madâris*. At the same time, many appointments are mentioned in the chronicles, but the presentation of these appointments is by no means consistent. Often there are gaps, when, for instance, no teaching appointments for a given *madrasa* will be mentioned for many years, thus preventing us from compiling a detailed list of teachers. By the same token, the sources do not always tell us what subjects a particular person taught at any given institution. They usually say *"darrasa"* or some variant construction of this verb, which is a general term for teaching, with no special technical meaning. In spite of these difficulties there is considerable information available concerning the bureaucratic and teaching posts which the chief judges held during their careers, and this information points up the wide variety of jobs which the *quḍât* held.

Wazîr

The office of *wazîr* was among the highest ranking offices in the civil bureaucracy. It went through great changes in the Baḥrî period; at a time it disappeared and its duties were divided among four functionaries, and sometimes it was not even held by a civilian, but rather by a high ranking *amîr*. In the earlier years of the present study, this post was held by several of the Shâfiʿî chief judges. Two of them were from the family of Ibn Bint al-Aʿazz and the other was Burhân al-Dîn al-Sinjârî.

Of these three Burhân al-Dîn enjoyed the shortest judicial career. In the years 659-660, prior to the establishment of the four chief judgeships, he and his brother had shared the judgeship of Egypt; Burhân al-Dîn being the judge of Fusṭâṭ. He did not return to the judgeship until the year of his death, 686, when he was appointed judge of al-Qâhira, but he lived for less than a month after assuming office. He held the post of *wazîr* twice. The first time was for about a year (677-678) after the death of Bahâʾ al-Dîn Ibn Ḥannâ, but he was deposed at the instigation of al-Shujâʿî. He managed to return in 679-680, after the death of the *wazîr* al-Asfûnî,[1] but was forced out of office again by al-Shujâʿî. After both depositions, he and his son were jailed and beaten. In between times, he held one or more teaching posts.[2] Al-Sinjârî's problem was that he was never strong enough to overcome his opponents, Ibn Ḥannâ and al-Shujâʿî, both of whom managed to conrol the wazirate and other high offices for much longer periods than al-Sinjârî ever could.

Tâj al-Dîn Ibn Bint al-A'azz, the first in the line of Shâfi'î chief judges in the present study, might be seen as a more successful version of al-Sinjârî. According to Ibn Kathîr, he held fifteen different offices in his lifetime.[3] He had been *wazîr* during the Ayyûbid period under al-Malik al-Kâmil[4] and during the Mamlûk period for the years 655-657,[5] which roughly coincides with the reign of Sultan al-Manşûr Nûr al-Dîn 'Alî. Ibn Bint al-A'azz never stayed very long in any one post, but he was able to stay at the top, and his shifting about among various posts was always at the highest levels. However, the important events in Tâj al-Dîn's career occurred before the period under study, and even before the Mamlûk era. Ibn Taghrî Birdî, looking back at the bureaucratic history of Egypt, considered him one of the great *wuzarâ)*.[6]

A much more interesting case, and one that falls entirely within the framework of the present study, is that of one of Tâj al-Dîn's sons, Taqî al-Dîn. He managed to hold seventeen posts in his lifetime,[7] but even this does not reflect the high status he achieved under Sultan Qalâ)ûn, because he held the posts of chief judge, *wazîr*, and *nâẓir al-khizâna* (see more below on this last office) all at the same time. As we have mentioned earlier, Tâj al-Dîn had assumed the judgeship of Fusţâţ in 685 after the death of Wajîh al-Dîn al-Bahnasî and worked to get the judge of al-Qâhira, Ibn al-Khuwayyî, transferred to Syria so that he could become chief judge of all Cairo. His plans were thwarted by the appointment of Burhân al-Dîn al-Sinjârî to replace Ibn Khuwayyî, but he finally achieved his goal when al-Sinjârî died. He was first offered the wazirate in 687, but refused it, and the *amîr* Baydarâ took it instead. However, Taqî al-Dîn was the real power. Not only did he still hold the office of *nâẓir al-khizâna*, but the new *wazîr* depended on him for advice. He used to go to Baydarâ every Thursday to decide with him what to do.[8] Eventually Baydarâ appointed Ḍiyâ) al-Dîn (Abd allâh al-Nashshâ)î[9] as his deputy and he helped him instead. Soon thereafter Taqî al-Dîn replaced Baydarâ as *wazîr* (same year, 687) in addition to his other duties. However, according to al-Maqrîzî, he kept himself too involved with the affairs of the *sharî(a*, and the wazirate became burdensome to him, so it was returned to Baydarâ.[10] Thus he was even more successful than his father, because he did not hold these high posts in rotation, but rather, incredibly, at the same time. It is most interesting that Taqî al-Dîn, an ambitious man who had probably grown up in court circles, should want to avoid the office of *wazîr*. He was single-minded and resolutely determined to become chief judge of all Cairo, even working to get Ibn al-Khuwayyî out of the way so he could advance more easily. Yet he was reluctant to become *wazîr*, and even resigned after only a brief term. He must have had considerable power, because even after his deposition as chief judge of Cairo in 690, Ibn Sal(ûs, the *wazîr* of the new sultan, al-Ashraf Khalîl, was afraid to allow Taqî al-Dîn to become chief judge of Damascus, lest he regain his old position and power.[11] Apparently, Ibn Bint al-A(azz felt himself powerful enough without the honorific of *wazîr*. On the other hand, the eleven year reign of Qalâ)ûn saw the appointment of six different *wuzarâ)*,[12] and perhaps the explanation of Tâj al-Dîn's actions lies in his desire to avoid a too prominent and too insecure office.

There was an opportunity for a Mâlikî judge to become *wazîr* during the sultanate of Qalâ'ûn, but Zayn al-Dîn Ibn Makhlûf, who was Mâlikî chief judge from 685 to 718, refused out of fear of ʿAlam al-Dîn al-Shujâʿî,[13] Qalâ'ûn's sometime *wazîr*.

Nâẓir al-khizâna, nâẓir al-khizâna al-kubrâ, nâẓir al-khâṣṣ, nâẓir khizânat al-khâss, nâẓir al-amlak al-ṣulṭâniyya, et. al.

In the year 729, al-Malik al-Nâṣir Muḥammad Ibn Qalâ'ûn abolished the wazirate, and "the function of the vizier passed to four lower officials, *nâẓir al-mâl, shâdd al-dawâwîn, nâẓir al-khâṣṣ,* and *kâtib al-sirr.* However, this division of power seems to have been merely theoretical. In practice, most of it was concentrated in the hands of the *nâẓir al-khâṣṣ,* who was the head of the *dîwân al-khâṣṣ,* and thus became the most important official in the Mamlûk sultanate."[14] "All the financial resources which had formerly flowed into *al-khizâna al-kubrâ,* that is, *bayt al-mâl* (the treasury), were diverted to the *khizânat al-khâṣṣ,* the private sultani treasury controlled by the *nâẓir al-khâṣṣ,* so that only minor financial matters were still subject to the authority of *al-khizâna al-kubrâ.*"[15]

The point to be made here is that before 729, the *nâẓir al-khizâna* was of great importance, apparently controlling the funds of the treasury. The *nâẓir bayt al-mâl* seems to have been charged with the more mundane duties of collection and distribution of revenue.[16] After that date, the *nâẓir al-khâṣṣ,* a post which had existed even earlier, became even more powerful, and most revenue went to the sultan's treasury over which the *nâẓir al-khâṣṣ* was in control. The *nâẓir al-khizâna* gradually lost influence, and was left in charge of the robes of honor. He began to be called *nâẓir al-khizâna al-kubrâ,* but the more grandiose title was, in fact, hollow.[17] Another official, the *nâẓir khizânat al-khâṣṣ,* was a subordinate of the *nâẓir al-khâss.*[18]

No judge is described as having held the post of *nâẓir al-khâṣṣ,* but several of them were appointed to the other posts. Sharaf al-Dîn al-Ḥarrânî al-Ḥanbalî (in office 696-709) held the post of *nâẓir al-khizâna* for a long time, and upon his appointment to the chief judgeship combined both offices[19] and apparently held both of them until he died. Taqî al-Dîn Ibn ʿAwaḍ al-Ḥanbalî (in office 712-738) was appointed *nâẓir al-khizâna* in 716, and thus held the two posts concurrently.[20] Our information on the holders of this office in the years between al-Ḥarrânî's death and Ibn ʿAwaḍ's appointment is somewhat sketchy. Ḍiyâʾ al-Dîn al-Nashshâʾî[21] held it from 714 until his death in 716, and he had assumed it at the death of Saʿd al-Dîn Muḥammad al-Aqfahsî in 714,[22] but we do not know who held it after al-Ḥarrânî died and before al-Aqfahsî took over. There is no evidence that Saʿd al-Dîn or Ḍiyâʾ al-Dîn were Ḥanbalîs. Ibn ʿAwaḍ was deposed from the chief judgeship in 738, but there is no indication if he was still *nâẓir al-khizâna* at that time nor who succeeded him as *nâẓir.*

At an earlier date the Mâlikîs were also given access to this office. Ibn Makhlûf (in office 685-718) was already *nâẓir al-khizâna* at the time of his appointment as chief judge, and there is reason to believe that he gained that post very soon after Qalâʾûn became sultan in 678 and held it until he died.[23] He was also *nâẓir al-amlâk al-sulṭâniyya.* This was a most privileged position, since it involved the administration of some of the sultan's personal properties.[24] In his role as *nâẓir al-amlâk* Ibn Makhlûf was responsible for organizing the finances which would support the *madrasa* the sultan was building, al-Nâşiriyya, which was completed in 703.[25]

We have mentioned above in our discussion of the wazirate that at one time, in the year 687, Taqî al-Dîn Ibn Bint al-Aʿazz held three posts simultaneously: *qâḍî al-quḍât, wazîr,* and *nâẓir al-khizâna.*[26] This would mean that Ibn Makhlûf, whom we have been told was *nâẓir al-khizâna* at the time of his becoming Mâlikî *qâḍî al-quḍât* in 685, probably gave it up around the time he became chief judge. However, al Nuwayrî had indicated that he held both posts until he died. Also, this post of *nâẓir al-khizâna* is sometimes called *nâẓir al-khizâna al-sulṭâniyya* in the biographies of Taqî al-Dîn Ibn Bint al-Aʿazz[27] and Sharaf al-Dîn al-Ḥarrânî.[28] Is this simply an elaborate way of saying *nâẓir al-khizâna* or does it refer to the *nâẓir al-khâşş* or an early version of the *nâẓir al-khâşş?* Taqî al-Dîn Ibn ʿAwaḍ is called *nâẓir al-khizâna al-kubrâ,*[29] which we know to be what the *nâẓir al-khizâna* was called after 729. These inconsistent uses of titles are confusing and leave us in doubt as to what offices these judges really held and what duties they performed in them.

Also, in the year 680 al-Maqrîzî records that Taqî al-Dîn Ibn Bint al-Aʿazz was put in charge of the *madrasa* and *al-turba* al-Şâliḥiyya, which posts his brother Şadr al-Dîn was forced to relinquish when he became Shâfiʿî chief judge in that year. These posts were to be in addition to the post he already held, that of *nâẓir al-khazâʾin al-maʿmûra.*[30] This post is not mentioned in any of the secretarial literature. Quatremère, in a footnote to his translation of al-Sulûk, mentions *al-makhzan al-maʿmûr,* which he translates as "les magasins du prince,"[31] and this may mean, therefore, that Taqî al-Dîn was the overseer of some of the sultan's warehouses. However, later we learn that in the year 690, Taqî al-Dîn was stripped of all his posts. There had been seventeen of them, including teaching posts, and all except these teaching posts are listed, but only the office of *nâẓir al-khizâna* is mentioned, not that of *nâẓir al-khazâʾin al-maʿmûra.*[32] Does this mean that the two titles are synonymous? The question, unfortunately, must remain unanswered until someone has classified all the bureaucratic titles of the Baḥrî period.

The office of *nâẓir khizânat al-khâṣṣ,* supposedly one of the subordinates of the *nâẓir al-khâṣṣ,* was held by three Mâlikî chief judges at some stage in their career; all of them were members of the al-Akhnâʾî family. Tâj al-Dîn al-Akhnâʾî (in office 750-763) was first made *nâẓir khizânat al-khâṣṣ* in 753, when he was already a *qâḍî al-quḍât,* but he resigned as *nâẓir* the same year and was replaced by Tâj al-Dîn al-Jawjarî.[33] In 756 he was removed very briefly as chief judge, and was replaced by Nûr al-Dîn al-Sakhâwî. Al-Akhnâʾî was then returned to the office of *nâẓir khizânat al-khâṣṣ* and his brother, the future chief judge Burhân al-Dîn, was made his assistant.[34] When al-Sakhâwî died a few months later, Tâj al-Dîn al-Akhnâʾî was returned to the chief judgeship, and he held both posts until his death in 763.[35] Although Burhân al-Dîn (in office 763-777) had been his brother's assistant as *nâẓir,* he lost that post when he himself became chief judge.[36] Burhân al-Dîn's nephew, Badr al-Dîn, who succeeded his uncle as chief judge in 777 (in office 777-778; 779), had also been *nâẓir khizânat al-khâṣṣ* early in his career, but we do not know the exact date, although it was probably sometime prior to 772 when he became *muftî* in the *dâr al-ʿadl.*[37]

Yet even with the office of *nâẓir khizânat al-khâṣṣ* the biographers and historians create some confusion. For example, al-Maqrîzî says that Tâj al-Dîn al-Akhnâ'î was *nâẓir khizânat al-khâṣṣ* and even gives the dates of his appointments.[38] However, Ibn Ḥajar al-ʿAsqalânî calls him *nâẓir al-khizâna al-sulṭâniyya* in this judge's biography in Rafʿ al-iṣr[39] and simply *nâẓir al-khizâna* in al-Durar al-kâmina.[40] Once again, the matter is extremely confusing, and the combination of a tendency in the biographies to abbreviate titles plus the lack of data in the chronicles every time a new candidate occupied a bureaucratic post makes a final solution of the problem of such titles impossible.

Finally, there is the case of ʿIzz al-Dîn Ibn Jamâʿa, who is described by al-Asnawî as having been *wakîl al-khâṣṣa wa-al-ʿâmma.*[41] This is apparently another way of saying that he had held the posts of *wakîl* both in the *dîwân al-khâṣṣ* and in the *bayt al-mâl.* In 731 he succeeded a certain al-Tâj Isḥâq as *wakîl bayt al-mâl.*[42] He seems to have lost this post prior to 734, but was reinstated in 737.[43] This reappointment in 737 was in addition to his earlier appointment as *wakîl al-khâṣṣ,* but the original date of this latter appointment is unknown. Probably, the *wakîl al-khâṣṣ* was also a subordinate of the *nâẓir al-khâṣṣ,* although the secretarial encyclopaedias do not mention it. These appointments were made prior to his assuming office as chief judge, and there is no indication if he continued to hold them afterwards. It is interesting to note that also in 731 he was appointed *nâẓir* of the mosque of Ibn Ṭûlûn and *al-madrasa al-Nâṣiriyya.*[44] Ibn Jamâʿa was well thought of by Sultan al-Malik al-Nâṣir Muḥammad, and all these appointments, culminating in his appointment to the chief judgeship in 738, were undoubtedly signs of approval.[45]

Nâẓir al-awqâf

The title of this section should be taken in its most general meaning, so as to include the management or controllership *(naẓar)* of any sort of *awqâf*, including those used to support mosques, colleges, etc. As with the posts previously discussed, an individual might have held one or more of these posts before, after, or during his judgeship.

The first time we hear of the post of controller of the funds of the orphans *(al-naẓar fî mâl al-aytâm)* is with Tâj al-Dîn Ibn Bint al-Aʿazz at the time of the establishment of the four chief judgeships, although this was probably the office of *nâẓir al-aḥbas*.[46] This particular office was lost to the Shâfiʿî chief judge at this judge's death, but Lâjîn gave the Shâfiʿî chief judge a special fund for orphans later, as we have mentioned in chapter I. Later in the Baḥrî period two Ḥanafî chief judges attempted to upgrade the status of the Ḥanafî chief judgeship, and one of the new areas over which they sought jurisdiction was the control of the funds of the Ḥanafî orphans. The Ḥanafîs had no lasting success in these attempts, and thus the Shâfiʿî chief judge controlled a special fund for the orphans throughout most of the Baḥrî period.[47]

After the restoration of the mosque of Ibn Ṭûlûn in the sultanate of al-Mâlik al-Nâṣir Muḥammad, it was managed both by *ʿulamâʾ* and *umarâʾ*. However, at certain times it was assigned exclusively to the Shâfiʿî *qâḍî al-quḍât*. The first *nâẓir* was Sultan Lâjîn's *dawâdâr*,[48] ʿAlam al-Dîn Sinjâr al-Jawâlî, and he was followed by the Shâfi'î chief judge, Badr al-Dîn Ibn Jamâ'a.[49] We do not know the date of Badr al-Dîn's appointment, but it could not have been earlier than 702, because he was living in Damascus during the sultanate of Lâjîn (696-702) and did not return to Egypt until he was summoned to the chief judgeship of Cairo at the death of Ibn Daqîq al-'Îd in Ṣafar, 702.[50] He was followed in this controllership by another *amîr*, at whose death Badr al-Dîn's son, 'Izz al-Dîn, was made its *nâẓir*.[51] 'Izz al-Dîn lost the post to Karîm al-Dîn al-Kabîr, but when the latter fell out of favour, the post was returned to the office of the Shâfi'î chief judge, where it remained until the days of Sultan al-Nâṣir Ḥasan (ruled 748-752, 755-762).[52] During his sultanate the amîr Ṣarghitmish became *nâẓir*,[53] apparently at the expense of the new chief judge,'Izz al-Dîn Ibn Jamâ'a (in office 738-766), but the *amîr* was imprisoned in 759.[54] After this, the Shâfi'î chief judge became *nâẓir* again, until the year 792, when Sultan Barqûq appointed an *amîr*.[55] This would mean that all the Shâfi'î chief judges from 759 until the end of the Baḥrî period (except for the year 764-766 when 'Izz al-Dîn Ibn Jamâ'a lost it)[56] held this post.[57] Thus Bahâ' al-Dîn al-Subkî (in office 766-773), Burhân al-Dîn Ibn Jamâ'a (773-779, 781-784) and Badr al-Dîn al-Subkî (in office 779-781) were also controllers of the mosque of Ibn Ṭûlûn while they held the office of Shâfi'î *qâḍî al-quḍât*.

Such detailed chronicles of the controllership of other mosques and colleges are not so readily available. However, the evidence is clear that the judges did hold the controllerships of others of them. One such college was the *madrasa* Zayn al-Tujjâr.[58] Tâj al-Dîn Ibn Bint A'azz had been a *mu'îd* there under its teacher and *nâẓir*, Al-Armâwî. He substituted for al-Armâwî as its *nâẓir* while the latter was on the pilgrimage, but this appointment never became permanent.[59] This occurred while Tâj al-Dîn was still quite young, and before he had held any other posts. Burhân al-Dîn al-Sinjârî (in office for a few weeks in 686) became both *nâẓir* and professor at the *madrasa* al-Shâfʿiyya (i.e., *al-madrasa* al-Nâṣiriyya bi-al-Qarâfa) in 682.[60] This appointment came after his second deposition from the wazirate, and may have been some sort of consolation for its loss. Ṣadr al-Dîn Ibn Bint al-Aʿazz had been teacher and *nâẓir* at the *qubba* and *madrasa* al-Ṣâliḥiyya, and in the year 680 when he died, these posts went to his brother, Taqî al-Dîn,[61] who lost them when he lost the chief judgeship himself in 690.[62] These appointments certainly did not belong to the Shâfiʿî chief judge by custom, and in fact, a eunuch became *nâẓir* at the mausoleum at al-Ṣâliḥiyya for a brief period between the controllerships of Ṣadr al-Dîn and Taqî al-Dîn.[63] Ṣadr al-Dîn also lost the controllership of *al-mashhad* al-Ḥusaynî[64] at that time, and it passed first to one of the chancery scribes and then to the *ustâdâr*.[65]

The Mâlikî chief judge Ibn Makhlûf (in office 685-718) was instrumental in the establishment of the *madrasa* al-Nâṣiriyya, which was built by al-Malik al-Nâṣir Muḥammad. In fact, he drew up the deed and made himself its *nâẓir* for life, in addition to holding the teaching post in *fiqh* in the section reserved for the Mâlikîs. The controllership and the teaching post were supposed to remain in his family, and if it died out, it was to pass to the Mâlikî chief judge. However, he had earned the enmity of Shihâb al-Dîn Ibn ʿUbâda, whom he had put to work as his assistant in drawing up the *awqâf* to support this *madrasa* and as deputy judge.[66] Shihâb al-Dîn was angry that he himself had not received any post in the new *madrasa* and told the sultan that Ibn Makhlûf had done all this work for himself and his progeny, not for the sultan. The sultan was sympathetic to this argument and changed the *waqf,* giving the controllership to one of his eunuchs, to be followed by others like him in the future.[67]

ʿIzz al-Dîn Ibn Jamâʿa was also the *nâẓir* of the *awqâf* for the *madrasa* al-Nâşiriyya bayn al-Qaşrayn (i.e., the one just discussed; obviously eunuchs did not monopolize the post of *nâẓir* there) and at *jâmiʿ* al-Qalʿa.[68] He lost both these posts in the year 743, because some of the sultan's eunuchs *(khuddâm)* slandered him for his administration of *awqâf,* and he lost the offices to eunuchs appointed by the sultan. ʿIzz al-Dîn was very upset at this and appealed to the amîr Arghûn al-ʿAlâʾî for help, but to no avail.[69]

The judges were controllers of other funds as well, but references to these are very scattered. In 749 ʿIzz al-Dîn Ibn Jamâʿa, still holding the office of chief judge, authorized the expenditure of funds from the *mâl al-ḫaramayn* for the construction of a well at Mecca.[70] In our discussion of the establishment of the four chief judgeships, we mentioned the complaint of the *amîr* of Medina against Tâj al-Dîn Ibn Bint al-Aʿazz, who controlled some *waqf* from which the *amîr* wanted to draw some funds.[71] Obviously, in both cases the chief judge was the *nâẓir* of these funds, and they may have been under the permanent jurisdiction of the Shâfiʿî *qâḍi al-quḍât*. The Ḫanbalî chief judge was also in charge of a number of *awqâf* for the benefit of orphans and others, and apparently their controllerships were part of his duties as chief judge.[72] Taqî al-Dîn Ibn Bint al-A'azz was the controller of the will *(tarika)* of Sultan al-Ẓâhir Baybars as regards the (legacies) of his children, *awqâf*, and properties. The only reason we know this is because it is contained in the list of posts which he lost in 690, when he was deposed from the chief judgeship.[73] Similarly, the Mâlikî chief judge Taqî al-Dîn al-Akhnâ'î was in charge of the funds which the *amîr* Arghûn had left his children.[74] Although these must have been extremely large and lucrative estates, there is no indication of the original appointments in the chronicles.

Qâḍî al-'askar

The *qâḍî al-'askar* was responsible for handling judicial cases which arose while the army was on campaign. All but the Ḥanbalîs were allowed to have such judges in Egypt, and when not travelling with the army these judges would attend the sessions of the *dâr al-'adl*, sitting a rank below the chief judges.[75] A few of the chief judges held this post at some time in their careers, and in one case, even concurrently with the chief judgeship. This post was held by Sirâj al-Dîn al-Hindî al-Ḥanafî, who originally acquired it through the aid of the *amîr* Ṣarghitmish, when the previous holder of the office died. He had first sought the help of Shaykhû, but was offered an *iqṭâ* instead. He was not satisfied with this and managed to gain Ṣarghitmish's help instead.[76] We do not know if this post was financially lucrative, but certainly its holder came into close contact with the sultan and important *umarâ'*, and this may explain why al-Hindî preferred it to an *iqṭâ'*. He held this office until he became chief judge in 769.[77] At that time, he passed this lesser judgeship to Ṣadr al-Dîn Ibn al-Turkumânî (in office 773-776), who held it until he too became chief judge.[78] The next Ḥanafî to hold this post was Sharaf al-Dîn Ibn Manṣûr (in office 777-778), who also gave it up when he became chief judge.[79] He was the last of the three who held the Ḥanafî chief judgeship for extremely brief terms after the death of Ṣadr al-Dîn Ibn al-Turkumânî.

Ṣadr al-Dîn al-Adhra'î (in office 663-677) is another Ḥanafî who seems to have held this post, but he is only rarely called *qâḍî al-'askar.*[80] Rather, the sources say that the sultan allowed him to judge wherever the army dismounted.[81] All this may simply be a circumlocution amounting to the same thing, but we do know that there was not an official Ḥanafî *qâḍî al-'askar* until 749, at least according to al-Maqrîzî.[82]

Mu'izz al-Dîn al-Khaṭîbî al-Ḥanafî (in office 677-692) was *qâḍî al-'askar* in al-Manṣûra in Lower Egypt[83] and *qâḍî al-juyûsh* in Damascus.[84] Apparently *qâḍî al-juyûsh* was a synonym for *qâḍî al-'askar,* but this term does not appear in any of the secretarial literature. References to the post of *qâḍî al-'askar* in rural Eygpt are rare, but it did exist in rural Syria, being part of the retinue of the local governor.[85] He held both these posts after he left the chief judgeship of Cairo.[86] Here again a Ḥanafî held this post prior to the date which al-Maqrîzî has given for the installation of the first Ḥanafî *qâḍî al-'askar.* These examples point to at least some form of this office being in existence prior to 749.

Obviously this judgeship was more important towards the end of the Baḥrî period than earlier, and three future Ḥanafî chief judges held it immediately prior to their assumption of the chief judgeship. For at least a brief time it seems to have competed with the post of *nuwwâb* as the best office for a candidate for the Ḥanafî chief judgeship to hold.

The only Shâfi'î to have held this post was Jamâl al-Dîn al-Zar'î (in office 710-711). Although we do not know the date of his original appointment, he was holding this judgeship when he became chief judge and continued to hold it during and after his term as chief judge,[87] relinquishing it only in 713 when he became chief judge of Damascus.[88] He lost this post in Damascus to Jalâl al-Dîn al-Qazwînî,[89] and eventually returned to Egypt and the post of *qâḍî al-'askar,* which he held until his death.[90]

In general, there is thus no evidence that any training and experience an individual might have gained as *qâḍî al-'askar* would help him advance to the chief judgeship, an office which drew candidates from elsewhere.

Khaṭîb

A few of the chief judges also held the post of *khaṭîb* at some point in their careers, but this occurred only rarely in Cairo. The Ḥanafî chief judge, Zayn al-Dîn al-Bisṭâmî (in office 742-748), was *khaṭîb* at the mosque of Ibn Ṭûlûn at the time of his death in 771,[91] but we are ignorant of the date of his appointment. Similarly, Tâj al-Dîn Ibn Bint al-A'azz (in office 663-665) held the post of *khaṭîb* somewhere at some time, but details are lacking.[92] One of his sons, Taqî al-Dîn (in office 686-690; 693-695) was *khaṭîb* at al-Azhar during his first term as chief judge of Cairo, but lost it with his other posts in 690.[93]

Badr al-Dîn Ibn Jamâ'a (in office 690-694; 702-710; 711-727) took over Taqî al-Dîn's post at al-Azhar when he himself became chief judge in 690.[94] During his second term (in 708) he was *khaṭîb* of the mosque in the citadel, but lost it a year later, because, says al-Maqrîzî, the sultan had turned against him.[95] There is no indication that he regained this post after the beginning of his third term, but he was made *khaṭîb* of *al-jâmiʿ al-jadîd* al-Nâṣirî in 712.[96] During the periods when he was judge in Jerusalem and Damascus, he also held the post of *khaṭîb* concurrently with the judgeship. In Damascus, the post of *khaṭîb* was at the Umayyad mosque, and he added to it that of *shaykh al-shuyûkh*.[97] His son, ʿIzz al-Dîn (in office 738-759; 759-766) had been assistant *khaṭîb* to his father at *al-jâmiʿ al-jadîd* and eventually gained that post for himself.[98]

Jalâl al-Dîn al-Qazwînî al-Shâfiʿî (in office 727-738) held the post of *khaṭîb* at the Umayyad mosque when he was chief judge in Damascus, and even before.[99] When he came to Cairo in 726, he was given a share in the post of *khaṭîb* in the mosque in the citadel and apprently held this post throughout his term as chief judge.[100]

The post of *khaṭîb* was undoubtedly a prestigious one, since it placed the individual who held it in the public view, and could easily work to his advantage in furthering or strengthening his career. However, there was no special relationship between the chief judgeship and the office of *khaṭîb* in any institution, even though some of those under study held the two posts simultaneously.

Miscellaneous Posts

There are a number of other posts which the chief judges held at some point in their careers. References to them are few and scattered, and indicate no special patterns. The Mâlikî chief judge, Burhân al-Dîn al-Akhnâ)î was made *muḩtasib* of al-Qâhira in 762,[101] but was forced to relinquish it, as well as the controllership of the hospital *(naẓar al-mâristân)*,[102] when he became chief judge in 763.[103] His nephew, Badr al-Dîn al-Akhnâ)î (in office 777-778, 779), had been appointed the *muftî* in the *dâr al-(adl* in 772,[104] perhaps with his uncle's help.[105] According to Ibn Tahgrî Birdî, the Ḩanafî Sirâj al-Dîn al-Hindî (in office 769-773) took the post of Ḩanafî *muftî* in the *dâr al-(adl*, as well as the chief judgeship from Jamâl al-Dîn Ibn al-Turkumânî (in office 750-769).[106] Finally, on a different note, Bahâ) al-Dîn al-Subkî al-Shâfi(î (in office 766-773) was made *amîn al-ḩukm* after he lost the chief judgeship. This post was concerned with accounting and investing the funds and endowments reserved for orphans.[107] The Mâlikî Zayn al-Dîn Ibn Makhlûf had also held this post early in his career.[108] Tâj al-Dîn Ibn Bint al-A(azz also held the post of *nâẓir al-dawâwîn*, which was the same as *nâẓir al-dawla*, at some point in his career. This officer was the *wazîr's* aide and was even authorized to use his signature.[109]

Thus the chief judges served in a wide variety of posts during their careers and often held such bureaucratic posts in conjunction with the chief judgeship. The more political posts such as *wazîr* or *nâẓir al-dawâwîn* generally fell only to the Shâfi(î chief judges during the early Baḩrî period, while posts relating to governmental or royal *(sulţânî)* finances can be found scattered throughout the time period under study. Prominent judicial or religious posts, like *qâḑî al-(askar* or *khaţîb*, were of little help, as a rule, for someone interested in acquiring a chief judgeship in Cairo. In short, aside from the office of deputy judge which we discussed in an earlier chapter, there is no significant relationship between any non-teaching post and the chief judgeship of Cairo.

B. Teaching Posts

The information available on the teaching posts which the judges held is quite abundant. However, the aim of the historians and biographers does not seem to have been comprehensive, but rather to indicate the highlights of their teaching careers. Thus, we can never be sure that we know all the teaching posts which the judges held in their lifetimes, and it is impossible to know the order in which they held all their appointments and, in most cases, their duration. Nevertheless, the considerable data which are available do allow us to gain some insight into their careers and perhaps discern some pattern in the system of appointments to the various colleges and mosques.[110] It seems that the chief judges were often in competition with other *ʿulamâʾ* for these teaching appointments, and neither their personal status nor that of their high office was any guarantee of a teaching appointment.

al-Ṣâliḥiyya

The *madrasa* al-Ṣâliḥiyya was the principal college in Egypt, especially during the early Baḥrî period. It had been built by al-Malik al-Ṣâliḥ Najm al-Dîn Ayyûb, who had made the unique provision of establishing in it a chair of *fiqh* for each of the four *madhâhib*. When the four chief judgeships were established, it was apparently the four professors of *fiqh* at this *madrasa* who were selected to fill the newly created positions, in addition to their teaching duties. They lived in quarters at al-Ṣâliḥiyya and held court there as well. Their successors in the chief judgeship seem almost always to have held the teaching posts there, but the information is often spotty.

The sources indicate that the Ḥanbalî chief judges managed to hold onto their teaching post more consistently than the judges of the other schools of law. After the Ḥanbalî judge, Shams al-Dîn Ibn al-ʿImâd, was put in jail in 670, his *nâʾib*, ʿIzz al-Dîn Ibn ʿAwaḍ, took his place, unofficially, as chief judge, finally receiving formal appointment in 679.[111] He may have taken his teaching post as well, but some sources say that Ibn al-ʿImâd taught there until his death.[112] In any case, it finally passed to the third Ḥanbalî chief judge, Sharaf al-Dîn al-Ḥarrânî, who took over in 696.[113] He probably held the post for life, and was followed in it by the next chief judge, Saʿd al-Dîn al-Ḥârithî (in office 709-711)[114] There is no indication that any of the three other Ḥanbalî chief judges of the Baḥrî period taught at al-Ṣâliḥiyya, but one of them, Muwaffaq al-Dîn al-Maqdisî (in office 738-769) was living there, at least in 742,[115] and this probably means that he was teaching there also. On the other hand, we do not know of any other Ḥanbalî *ʿulamâʾ* teaching there in that period, and it may very well be that the appointment to the teaching post there, and a residence in this *madrasa* as well, became such a normal procedure that mention of it dropped from the sources.

References to the Mâlikî professors there are almost non-existent. Sharaf al-Dîn al-Subkî (in office 663-669) was the first and only Mâlikî we have found who held the post there.[116]

Others may have followed him, but there is no information about them.

The first Ḥanafi chief judge, Ṣadr al-Dîn Adhra'î (in office 663-677), evidently held the teaching post at al-Ṣâliḥiyya throughout his term of office. There is no indication that his successor, Mu'izz al-Dîn al-Khaṭîbî, taught there, although he probably did, because the next judge, Shams al-Dîn al-Sarûjî (in office 692-696), certainly did.[117] After Ḥusâm al-Dîn al-Râzî (in office 696-698) came from Damascus to replace al-Sarûjî as chief judge and received his robe of honour, he went to al-Ṣâliḥiyya and found al-Sarûjî still living there. Instead of evicting him, al-Râzî went to another *madrasa* to live and to hold his court.[118] When Shams al-Dîn Ibn al-Ḥarîrî (in office 710-717) came to Cairo from Damascus to be chief judge, he was assigned the teaching post at al-Ṣâliḥiyya among others.[119] Al-Sarûjî, who had returned to office in 698, was not so lucky this time, and Ibn al-Ḥarîrî drove him out.[120] There is no further reference to Ḥanafîs teaching at al-Ṣâliḥiyya after this, but we do know that Jamâl al-Dîn Ibn al-Turkumânî (in office 750-769) resided there from the time of his installation as chief judge until his death in 769; his family lived there with him. Ibn Taghrî Birdî says that his residence there was according to custom,[121] and we are probably safe to say that all the Ḥanafî judges lived there, even if we do not have verification of this fact for each and every one of them.

Tâj al-Dîn Ibn Bint al-A'azz passed the Shâfi'î teaching post at al-Ṣâliḥiyya to his son, the future judge Ṣadr al-Dîn (in office 678-679) in 665, at his death, and Ṣadr al-Dîn continued teaching there until he died in 680.[122] It is interesting that he was able to keep this post even after he left the chief judgeship, and his is the only such case we have met. His brother Taqî al-Dîn, probably took the post when he first assumed office as chief judge in 685, if not earlier, but this is difficult to prove. Badr al-Dîn Ibn Jamâʿa was awarded the post when he became chief judge for the first time in 690,[123] but had to give it up when he left office in 694, but he regained it at the beginning of his third term in 711.[124] Jalâl al-Dîn al-Qazwînî, Ibn Jamâʿa's successor (in office 727-738), received this teaching appointment at the time he became chief judge and apparently held it throughout this term.[125]

After al-Qazwînî there is no mention of any chief judge holding a teaching post in al-Şâliḫiyya. There are a number of possible explanations for this. One is that the teaching posts fell vacant, or were handled by *muʿîdîn* or the like due to a lack of funds. On the other hand, the sources might have lost interest in this *madrasa*, because it had lost status to another *madrasa*, and since they had never reported every teaching post which an individual held anyway, other *madâris* took al-Şâliḫiyya's place of prominence. It is more likely, however, that this teaching post became indentified with the office of chief judge, since the judges' residences were there, and it was not necessary to report what was common knowledge: that the chief judge also held the teaching post of his *madhhab* at al-Şâliḫiyya. This seems the most likely explanation, since al-Şâliḫiyya was still flourishing throughout the eighth and ninth centuries. In 730 new endowments were established for the posts of *khaţîb* and *imâm*, and al-Maqrîzî considered it one of the wealthiest *madâris* of his day.[126]

Al-Nâşiriyya bayn al-Qaşrayn

This *madrasa* was completed by al-Malik al-Nâşir Muḥammad in the year 703, and all four schools of law were represented there. At the time of its foundation, three of the four chief judges, but not the Shâfiʿî, took the respective posts for the teaching of *fiqh,* while Şadr al-Dîn Ibn al-Muraḥḥil,[127] a noted *ʿâlim,* took the post which logically should have gone to the Shâfiʿî chief judge, Badr al-Dîn Ibn Jamâʿa. The other three were Ibn Makhlûf for the Mâlikîs (he was supposed to have been the *nâẓir* as well, and he organized the *awqâf* for the college's maintenance, as we have noted above; in office 658-718), Sharaf al-Dîn al-Ḥarrânî for the Ḥanbalîs (in office 696-709), and Shams al-Dîn al-Sarûjî for the Ḥanafîs (in office 692-696), 698-710).[128] There is no mention of which other Mâlikîs followed Ibn Makhlûf as the Mâlikî professor there, but we do know that the terms of the original charter established him and his descendants as the holders of both the controllership and the Mâlikî teaching post, and if the family died out, it was to pass to the Mâlikî chief judge.[129] He and his family lost the controllership, and may well have lost the teaching post after Ibn Makhlûf's death, but we do not know the names of the later Mâlikî teachers there. Sharaf al-Dîn al-Ḥarrânî's successor as Ḥanbalî *qâḍî al-quḍât,* Saʿd al-Dîn al-Ḥârithî (in office 709-711), also taught at al-Nâşiriyya, probably by virtue of his appointment as chief judge,[130] but he is the last Ḥanbalî we know to have taught there. Al-Sarûjî's successor to the chief judgeship and the Ḥanafî chair of *fiqh* at al-Nâşiriyya was Shams al-Dîn Ibn al-Ḥarîrî (in office 710-728).[131] He was appointed to several teaching posts, including this one, at the time of his appointment to the chief judgeship.[132] Here again he is the last of his *madhhab* whom we know to have held this post. Ibn Muraḥḥil's appointment to the Shâfi'î teaching post can probably be explained by his high status as an *'âlim;* during his residency in Damascus he had had many debates with Ibn Taymiyya.[133] He died in 716,[134] but the only successor of his that we know is Jalâl al-Dîn al-Qazwînî, the Shâfi'î chief judge from 727 to 738, who received this post when he became chief judge and probably held it throughout his term.[135] Since the first Shâfi'î teacher there was not a chief judge, there is no reason to suppose that this teaching post necessarily followed the office of chief judge. This *madrasa* survived into the Burjî period, and al-Maqrîzî considered it an important one.[136] Finally, it may very well be that here again what we have said about the teaching posts at al-Ṣâliḥiyya probably going to all the chief judges by custom may also apply, and this is why information on the later teachers there is lacking.

Al-Nâṣiriyya bi-al-Qarâfa

This *madrasa,* located near the tomb of the Imâm al-Shâfi'î, was built by al-Nâṣir Ṣalâḥ al-Dîn Yûsuf ibn Ayyûb (Saladin; ruled 564-589) for the teaching of Shâfi'î *fiqh* exclusively. From the end of the Ayyûbid period until 678 the professorship remained vacant, and teaching duties were carried out by *mu'îdûn.* In that year Taqî al-Dîn Ibn Razîn (in office 665-676, 676-678) was appointed professor of *fiqh* there; this was after his deposition from the chief judgeship. When he died in 680, the job went to Ibn Daqîq al-ʿÎd, who would serve as chief judge from 695 to 702. He lost it in 682 to Burhân al-Dîn al-Sinjârî (in office 686), who apparently held the post until he died in 686.[137] Taqî al-Dîn Ibn Bint al-Aʿazz (in office 686-690, 693-695) was the next teacher about whom we know, but he did not begin his duties there until 690, after his deposition from the judgeship. During the years 690 to 693 Taqî al-Dîn was constantly being harassed by the *wazîr* Ibn Salʿûs, and it was only through the influence of the *amîr* Baydarâ, whom Taqî al-Dîn had helped when the *amîr* was *wazîr*, was he able to obtain this post.[138] For approximately the next sixty years the tenure of this post is vague. We know that Ḍiyâʾ al-Dîn Muḥammad ibn Ibrâhîm al-Munâwî (d. 764) followed (Shams al-Dîn) Ibn al-Qummâḥ (d. 741).[139] At al-Munâwî's death, Shams al-Dîn Muḥammad Ibn al-Labbân was able to secure the post at this *madrasa* with the help of some *umarâʾ*, including Jankalî Ibn al-Bâbâ.[140] There had been a struggle as to who would succeed Ḍiyâʾ al-Dîn al-Munâwî, and the Shâfiʿî chief judge, ʿIzz al-Dîn Ibn Jamâʿa, had worked to get his own deputy (and Ḍiyâʾ al-Dîn's newphew), Tâj al-Dîn al-Munâwî, installed in the post. Ibn Jamâʿa was briefly successful in this, but Ibn al-Labbân's powerful friends finally won him the post.[141] Bahâʾ al-Dîn Aḥmad al-Subkî was appointed here at some point,[142] and in 763 the post went to his brother, Tâj al-Dîn ʿAbd al-Wahhâb, along with several other offices which his brother had held.[143] The teaching post at this *madrasa* continued to stay with the al-Subkî family, when another of its members, Bahâʾ al-Dîn Muḥammad al-Subkî (chief judge 766-773) took this post in 773, after his deposition from the chief judgeship.[144] In the middle of his term as chief judge, in 775,

Burhân al-Dîn Ibn Jamâ'a (in office 773-779) became professor of *fiqh* there when his predecessor, al-Subkî, went to Damascus.[145] In 779 Sirâj al-Dîn al-Bulqînî received the teaching post there,[146] and held it until 781 when Burhân al-Dîn Ibn Jamâ'a, who had now started serving his second term as chief judge (781-784) persuaded him to give it up in exchange for the controllership of two *awqâf*.[147] In short, this was a minor teaching post for most of the Baḥrî period, rarely held by a chief judge in office. Most of the time it was held by people who had lost high offices, such as Taqî al-Dîn Ibn Bint al-A'azz and Ibn Razîn after they had been deposed from the chief judgeship, and Burhân al-Dîn al-Sinjârî after he lost the wazirate. The frequent mention of this post in the late Baḥrî period is probably due to the fact that it was held by so many members of the Subkî family. On the other hand, it may have become a more prestigious or lucrative post towards the end of the Baḥrî period, when Burhân al-Dîn Ibn Jamâ'a was willing to buy it from al-Bulqînî, and Ibn al-Labbân and Tâj al-Dîn al-Munâwî competed for it.

The Mosque of Ibn Ṭûlûn

This mosque was one of the oldest in Cairo and was renovated in 697 during the sultanate of Lâjîn. Provisions were made for the teaching of *fiqh* according to all four schools of law, as well as for professorships in Quran, *ḥadîth*, and medicine. In the year 767 the *amîr* Yalbughâ al-Khâṣṣakî al-'Umarî established seven Ḥanafî teaching posts there, which, according to al-Maqrîzî, induced many Shâfi'îs to change *madhhab*.[148] Even before this, however, the Ḥanafîs seemed to have had a special fondness for this institution, and most of the references to it among the individuals we are studying are to the Ḥanafî chief judges.

Shams al-Dîn al-Sarûjî (in office 692-696, 698-710) was the first of these Ḥanafîs to hold a teaching post there, probably in *fiqh*. This was one of a number of teaching posts which he held during his career,[149] and although we do not know the exact dates he held it, we do know that he lost all his teaching posts when he was deposed from the chief judgeship in 710; he died the same year.[150] Zayn al-Dîn al-Bisṭâmî (in office 742-748) is the next chief judge to have held this post. He received the appointment as teacher of Ḥanafî *fiqh* there in 750, two years after his deposition from the chief judgeship, when Jamâl al-Dîn Ibn al-Turkumânî (in office 750-769), the current chief judge, assigned al-Bisṭâmî this post. Ibn al-Turkumânî may have been holding this post at the time he transferred it to al-Bisṭâmî, but the matter is not clear, although Ibn Ḥajar al-ʿAsqalânî praises Ibn al-Turkumânî, calling it a sign of Jamâl al-Dîn's nobility.[151] Sirâj al-Dîn al-Hindî (in office 769-773) succeeded al-Bisṭâmî in that post when the latter died in 771.[152] Although Jamâl al-Dîn Ibn al-Turkumânî may or may not have taught *fiqh* there, he certainly did teach *tafsîr* at the mosque, and perhaps he had found the two teaching posts burdensome and thus gave it to his predecessor.[153] Al-Hindî served for two years, and when he died in 773, he was followed by Shams al-Dîn Ibn Ṣâyigh, an *ʿâlim* of some repute.[154] Finally, Jâr Allâh (in office 778-782) succeeded Ṣadr al-Dîn Ibn al-Turkumânî (in office 773-776) in a teaching post there when the latter died in 776.[155] Both Ibn Ṣâyigh and Ṣadr al-Dîn Ibn al-Turkumânî died in 776, thus vacating two chairs of *fiqh*. This was possible only because of the additional endowments for Ḥanafî teachers established by the *amîr* Yalbughâ.

Sa'd al-Dîn al-Ḥârithî, the Ḥanbalî chief judge from 709-711, taught *fiqh* there.[156] Badr al-Dîn Ibn 'Aqîl, chief Shâfi'î judge for a few months in 759, taught *tafsîr* there for a good many years.[157] As we can easily see, the teaching posts in this mosque, though apparently numerous, are not very well documented, even though it was obviously a favourite of the Ḥanafîs. About one-third of the Ḥanafî chief judges of the Baḥrî period held a post there at some time during their careers, but beyond this there is no special relationship between the teaching posts here and the chief judgeship.

The College and Shrine (qubba) *of al-Manṣûriyya*

Both these structures were built by Sultan al-Malik al-Manṣûr Qalâ'ûn, and were finished in 684. *Fiqh* according to the four *madhâhib* were taught in both places; *ḥadîth* and Quran were taught at the tomb. There was also a hospital and a free school for orphans *(maktab al-sabîl)* in this complex.[158] Jâr Allâh (in office 778-782) became teacher of Ḥanafî *fiqh* in the *madrasa*, replacing Sirâj al-Dîn al-Hindî (in office 769-773), but this was almost five years before Jâr Allâh (in office 778-782) was appointed to al-Manṣûriyya when he first came to Egypt from Syria.[159] Sharaf al-Dîn Ibn Manṣûr spent some time in Cairo prior to becoming chief judge in 777,[160] and maybe then he received the post at al-Manṣûriyya. This post does not seem to have been that of professor of *fiqh*, but rather some lesser position concerned with verifying the recitation of the students in the subjects of *fiqh* and *uşûl al-fiqh*.[161] The Ḥanabalî chief judge, Sa'd al-Dîn al-Ḥârithî (in office 709-711), held a post at al-Manşûriyya at some point in his career.[162] Later, in 761, Muwaffaq al-Dîn al-Maqdisî (in office 738-769) assumed the teaching post there in the middle of his term as chief judge, after the death of Şadr al-Dîn Muḥammad Ibn 'Awaḍ, the son of the chief judge, Taqî al-Dîn Ibn 'Awaḍ (in office 712-738).[163] This may, however, refer to the post of professor of *ḥadîth* in the Qubba al-Manşûriyya, which, according to another source, he held at some time.[164] What is especially interesting about this appointment is that Şadr al-Dîn vacated two posts by his death, but only one of them went to the then Ḥanbalî chief judge; the other went to his son-in-law and successor, Naşr Allâh (in office 769-795).[165] Most likely, Muwaffaq al-Dîn helped secure the job for his son-in-law. The only Mâlikî chief judge to have taught there was Taqî al-Dîn Ibn Shâs (in office 680-685), but it is not certain at what point in his career he held the post.[166]

Al-Shaykhûniyya

This complex of *khânqâh* and mosque was completed by the *amîr* Shaykhû in 756, and all four schools of law were represented.[167] The Mâlikî chief judge, Nûr al-Dîn al-Sakhâwî (in office briefly in 756), was a protege of this *amîr*, and he was appointed teacher of Mâlikî *fiqh* in this mosque in 753. (Obviously, classes started here before all construction had ceased.) Al-Sakhâwî was thus one of the original appointees.[168] Muwaffaq al-Dîn al-Maqdîsî (in office 738-769) was the first Ḥanbalî professor of *fiqh* in the *khânqâh*.[169] His son-in-law and successor, Naşr Allâh (in office 769-795) also taught in the Shaykhûniyya complex, probably succeeding his father-in-law.[170] The Shâfi'î post went to a junior member of the Subkî family, Bahâ' al-Dîn Aḥmâd, and the Ḥanafî post, combined with that of shaykh of the *khânqâh*, went to a non-judge, Akmal al-Dîn Muḥammad ibn Maḥmûd.[171] Clearly, the Ḥanafî *madhhab* was the favored one in this *khânqâh*, but the chief judges were not especially well represented in this complex. Neither had the judges been very well represented in al-Manṣûriyya, but there do not seem to be any particular reasons for this poor representation in either complex, and such evidence merely points up the fact that the chief judges, even in office, had to compete with other *'ulamâ'* for teaching posts.

Al-Jamâliyya

This institution was a combination of a Ḥanafî *madrasa* and Sufi *khânqâh*, and was founded by the *amîr* 'Alâ' al-Dîn Mughlâṭây al-Jamâlî in 730. The posts of teacher of Ḥanafî *fiqh* and *shaykh* of the *khânqâh* stayed in the family of Ibn al-Turkumânî. The first was 'Alâ' al-Dîn Ibn al-Turkumânî (in office 748-750), who passed it to his son Jamâl al-Dîn (in office 750-769), who passed it in turn to his son, Ṣadr al-Dîn (in office 773-776). It then went to one of their relatives *(qarîbuhum)*, Ḥamîd al-Dîn, who eventually passed it to his own son.[172] Apparently 'Alâ' al-Dîn Ibn al-Turkumânî was given this post before he became chief judge, since the *madrasa* was built almost twenty years before he became chief judge, but we do not know the exact date he took the post. We cannot be sure if it were the prestige of the office of chief judge or nepotism which allowed this post to be passed from father to son for several generations, but after a while this *madrasa* seems to have become the fief of the Ibn al-Turkumânî clan.

Other Teaching Posts

There are numerous other teaching posts which the chief judges in our study held, sometimes by virtue of the fact that they held this high office, and other times for no special reason that we know. In 703 the famous mosque of al-Ḥâkim was renovated, and provisions made for the teaching of *fiqh* according to all four schools of law, as well as instruction in *ḥadîth* and Quran. The four chief judges of the time were appointed to the teaching posts in *fiqh:* Badr al-Dîn Ibn Jamâʿa al-Shâfiʿî, Shams al-Dîn al-Sarûjî al-Ḥanafî, Zayn al-Dîn Ibn Makhlûf al-Mâlikî, and Sharaf al-Dîn al-Ḥarrânî al-Ḥanbalî. Saʿd al-Dîn al-Ḥârithî was named professor of *ḥadîth,* and this may well have been the future Ḥanbalî judge (in office 709-711).[173] Shams al-Dîn Ibn al-Ḥarîrî followed al-Sarûjî as teacher of Ḥanafî *fiqh* at the latter's death.[174]

On the other hand, when Sultan Baybars finished his Ẓâhiriyya *madrasa* in 662, he only established professorships of *fiqh* there for the Shâfiʿîs and the Ḥanafîs. The future chief judge Ibn al-Razîn received an appointment there at the time of the college's founding.[175] The Shâfiʿî chief judge Bahâʾ al-Dîn Ibn ʿAqîl was the first to teach *fiqh* at the mosque in the citadel, but this was in 731, long before he became chief judge, and after the mosque itself had been completed.[176] He also taught at *al-madrasa* al-Quṭbiyya, having been appointed there in 734, and was still teaching there in 745, when Khalîl ibn Aybak al-Ṣafadî received an *ijâza* from him.[177] He also taught at al-Khashshabiyya, which was located in the mosque of Ibn Ṭûlûn;

he had taken this post from ʿIzz al-Dîn Ibn Jamâʿa and continued to hold it until his own death in 769.[178]

Shams al-Dîn al-Sarûjî al-Ḥanafî (in office 692-696, 698-710) taught at al-Suyûfiyya. It received its name from a nearby market, which existed at the time Ṣalâḥ al-Dîn Ibn Ayyûb (Saladin) established it as an exclusively Ḥanafî *madrasa*. We do not know the exact dates during which al-Sarûjî taught there, but he died there in 710.[179] Saladin established another *madrasa* called al-Qamḥiyya, completed in 566, but devoted exclusively to the Mâlikîs. Taqî al-Dîn Ibn Shâs (in office 680-685) was appointed there near the end of his term of office in 684,[180] and ʿAlam al-Dîn al-Bisâṭî (in office 778-779, 779-783) also taught there for an unknown period of time, but he was teaching there at the time of his death, some three years after he lost the chief judgeship.[181] Similarly, Zayn al-Dîn al-Bisṭâmî (in office 742-748) taught Ḥanafî *fiqh* at al-Azhar at some point in his career.[182]

The mass of information which the literary sources provide on the teaching careers of the chief judges is impressive and almost overwhelming. Since the aim of the present study is to examine the careers of the chief judges, we could not ignore such teaching appointments, which, in many cases, judges held for long terms. However, there is little correlation between teaching careers and judicial careers. Unlike the Ottoman case where an aspirant to the chief judgeship had to have held a graded series of teaching appointments before he was even considered for the chief judgeship, there was no *cursus honorum* for a would-be chief judge of Cairo during the Mamlûk period. Once appointed to office, however, the chief judge seems to have always held a number of teaching posts. Often he would simply take over the post vacated by his predecessor, and, if a new *madrasa* were inaugurated during his tenure, for example, he would often, though not always, be awarded the professorship of *fiqh* in his *madhhab* there. It seems that the teaching posts at al-Şâliḫiyya *madrasa*, where the chief judges normally held court, were usually reserved for the chief judges. However, the limits which we must place on even these generalizations point up the fact that in spite of their status as the leading judicial arbitors in the capital, the chief judges had to compete with other *ʿulamâʾ* for teaching appointments. All this may indicate that the chief judges did not really enjoy much prestige, and this is why they seem to have been treated pretty much like other *ʿulamâʾ* when a teaching position fell vacant. Yet the judges did enjoy a certain status, at least, because of their roles as judicial arbitrators among the masses of the people. A simpler explanation is probably called for; namely, that the *ʿulamâʾ* of Cairo did not form a stratified institution where teaching posts were strictly ranked. Although it is likely that certain teaching posts were more prestigious than others, we should not search too deeply for a structured religious institution where every teaching appointment carried some special significance. Rather, teaching, especially the teaching of *fiqh,* was an important part of a judge's career, both before and after he assumed the chief judgeship, but there is no evidence that the location of such appointments was critical.

The Qâḍî *as* Shaykh

The term *shaykh* is, of course, a common term of respect in

Arabic, but in the period under study one of its technical meanings was the individual who was in charge of a group of Sufis; in particular, the leader of a Sufi *khânqâh*. A number of the judges held such positions, and several of them also held the post of *shaykh al-shuyûkh*. This last title referred, at first, to the *shaykh* of the *khânqâh* Sa⁽id al-Su⁽adâ⁾, also known as al-Ṣalâḥiyya, then later to the shaykh of the *khânqâh* at Siryâqûs built by al-Malik al-Nâṣir Ibn Qalâ⁾ûn; eventually it lost its specific meaning and simply became an honorific for the *shaykh* of any *khânqâh*.[183] According to al-Qalqashandî, the *shaykh al-shuyûkh*, in its strictest sense, also had a general jurisdiction over all the *khawâniq* and Sufis of Egypt.[184] This post, which then meant *shaykh* of Sa⁽îd al-Su⁽adâ⁾ as well, was held by the Shâfi⁽î Tâj al-Dîn Ibn Bint al-A⁽azz (in office 663-665),[185] and later by his son, Taqî al-Dîn, who lost it along with his other appointments in 690.[186] The Ḥanablî chief judge, Shams al-Dîn Ibn al-⁽Imâd (in office 663-670), also held this post after Tâj al-Dîn Ibn Bint al-A⁽azz died in 665.[187] Much later in the Baḥrî period the Ḥanafî Jâr Allâh (in office 778-782) was also *shaykh* of this *khânqâh*, but he was forced from office by its residents in 778, prior to his becoming chief judge.[188] He never returned to it, but did manage to have his nephew appointed instead.[189] By the time Jâr Allâh had become *shaykh*, this *khânqâh* had already fallen into second place behind the one at Siryâqûs, and its *shaykh* did not have the wide powers of an earlier day.

Other chief judges also became *shuyûkh* of *khawâniq*. We have noted above the domination of al-Jamâliyya complex by the Ḥanafî Ibn al-Turkumânî clan. Each of them combined the post of teacher in the *madrasa* and *shaykh* of the Sufis in its *khânqâh*.[190]

Before leaving the discussion of this title, there are two questions which must be answered, at least in part. First, what were the responsibilities of the *shaykh* of a *khânqâh*, and, secondly, were any of the chief judges Sufis? It is not possible to answer these questions in detail without a great deal of research on the institution of the *khânqâh* (and other Sufi institutions) in Egypt, as well as an in-depth study of Sufism in the Mamlûk Empire during the Baḫrî period. This is obviously impossible within the limits of the present study, but we do have some answers. The *shaykh* may have been, but was not necessarily, the *nâẓir* of the *khânqâh*. In the description of the *khânqâh* of Shaykhû it is explicitly stated that the duties of *shaykh* and *nâẓir al-awqâf* would go to one man.[191] In the earlier case of al-Jamâliyya, the *nâẓir* is not even mentioned, and the *shaykh* may have assumed these duties as well. The data are insufficient for generalization, but in the case of the *khânqâh* of Shaykhû, its founder was probably afraid that an *amîr* might be made *nâẓir*, and the *awqâf* would be dissipated; in fact, Sultan al-Malik al-Nâşir Faraj did exactly that in the Burjî period.[192] Was the *shaykh* of a *khânqâh* necessarily also a Sufi? Perhaps, but this aspect of the judges' interests is not well documented. Only Badr al-Dîn Ibn Jamâ'a was known to have been well versed in the ways of the Sufis,[193] but he was never the *shaykh* of a *khânqâh* in Egypt, only in Syria, where the Sufis of a particular *khânqâh* requested he be appointed their *shaykh*.[194] We must also remember that when Ibn Taymiyya's disciple, Ibn Murrâ, was arrested in Cairo for, among other things, criticizing Sufism, Ibn Jamâ'a was one of his adversaries; this may indicate some support for Sufism, but the matter is hardly decisive. If we interpret the post of *shaykh* of a *khânqâh* or *shaykh al-shuyûkh* as basically an administrative one, to oversee *awqâf* and see that the Sufis were cared for, then it certainly was not necessary for the *shaykh* to be a Sufi, and this can be seen as just another administrative appointment. Since information on the judges as Sufis is virtually non-existent, we are led to assume that these posts were mainly administrative and did not mean that their holders were Sufis.

Obviously the judges held quite a number of posts besides that of chief judge during their career. All of them held teaching posts, and most of them held other posts in the bureaucracy and the judicidal administration. We might have expected that a chief judge of Cairo would have been kept so busy by his official and cermonial duties that he would not have had any spare time for teaching. Of course, we cannot know their schedule of lectures, and the judges may have lectured only rarely. However, there is evidence that they really did lecture, because when Sirâj al-Dîn al-Hindî arrived in Cairo in 743, he attended the lectures of the Ḥanafî chief judge, Zayn al-Dîn al-Bisṭâmî (in office 742-748) and later those of ʿAlâʾ al-Dîn Ibn al-Turkumânî (in office 748-750).[195] Undoubtedly it was an honor to receive a teaching post in a *madrasa*, and it is logical to assume that students of *fiqh* would want to study with the highest ranking jurist in the capital.

Nevertheless, we must never forget that the chief judgeship and the teaching posts were paid positions. According to al-Maqrîzî, the salary of the chief judge was fifty dinars per month,[196] which, assuming an average ratio of twenty dirhems[197] to the dinar, was equal to 1,000 dirhems per month. The average monthly salary of a teacher of *fiqh* in a *madrasa* was ten dinars,[198] but many professors earned more. Burhân al-Dîn al-Sinjârî earned forty dinars a month when he was made *mudarris* at al-Nâşiriyya bi-al-Qarâfa, although earlier the Shâf'îs Taqî al-Dîn Ibn Razîn and Ibn Daqîq al-'Îd had earned only one-half and one quarter of that amount respectively.[199] At al-Nâşiriyya bayn al-Qaşrayn the professors earned 200 dirhems (approximately ten dinars) per month,[200] as did the professors at al-Manşûriyya.[201] At the mosque of Ibn Ţûlûn the professors received only 100 dirhems (i.e. approximately five dinars) for their teaching duties.[202]

In addition we have seen that many of the chief judges held the controllerships of *awqâf*, for which they also received a salary. For example, when Burhân al-Dîn al-Sinjârî was receiving forty dinars per month as teacher at al-Nâşiriyya bi-al-Qarâfa, as the *nâẓir* of the same institution he received only ten dinars plus a ration of bread and water.[203] Assuming the difference between the two salaries to be typical, the *nâẓir* of such an institution was clearly a more poorly paid official. Of course, we know that the chief judges were the overseers of other *awqâf* and the executors of estates, for which services they must have received salaries. We have learned that the Shâfi'î chief judge was also the controller of a special fund for orphans, and the other judges probably had some similar fund, although perhaps not as large a one. The Mâlikî chief judge, Zayn al-Dîn Ibn Makhlûf, had been an *amîn al-ḩukm*, an official who helped administer a *mawda' al-ḩukm* on behalf of orphans and others,[204] and the Ḩanbalî chief judge, Taqî al-Dîn Ibn 'Awaḑ, was deposed; in part, because he mishandled the *awqâf* reserved for orphans and others.[205] Although two of the later Ḥanafî chief judges worked unsuccessfully to have a permanent special fund for orphans like the Shâfiʿî chief judge, it is reasonable to assume that they controlled some sort of *awqâf* for orphans, since the Ḥanbalî and Mâlikî chief judges evidently did.

Although we do not know the salaries which the chief judges received as controllers of such *awqâf* or funds, it is not the question of salaries which should concern us, but rather the problem of corruption. It is incorrect to say that all the chief judges were corrupt in their dealings with the *awqâf*, but there are many hints as well as strong evidence in the sources that personal enrichment at the expense of the *awqâf* was a recurring problem. The Shâfiʿî chief judge, Jamâl al-Dîn al-Zarʿî (in office 710-711) is pointedly lauded by Ibn Ḥajar al-ʿAsqalânî who says that during his tenure the *awqâf* flourished, profits increased, and the profits were transferred to the proper beneficiaries of the *awqâf*.[206] The major cause for the deposition of three of the four chief judges in 738 was the mishandling of *awqâf* funds. Before the Shâfiʿî chief judge al-Qazwînî, who was deposed that year, could leave Cairo he had to pay back the sum of 230,000 dirhems (see next chapter for more details). Obviously the controllerships of *awqâf* which went along with the chief judgeship could prove to be extremely lucrative. Unfortunately, we do not know of all the *awqâf* which the *quḍât* controlled; e.g., Ibn ʿAwaḍ, the Ḥanbalî chief judge who was deposed in that year, was accused of selling the *awqâf* of orphans and others, but we have no details concerning these *awqâf*. Possibilities for such corruption probably help explain al-Sakhâwî's charge that Badr al-Dîn al-Subkî al-Shâfiʿî became chief judge through bribery.[207] It is highly unlikely that he would have spent money to become chief judge, unless he had hopes of acquiring even more money once he held that office. Of course, accepting bribes might have been another way in which a chief judge could enrich himself, but here the evidence is quite indirect; the Ḥanafî Shams al-Dîn al-Sarûjî is praised for never having accepted a bribe.[208] If he were singled out for such praise, obviously other judges did accept bribes.

However, the weight of evidence points to corruption in the administration of *awqâf*. In 713 the *amîr* Badr al-Dîn Ibn al-Wazîrî became *nâʾib* in the *dâr al-ʿadl* and *shâdd al-awqâf*.[209] A petition reached the *dâr al-ʿadl* concerning some matter relating to *awqâf* and the *amîr* started demanding an accounting of the *awqâf* for the previous twenty years, as well as (an accounting of the) *mawâdiʿ al-ḥukm*. He was harsh on the *awqâf* secretaries, beating them because of the corruption of their accounts. The (chief) judges became very upset at this, and the Shâfiʿî chief judge, Badr al-Dîn Ibn Jamâʿa, managed to get some influential people, such as the *nâẓir al-jaysh*[210] and the *kâtib al-sirr*,[211] to join him to stop these inquiries. Finally, the sultan put an end to the investigation, saying that it was an insult to the judges and the people of knowledge. Not everyone was happy with the sultan's decision, but the investigation of the *awqâf* ceased.[212] Obviously, if the accounts had been in order, and there was no danger of high ranking officials, including the chief judges, being accused of corruption, Ibn Jamâʿa and the others would not have been so adamant in their opposition. It is interesting to note that a few years after this incident Ibn Jamâ'a stopped accepting a salary for his services as chief judge. He had become so wealthy that he no longer needed this salary.[213]

In short, we have seen that many of the chief judges were honest and righteous men who suffered chastisement and even loss of part or all of their jurisdiction out of defense for their beliefs. Yet many other chief judges took advantage of their high office and their controllership of *awqâf* for the sake of personal enrichment. It seems almost unbelievable that any *awqâf* survived the attacks from without by the Mamlûks and the pilfering from within by the chief judges (and probably others). It may have been the case, sometimes, that the chief judges cooperated with the Mamlûks in the modification or annullment of certain *awqâf* so that they, the judges (or certain judges), could do as they pleased with the other *awqâf*. However, there is no evidence of such coordinated plotting. Rather, the extent of the *awqâf* in the Mamlûk empire must have been so great that both Mamlûks and civilians could chip away at them for their own benefit and still leave enough of these endowments untouched so that most of the personnel and institutions which benefited from the *awqâf* could still be supported. Although there is some evidence that the chief judges could increase their personal wealth by accepting bribes for favorable verdicts, the access to the wealth of the *awqâf* which the chief judgeship afforded was probably an even stronger incentive for many individuals to seek this office. Similarly, some men who had led pious and apparently frugal lives prior to becoming chief judge of Cairo, such as Jalâl al-Dîn al-Qazwînî who had gone into debt as a result of his charity, seem to have been overwhelmed and easily led astray by the enormous possibilities and ease of corruption in office. Numerous judges, and perhaps even a majority of them, did not indulge in corrupt practices, but there is no doubt that such illegal manipulations provided a considerable supplement to the salaries of many of the chief judges.

ENDNOTES

[1]See Rabie, Financial System, p. 139 and references there.

[2]Manhal MS, fols. 299b-300a.

[3]Ibn Kathîr, XIII, 250.

[4]Al-Asnawî, I, 148.

[5]Raf‘, II, 337.

[6]As quoted in Popper, Notes, I, 96.

[7]Sulûk, I, 773.

[8]Ibid., p. 741.

[9]Perhaps this should read Ḍiyâ’ al-Dîn Abû Bakr ibn ‘Abd Allâh al-Nashshâ’î (Durar, I, 474-75).

[10]Sulûk, I, 742.

[11]For details, see chapter VI.

[12]Rabie, Financial System, p. 140.

[13]Al-‘Aynî, Ahmet III 2912/4, fol. 321b. See also al-Nuwayrî, Leiden Or. 20, fols. 103a-b.

[14]Rabie, Financial System, p. 143.

[15]Ibid., p. 144. [16]Ibid., p. 147.

[17]Al-Qalqashandî, Ṣubḥ, IV, 31, which is on the authority of Masâlik al-abṣâr by Ibn Faḍl Allâh al-‘Umarî (d. 748).

[18]La Syrie, p. LXXI.

[19]Al-ʿAynî, Ahmet III 2912/4, fol. 273b; Wâfî, Aya Sofya MS, XIX, 35a-b.

[20]Sulûk, II, 169. Al-Şafadî (Aʿyân, fol. 46b) calls him *nâẓir al-khizâna al-kubrâ*.

[21]See note 9. This time it is definitely Abû Bakr ibn ʿAbd Allâh.

[22]Sulûk, II, 142; this is Muḥammad ibn ʿAbd Al-Majîd (Durar, IV, 145).

[23]Al-Nuwayrî, BN 1579, fol. 87a.

[24]La Syrie, p. LXXIV.

[25]Sulûk, I, 1040. This is actually a section from al-Nuwayrî, which the editor of Sulûk has appended to al-Maqrîzî's chronicle.

[26]Sulûk, I, 742.

[27]Wâfî, Ahmet III 2920/18, fol. 64b.

[28]Rafʿ, II, 365; Ibn Rajab, II, 358.

[29]Aʿyân, fol. 46b.

[30]Sulûk, I, 687.

[31]Quatremère, Histoire, I, a, 22.

[32]Sulûk, I, 773.

[33]Ibid, II, 885.

[34]Ibid, III, 19.

[35]Ibid, III, 74.

[36]Ibid, III, 73.

[37]Raf', II, 384; Sulûk, III, 191.

[38]See above notes 33, 34, and 35.

[39]Raf' MS, fol. 126a.

[40]Durar, V, 12.

[41]Al-Asnawî, I, 389.

[42]Sulûk, II, 340; La Syrie, LXXVII.

[43]In 737 he succeeded Najm al-Dîn al-As'ardî as *wakîl bayt al-mâl* (Sulûk, II, 424). Al-As'ardî had taken over the post in 734 from a third party, whose date of appointment is unknown (Sulûk, II, 375).

[44]Sulûk, II, 337.

[45]Cf. the comments on Ibn Jamâ'a by the sultan when he appointed him (Sulûk, II, 242).

[46]Sulûk, I, 1534. See chapter I, p. 24.

[47]See chapter I, p. 25.

[48]La Syrie, pp. LVII-LVIII; Popper, Notes, I, 92.

[49]Khiṭaṭ, II, 269.

[50]Sulûk, I, 828, 889, 929; Ibn Kathîr, XIV, 21, 27.

[51]Khiṭaṭ, II, 269.

[52]This chronology is based on Khiṭaṭ, II, 269, but there seems to be something wrong with it. Karîm al-Dîn al-Kabîr was apparently made *nâẓir* in 721, but fell from favor, was jailed in 723, and was soon afterwards sent into exile (Durar, I, 430-32). Al-Maqrîzî (Sulûk, II, 337) says that 'Izz al-Dîn became *nâẓir* in 731, not long after Karîm al-Dîn's departure. I think that it

was not ʿIzz al-Dîn who became *nâẓir* after the death of the *amîr*, but rather Badr al-Dîn, and it was he who lost the post of Karîm al-Dîn. Badr al-Dîn was chief judge from 711 to 727. His son, ʿIzz al-Dîn, became a teacher in the Mosque of Ibn Ṭûlûn in 719, but he was only twenty-three years old at the time. This still leaves a gap between Karîm al-Dîn's departure in 723 and ʿIzz al-Dîn's alleged assumption of the post in 731. Perhaps his father transferred the controllership to him at that date. In any case, this is the best hypothesis I can produce in the light of the sketchy evidence.

[53]Khiṭaṭ, II, 269.

[54]Durar, II, 305-306.

[55]Khiṭaṭ, II, 269.

[56]Sulûk, II, 99.

[57]Khiṭaṭ, II, 269.

[58]It was also known as al-Nâṣiriyya and al-Sharîfiyya (Khiṭaṭ, II, 363-64). In the index and notes to Sulûk, the editor has mentioned these various names, but he has made some mistakes. He has classified *al-madrasa* al-Nâṣiriyya (Ṣalâh al-Dîn) *bi-jiwâr qabr al-imâm* al-Shâfiʿî, *madrasa* Zayn al-Tujjâr, and *madrasa* al-Shâfiʿiyya as one and the same institution.
There were several *madâris* known as al-Nâṣiriyya, and he has confused them. The *madrasa* known as Zayn al-Tujjâr was also known as al-Nâṣiriyya and al-Sharîfiyya, but it was not located in the neighborhood of the tomb of al-Shâfiʿî, but rather near *al-jâmiʿ al-ʿatîq* or the Mosque of ʿAmr ibn al-ʿÂṣ as Khiṭaṭ clearly states. The *madrasa* al-Nâṣiriyya located near the tomb of al-Shâfiʿî is listed separately in Khiṭaṭ as *al-madrasa* al-Nâṣiriyya bi-al-Qarâfa, and is described as "*bi-jiwâr qubbat al-imâm...al-Shâfiʿî*" (Khiṭaṭ, II, 400-401). It is not referred to as al-Shâfiʿiyya here, but I am sure that the two were identical. Al-Jazarî's description of al-Shâfiʿiyya in al-Qarâfa, the salaries, and persons who taught there is identical to Khiṭaṭ's description of al-Nâṣiriyya near the tomb of al-Shâfiʿî (Haarmann, Quellenstudien, Arabic text, p. 20).

[59]Rafʿ, II, 376.

[60]The version in Rafʿ al-iṣr is wrong; it say 681, and the salaries are reversed (Rafʿ, II, 222). See also Ibn al-Furât, Târîkh, VII, 272; Khiṭaṭ, II, 401; Haarmann, Quellenstudien, Arabic text, p. 20.

[61]Ibn al-Furât, Târîkh, VII, 208.

[62]Sulûk, I, 773.

[63]Ibid., p. 687; Ibn al-Furât, Târîkh, VII, 208.

[64]Khiṭaṭ, I, 427-30.

[65]Ibn al-Furât, Târîkh, VIII, 208. On the ustâdâr, see Popper, Notes, I, 93.

[66]Sulûk, I, 955.

[67]Ibid., p. 1041.

[68]Khiṭaṭ, II, 325.

[69]Sulûk, II, 624. For his original appointment, see Sulûk, II, 337. A brief biography of this *amîr* is to be found in Durar, II, 376.

[70]Sulûk, II, 766.

[71]See chapter I, p. 21.

[72]Al-ʿAynî, Ahmet III 2911/c34, fol. 65b; Durar, II, 404.

[73]Sulûk, I, 773.

[74]Ibid., II, 393.

[75]La Syrie, p. LXVII; Popper, Notes, I, 100.

[76]Inbâʾ al-ghumr, I, 30: See also Sulûk, III, 33.

[77]Sulûk, III, 158.

[78]Manhal MS, fol. 695b.

[79]Inbâʾ al-ghumr, I, 152-53.

[80]Al-Lakhnawî, al-Fawâ'id, pp. 80-81.

[81]Wâfî, BN 2065, fol. 67b; al-Nu'aymî, Dâris, I, 532. Al-Lakhnawî (al-Fawâ'id, pp. 80-81) quotes al-Ṣafadî on this point, but apparently summarizes, rather than quotes verbatim.

[82]See chapter II, note 51.

[83]Ibn Abî al-Wafâ, al-Jawâhir, II, 201.

[84]Wâfî, British Museum MS Add. 23359, fol. 147b.

[85]La Syrie, pp. 161-62, 209, 224, 231.

[86]Wâfî, British Museum MS Add, 23359, fol. 147b.

[87]A'yân, fol. 201b; Manhal MS, fol. 336a.

[88]Durar, II, 256.

[89]Ibid.

[90]Ibn Taghrî Birdî, al-Nujûm al-zâhira, IX, 304.

[91]Durar, III, 245.

[92]Al-Asnawî, I, 148.

[93]Sulûk, I, 773.

[94]Raf' MS, fol. 104a.

[95]Sulûk, II, 43, 83.

[96]Sulûk, II, 114.

[97]Al-Asnawî, I, 386-87; Durar, III, 367-68.

[98]Al-Asnawî, I, 389; Durar, II, 489.

[99]Ibn Kathîr, XIV, 185.

[100]Sulûk, II, 283.

[101]Sulûk, III, 60; La Syrie, pp. LXXVII-LXXVIII; Popper, Notes, I, 101.

[102]La Syrie, p. LXXX; Popper, Notes, I, 101.

[103]Sulûk, III, 73.

[104]There were four *muftûn* there, and they sat a rank below the *quḍât al-ʿaskar;* La Syrie, p. LXXVII; Popper, Notes, I, 101.

[105]Sulûk, III, 191.

[106]Manhal MS, fol. 542b.

[107]Inbâʿ al-ghumr, I, 11.

[108]Rafʿ, II, 405; Durar, III, 202; al-Nuwayrî, BN 1579, fol. 80b.

[109]Ibn Kathîr, XIII, 249; La Syrie, pp. LXII, LXVIII.

[110]Here again I am concentrating on the teaching appointments in Cairo, not elsewhere in the Mamlûk empire.

[111]Sulûk, 657.

[112]Ibn Kathîr, XIII, 277; al-Yûnînî, III, 280.

[113]Rafʿ, II, 365.

[114]Aʿyân, fol. 589a.

[115]Sulûk, II, 591.

[116]Al-Yûnînî, II, 461.

[117] A'yân, fol. 21b; Durar, I, 96.

[118] Ibn Ṭûlûn, Quḍât, p. 191.

[119] A'yân, fol. 484a; Durar, IV, 158; al-'Aynî, Ahmet III 2912/4, fol. 275b; Ibn Kathîr, XIV, 58.

[120] Raf', I, 51.

[121] Manhal MS, fol. 422b; See also Sulûk, II, 797, and Raf', II, 286.

[122] Shadharât, V, 367; al-Yûnînî, II, 362; al-Asnawî, I, 150; al-Nuwayrî, BN 1578, fol. 36a.

[123] Raf' MS, fol. 104a.

[124] Sulûk, I, 771; Durar, III, 368.

[125] Al-Nuwayrî, Leiden Or. 19b, fol. 121b; Sulûk, II, 283.

[126] Khiṭaṭ, II, 382.

[127] Muḥammad ibn 'Umar (Durar, IV, 234-41).

[128] Khiṭaṭ, II, 382.

[129] Sulûk, I, 1041. This is an edition of part of al-Nuwayrî.

[130] A'yân, fol. 589a; Raf' MS, fol. 133a.

[131] Durar, IV, 158; Ibn Kathîr, XIV, 58; al-'Aynî, Ahmet III 2912/4, fol. 275b.

[132] A'yân, fol. 484a.

[133] Durar, II, 234.

[134] Ibid., p. 241.

[135] Sulûk, II, 283; al-Nuwayrî, Leiden Or. 19b, fol. 121b.

[136] Khiṭaṭ, II, 382.

[137] Ibid., pp. 400-401; Ibn al-Furât, Târîkh, VII, 272.

[138] Sulûk, I, 773.

[139] Durar, III, 372. Shams al-Dîn's biography can be found in Durar, III, 391.

[140] Sulûk, II, 691.

[141] Durar, III, 470.

[142] Sulûk, III, 74-75.

[143] Ibid.

[144] Ibid., p. 199.

[145] Ibid., p. 223.

[146] Ibid., p. 320.

[147] Inbâʾ al-ghumr, I, 297.

[148] Khiṭaṭ, II, 268-69.

[149] Aʿyân, fol. 21b.

[150] Rafʿ, I, 51.

[151] Rafʿ, II, 286.

[152] Ibnâʾ al-ghumr, I, 30.

[153] Durar, II, 381.

[154]*Sulûk*, III, 198; a biography of Shams al-Dîn is to be found in *Durar*, IV, 119-20.

[155]*Inbâʾ al-ghumr*, II, 38.

[156]Al-ʿAynî, Ahmet III 2912/4, fol. 295a.

[157]*Durar*, II, 373.

[158]*Khiṭaṭ*, II, 379-80; *Sulûk*, I, 997-1001.

[159]*Sulûk*, III, 198-99.

[160]*Rafʿ*, I, 89.

[161]*Rafʿ*, I, 90-91.

[162]Ibn Rajab, *Dhayl*, II, 363.

[163]*Sulûk*, III, 56.

[164]*Durar*, II, 404.

[165]*Sulûk*, III, 56.

[166]*Rafʿ*, I, 205.

[167]*Khiṭaṭ*, II, 313-14.

[168]*Sulûk*, II, 864.

[169]*Khiṭaṭ*, II, 421.

[170]*Shadharât*, VI, 343.

[171]*Khiṭaṭ*, II, 421.

[172]*Ibid*., p. 392.

[173]Ibid., p. 278. Al-ʿAynî (Ahmet III 2912/4, fol. 295a) says that al-Ḥarrânî was *shaykh* of the *dâr al-ḥadîth* at this mosque. Al-Nuwayrî (Leiden Or. 20, fol. 15b) calls him Ibn Masʿûd, but his own ism was Masʿûd; see Durar, V, 116.

[174]Ibn Kathîr, XIV, 58; al-ʿAynî, Ahmet III 2912/4, fol. 275b.

[175]Al-Yûnînî, I, 551.

[176]Wâfî MS, Sulaymâniyya, XVII, 38b. It was completed by al-Malik al-Nâṣir Muḥammad in 718 (Khiṭaṭ, II, 325).

[177]Wâfî, op. cit., fol. 39b.

[178]Durar, II, 373.

[179]Manhal, I, 191; Khiṭaṭ, II, 365-66.

[180]Rafʿ, I, 205.

[181]Sulûk, III, 513.

[182]Durar, III, 245.

[183]Khiṭaṭ, II, 415; La Syrie, p. LXXIX. See also Sulûk, III, 273-74 for an example of how this title was used in the later Baḥrî period.

[184]Al-Qalqashandî, Ṣubḥ, IV, 193; La Syrie, p. 163.

[185]Al-Asnawî, I, 148; Khiṭaṭ, II, 415.

[186]Rafʿ, II, 328; Sulûk, I, 773.

[187]Al-Nuwayrî, BN 1578, fol. 36a.

[188]Inbâʾ al-ghumr, I, 191.

[189]Ibid., p. 269.

[190]*Khiṭaṭ*, II, 392.

[191]*Ibid.*, p. 421.

[192]*Ibid.*

[193]*Durar*, III, 369.

[194]Ibn Kathîr, XIV, 14.

[195]*Inbâʾ al-ghumr*, I, 29.

[196]*Khiṭaṭ*, II, 224.

[197]Popper, *Notes*, II, 52; E. Ashtor, *Histoire des prix et des salaires dans l'orient medieval* (Paris, 1969), p. 275.

[198]Ashtor, *Histoire*, p. 377.

[199]*Khiṭaṭ*, II, 400-401; the rate of exchange at that time was thirteen and one-third dirhems to the dinar.

[200]*Sulûk*, I, 1049.

[201]*Ibid.*, p. 1001.

[202]Al-Nuwayrî, Leiden Or. 20, fol. 15b.

[203]*Khiṭaṭ*, II, 400.

[204]See al-Nuwayrî, BN 1579, fol. 86b.

[205]Al-ʿAynî, Ahmet III 2911/c34, fol. 65b.

[206]*Rafʿ*, II, 250.

[207]Al-Sakhâwî, *al-Ḍawʾ*, IX, 89.

[208]*Durar*, I, 97.

[209]See Rabie, _Financial System_, pp. 150 ff.

[210]_La Syrie_, p. LXXII; Popper, _Notes_, I, 97.

[211]Popper, _Notes_, I, 97; _La Syrie_, p. LXIX.

[212]_Sulûk_, II, 126.

[213]_Durar_, III, 368; _Sulûk_, II, 181.

CHAPTER VI

The Judge Out of Office

The chief judgeship was the highest religious office to which an *ʿâlim* could aspire. Thus it often involved a lifetime of effort to reach this post. It will not be surprising, therefore, to find that most of the judges we have been studying died while in office. In addition, corruption and political machinations played a part in bringing a judge's term of office to an end.

Ḥanbalîs

The Ḥanbalî *madhhab* has been described as the most stable of the four in Egypt, because its chief judges, on the average, managed to stay in office longer than their contemporaries. The fact that there are fewer of them to discuss is a possible indicator of the lack of competitiveness for this office. This supposition is buttressed by the sparsity of evidence of their political involvement, unlike, for example, the Shâfiʿîs. These generalizations hold true under close scrutiny. Five of the seven Ḥanbalî judges died in office, and the last three were in office for more than twenty-five years each: Taqî al-Dîn Ibn ʿAwaḍ (in office 712-738) and Naṣr Allâh (in office 769-795), both for twenty-six years, while Muwaffaq al-Dîn al-Maqdisî (in office 738-769) held the record with thirty-one years as chief judge.[1] There is a direct correlation here between the lengths of their terms in office and their personal longevity. Taqî al-Dîn Ibn ʿAwaḍ died at the age of seventy-six and the other two at the age of seventy-eight. By the same token, the judge with the shortest term, Saʿd al-Dîn al-Ḥârithî (in office 709-711) died the youngest at the age of fifty-nine. Sharaf al-Dîn al-Ḥarrânî (in office 696-709) is a sort of intermediate case; he died at the age of sixty-three after thirteen years in office. His predecessor, ʿIzz al-Dîn Ibn ʿAwaḍ (in office 679-696), presents a problem for the statistician. Although his death at the age of eighty-six and his formal term of office of seventeen years would lead us to classify him as a case similar to that of al-Ḥarrânî, we must not forget that he was de facto chief judge after Shams al-Dîn Ibn al-ʿImâd's deposition in 670, which would make his full term twenty-five years. Thus, four of the seven Ḥanbalî judges did manage to hold office for twenty-five years of more.

The case of the first Ḥanbalî *qâḍî al-quḍât* is the most interesting case of all. Shams al-Dîn Ibn al-ʿImâd was deposed from office in 670 after only seven years in office and jailed for mishandling funds. The scandal arose strictly out of a personal grievance. During the first years after the establishments of the four chief judgeships, each of the judges was allowed to appoint deputies in the provinces of Egypt. One such deputy, in the town of Maḥalla,[2] was Najm al-Dîn Aḥmad ibn Ḥamdân,[3] the brother of the poet Taqî al-Din Shabîb ibn Ḥamdân.[4] When the chief judge Ibn al-ʿImâd dismissed his brother from his post, Shabîb became angry and wrote a letter to the sultan claiming that the judge had deposits of money *(wadâʾiʿ)* in his possession belonging to merchants from Baghdad, Ḥarrân and Damascus who had died.[5] The sultan summoned the judge and asked him about this, but he denied it; so the sultan had his house searched and found most of what Shabîb had claimed would be there. Some of the funds belonged to people who had died and left heirs, while others to people who were still alive.[6] The sultan levied the *zakât* for several years on what was found, and returned the deposits to those who were still living. He then ordered the judge jailed and his house confiscated.[7]

Shabîb was apparently not satisfied with this punishment and tried to have Ibn al-ʿImâd punished more severely, perhaps, even executed. Later the same year the sultan was in Syria, and Shabîb brought official charges against Ibn al-ʿImâd that he was a member of some heretical sect and that he had slandered the sultan.[8] This matter came before the *nâʿib al-sulṭân,* who ordered the convocation of an assembly to settle the matter. However, some of the witnesses withdrew their testimoney, and the *nâʾib* soon learned that Shabîb was prejudiced against Ibn al-ʿImâd. He became very angry at that, jailed Shabîb and confiscated his property. Ibn al-ʿImâd was no better off; he was returned to jail in the citadel, where he remained for two years.[9] After his release from prison, he stayed at his home in al-Ṣâliḥiyya *madrasa* teaching until he died.[10]

The sultan's judgement against him had been personal and severe. No majlis of *ʿulamâʾ* was convened, apparently because it was a matter of financial and not religious misconduct. The severity of the punishment is difficult to explain, and it was certainly the most severe punishment any judge suffered at the hands of any sultan in the Baḫrî period. The sultan had taken his side in earlier plots against him, but perhaps his lying had made the sultan extremely angry.

In the year 738 three of the four chief judges were deposed, almost at the same time. One of these was ʿIzz al-Dîn Ibn ʿAwaḑ. The *amîr* Jankalî Ibn al-Bâbâ, who was a Ḫanbalî himself, denounced Ibn ʿAwaḑ and the Shâfiʿî chief judge, al-Qazwînî, and especially their children, for bribery and corruption in the selling of *awqâf*.[11] The sultan summoned ʿIzz al-Dîn and asked him about the money from the sale of *awqâf* which had belonged to orphans[12] and others[13]. The judge gave some excuses and the sultan ordered that he be beaten until he produced the money. Ibn ʿAwaḑ also lost whatever teaching posts he held at this time, and may have suffered a brief imprisonment, but the matter is not certain. He died very soon after his deposition.[14]

In conclusion, the Ḫanbalî chief judges were generally a sober and upright group. Although two of the seven were brought down by scandal, the rest enjoyed very long terms in office, and the political in-fighting, which was part of the struggle to secure the favor of *umarâʾ* and sultans, does not seem to have touched them.

Mâlikîs

All but two of the eleven Mâlikî chief judges of the Baḫrî period died in office, generally at an advanced age. Yet they cannot be categorized and described as simply as the Ḫanbalîs. In order to discuss them more easily, I have divided the Mâlikî chief judges into four groups.

The first group consists of the first three Mâlikî judges.

All of them died in office, at a reasonably advanced age and after having served as judge for a respectable length of time. Unlike the Ḥanbalîs, there is no correlation with this group between the age at the time of death and the length of their terms. In fact, Nafîs al-Dîn Ibn Shukr who served the longest of the three, died at the earliest age. Ibn Shukr was dismissed with two of the other chief judges in 678, but he was returned to office the next year, when Qalâʾûn became sultan. There is no evidence that anyone else was appointed during that interval.[15]

The second group consists of only two individuals, ʿAlî Ibn Makhlûf and Taqî al-Dîn al-Akhnâʾî, who are noteworthy not only for their personal longevity, eighty-five and ninety years respectively, but also for the length of their service as judges, thirty-three and thirty-two years respectively. Both men died in office.

Ibn Makhlûf was deposed from office briefly in 711, but the circumstances surrounding this deposition are not perfectly clear. Ibn Ḥajar says that it happened because Ibn Makhlûf hesitated to certify a letter or deed *(maktûb)* at the sultan's request,[16] whereas al-ʿAynî says that the judge refused to allow the sultan to tear down some building.[17] The account in al-Nuwayrî is even less clear, but the point is that the judge would not reverse a decision he had made, in spite of the sultan's protests, and he was deposed.[18] According to al-Nuwayrî, no one replaced Ibn Makhlûf.[19] In another version, we are told that the sultan ordered the Shâfiʿî *qâḍî al-quḍât*, Badr al-Dîn Ibn Jamâʿa, to find a Mâlikî judge and make him his *nâʾib*, thus abolishing the Mâlikî chief judgeship. He chose Badr al-Dîn Muḥammad Ibn Rashîq, who had been judge in Alexandria from

692 to 708, but this did not last more than a few days, and Ibn Makhlûf was returned to office.[20] In Raf' al-iṣr Ibn Ḥajar claims that Ibn Makhlûf was also deposed the previous year for support of Baybars II.[21] However, there is no other evidence that Ibn Makhlûf was deposed at that time, and even in his other work, al-Durar al-kâmina, Ibn Ḥajar only mentions the deposition of 711.[22]

Taqî al-Dîn al-Akhnâ'î enjoyed a less dramatic tenure, and finally died in the plague of 750. It should also be noted that he was the only chief judge who survived the purge of 738, when the other three judges were deposed because of corruption.

The next three judges, Tâj al-Dîn al-Akhnâ'î, Nûr al-Dîn al-Sakhâwî, and Burhân al-Dîn al-Akhnâ'î, form the third group. These two members of the al-Akhnâ'î family were brothers and both served for almost the same length of time, Tâj al-Dîn for thirteen years from 750 to 763, except for a few months in 756, and Burhân al-Dîn for fourteen years from 763-777. We do not know their ages at the time of their deaths, but both died in office. Nûr al-Dîn al-Sakhâwî served for only a few months, and died at the age of eighty, at which time Tâj al-Dîn al-Akhnâ'î, who had been transferred to the post of *nâẓir khizânat al-khâṣṣ* when al-Sakhâwî was appointed, returned to the chief judgeship.[23]

The fourth and last group consists of the three remaining Mâlikî judges, all of whom had short and stormy careers. The first of these judges was Badr al-Dîn 'Abd al-Wahhâb al-Akhnâ'î, who served from 777 to 778, and for a few months in 779. He was the nephew of both Tâj al-Dîn and Burhân al-Dîn al-Akhnâ'î, and the last and weakest of this extended family to hold office.[24] He was on the pilgrimage with al-Ashraf Sha'bân when this sultan was murdered at ʿAqaba, but unlike the Shâfiʿî *qâḍî al-quḍât*, Burhân al-Dîn Ibn Jamâʿa, and the Ḥanbalî judge, Sharaf al-Dîn Ibn Manṣûr, both of whom retreated to Jerusalem until the ensuing power struggle was resolved, al-Akhnâʾî sided with the *amîr* Ṭashtamur.[25] Unfortunately, this was not the winning side, and he was forced from office the same year. He managed to regain the office for a few months the next year (779), but this came to nothing, and he died in 784 at the age of sixty-four without ever regaining a major post.[26] His successor, ʿAlam al-Dîn al-Bisâṭî, would remain in office for about seven years, losing his post only for those months in 779. Al-Bisâṭî was finally deposed because of an argument he had with Burhân al-Dîn Ibn Jamâʿa, who was then Shâfiʿî chief judge. The circumstances of this dispute are not clear. One version is that some clerks presented a will *(waṣiyya)* to al-Bisâṭî, and he approved it before Ibn Jamâʿa had seen it. The latter was angry at al-Bisâṭî's arrogance and worked to have him deposed.[27] Another story is that an argument arose between them during a majlis which was convoked to discuss a *waqf*. In any case the sultan sided with Ibn Jamâʿa, deposed al-Bisâṭî, and allowed Ibn Jamâʿa to choose the new Mâlikî chief judge.[28] He chose Ibn Khayr al-Anṣârî, whose three year term ended with his deposition in 786. Al-Maqrîzî says that he was deposed because he would not judge a case that he considered outside the knowledge of Mâlikî *fuqahâʾ*.[29]

The most striking feature of the Mâlikî chief judges as we are studying them in this chapter is that they suffered so many depositions from office. This is in sharp contrast to the Ḥanbalîs whose judges usually enjoyed long terms of office and, despite two noteworthy scandals, provided stable regimes. The

Mâlikî chief judgeships were more hectic and the Mâlikîs were clearly more politically ambitious. Badr al-Dîn al-Akhnâ'î lost the chief judgeship because he backed the wrong side in the struggle for the sultanate following the murder of al-Ashraf Sha'bân. We have seen in the earlier chapter on appointments how al-Bisâṭî became chief judge through the influence of an *amîr* and perhaps he thought that this backing would allow him to challenge the Shâfi'î chief judge. His miscalculation led to his dismissal. Ambition may also have played a large part in persuading members of the Akhnâ'î family to leave their native Shâfi'î *madhhab* to seek power within the less crowded Mâlikî *maddhab*, even though most of them managed to hold office until they died. Thus we find at the termination of their careers as chief judge, as we found at the beginning, at least some evidence of the political manipulations and amibitons of these Mâlikî *quḍât*. Most of them died in office, but their frequent depositions show that this fact is not an indicator of the stability of the Mâlikî chief judges in office as it had been for the Ḥanbalîs.

Ḥanafîs

Although half again the number of Ḥanafîs held their respective chief judgeship as did Mâlikîs, it is even easier to describe the end of their careers as *qâḍî al-quḍât*. Half of them died in office, and most of the others resigned to return to teaching careers outside Egypt. Scandal and changes in the political climate occasionally affected the termination of a Ḥanafî judgeship, but these were not very important factors.

Those judges who died in office provide us with no special

trends. Some had served for long terms while others died after only a short tenure. Muʿizz al-Dîn al-Khaṭîbî died after having served fifteen years (677-692) as the Ḥanafî chief judge and Shams al-Dîn Ibn al-Ḥarîrî died at the age of seventy-three after an eighteen year term (710-728). Sirâj al-Dîn al-Hindî (in office 769-773), Jalâl al-Dîn Jâr Allâh (778-782) and Ṣadr al-Dîn Ibn Manṣûr (782-786) all died after having served four year terms; the last two were eighty and seventy-nine years of age respectively at the time of their deaths. Similarly, ʿAlâʾ al-Dîn Ibn al-Turkumânî (in office 748-750) and Ṣadr al-Dîn Ibn al-Turkumânî (773-776) had only served two and three years respectively, and Sirâj al-Dîn al-Râzî died in 717 after a term of only a few months. The aforementioned Ṣadr al-Dîn Ibn al-Turkumânî was only thirty-two years of age when he died, the youngest of any chief judge to die in office. It is interesting to note that the Ḥanafî *qâḍî al-quḍât* with the longest term of office also died at a very early age; this was Jamâl al-Dîn Ibn al-Turkumânî, who died at the age of fifty after a nineteen year term (750-769). If he had lived, he might well have enjoyed the longest tenure of any chief judge of the Baḥrî period, regardless of *madhhab*.

Burhân al-Dîn Ibn ʿAbd al-Ḥaqq was deposed because of the misconduct of his children.[30] He, like the deposed Shâfiʿî judge, al-Qazwînî, returned to Damascus, but whereas al-Qazwînî became chief judge, Ibn ʿAbd al-Ḥaqq had to content himself with a teaching position. He died six years later in Damascus.[31] Zayn al-Dîn al-Bisṭâmî (in office 742-748) was deposed after a six year term under rather mysterious circumstances. His successor, ʿAlâʾ al-Dîn Ibn al-Turkumânî (in office 748-750), was appointed by the sultan al-Muẓaffar Ḥajjî ibn al-Nâṣir (ruled 747-748), but he was given the post before al-Bisṭâmî had been notified of his dismissal. When Ibn al-Turkumânî appeared before al-Bisṭâmî in his robe of honor, the latter was dumbfounded.[32] Apparently the sultan wanted to avoid any opposition to his new appointment, but the sources do not supply any details. We do know that al-Malik al-Nâṣir Ibn Qalâʾûn had disliked Ibn al-Turkumânî because of his friendship with *umarâʾ*,[33] but there is no evidence that al-Bisṭâmî really did have powerful friends. In any case, his subsequent career was rather nondescript. Some sources say that he stayed at home teaching until he died some twenty-three years later in 771,[34] while others credit him with the post of *khaṭîb* at the mosque of Ibn Ṭûlûn, to which he was appointed sometime after his deposition, perhaps in 752.[35] Judging from his subsequent behavior, it seems that Ibn Ḥajar al-ʿAsqalânî was correct in saying that al-Bisṭâmî was happy when his appointment as judge ended.[36]

The term of Ḥusâm al-Dîn al-Rûmî was roughly coterminous with the sultanate of Lâjîn (696-698). When Lâjîn was assassinated, al-Rûmî was deposed by al-Malik al-Nâṣir upon his return from Kerak. He returned to Damascus and resumed his old post as chief judge, which he had left in the care of his son.[37] He was lost and apparently killed soon after in the battle with the Mongols at Wâdî Khazandâr near Damascus.[38] The story is also told that he was not killed, but rather captured, sold as a slave to the Franks in Cyprus who were aware of his medical knowledge, and further that he managed to send word to his son Jalâl al-Dîn in the year 735 that he was alive in Cyprus and wanted to be rescued from his captivity. The story was not believed, especially since he would have been one hundred and four years old at that time)[39]

The two terms of Shams al-Dîn al-Sarûjî came before (692-696) and immediately after (698-710) that of Ḥusâm al-Dîn al-Rûmî. He lost the post the first time because Lâjîn brought his old friend al-Rûmî to Egypt to be in his administration. When al-Nâşir returned from Kerak in 710, he deposed al-Sarûjî from the judgeship and all his teaching posts because of his support of Baybars II. After his first deposition, his successor had been kind enough to allow him to keep his residence at the Şâliḥiyya *madrasa,* but he was not so fortunate the second time and was driven out. He died a few months later.[40] We have traced the controversial career of Ḥusâm al-Dîn al-Ghûrî (in office 738-742) in an earlier chapter. Although he managed to gain the support of some *umarâ)*, he had angered the other chief judges[41] as well as other people at court,[42] and he was finally forced to leave Egypt. He went first to Damascus, and then to his native Baghdâd, where he taught in the mausoleum of Abû Ḥanîfa.[43]

All the remaining Ḥanafî judges resigned from office and returned to Damascus. Şadr al-Dîn al-Ahra(î (in office 663-677) resigned his post at the age of eighty-three to become chief judge of Damascus.[44] He had been on extremely close terms with Sultan Baybars, who died in 676. Perhaps the sultan's death and a desire to spend his last years with his sons, who held teaching posts in Damascus, prompted his resignation. The last three Ḥanafî chief judges served a combined term of little more than a year (777-778). After Şadr al-Dîn Ibn al-Turkumânî died in office, the judgeship remained vacant for two and a half months while the authorities tried to attract someone to fill the post.[45] The first of the three to be appointed was Najm al-Dîn Ibn Abî al-ʿIzz, also known as Ibn al-Kishk. He lasted only one hundred days in 777 before he resigned and returned to Damascus.[46] He eventually became chief judge in Damascus in 792 and was assassinated by a mad man in 799 for no apparent reason.[47] He was followed by his cousin, Ṣadr al-Dîn ʿAlî Ibn Abî al-ʿIzz, who lasted about as long in office as his cousin before returning to Damascus, also to become chief judge there after a number of years.[48] He, in turn, was followed by Sharaf al-Dîn Ibn Manṣûr, who remained in office less than a year (777-778) before resigning and returning to Damascus. As chief judge he was pressured by some of the people at court to nullify certain *awqâf*, but he refused and eventually resigned rather than continue to be forced to resist their pressure.[49] On the other hand, al-Maqrîzî says that the sultan deposed him for not acting as the sultan wished,[50] maybe concerning these *awqâf*.

Certainly this comparatively large number of resignations makes the Ḥanafî chief judges of the Baḥrî period different from their contemporaries in the other *madhâhib*. Perhaps the pressures of being a chief judge in the capital drove them to resigning. Scandal and political machinations also had their effects, yet about one-half of these judges managed to hold office until they died.

Shâfiʿîs

In the discussion of these three *madhâhib* we have seen the careers of the chief judges ended by death, scandal, political intrigue and resignation. All these explanations exist for the termination of the Shâfi(î chief judgeship as well plus one more, which can be seen as an indication of the Shâfi(î *madhhab's* superior status: retirement with a pension. The existence of all these factors plus the division of the Shâfi(î judgeship between two judges, one with jurisdiction over al-Qâhira and the other over Fusţâţ, makes this *madhhab* the most variegated and complex of all to discuss.

Almost half the Shâfi(î chief judges died in office. Tâj al-Dîn Ibn Bint al-A(azz (in office 663-665) was the first Shâfi(î judge after the system of the four judgeships was established. His death at the age of sixty-one ended a brilliant career, which had included the offices of *wazîr* as well as the chief judgeship of Egypt several times prior to 663. Taqî al-Dîn Ibn Razîn was one of the two judges who divided the judicial authority following the death of Ibn Bint al-A(azz. He was first judge of al-Qâhira (665-676) and then promoted to full authority over Egypt (676-678). His career in Egypt was a second one, since he had been a successful *faqîh* in Damascus, but fled because of the invasion of Hûlâgû. He died at the age of seventy-seven. The career of Wajîh al-Dîn al-Bahnasî was somewhat the reverse of Ibn Razîn's. He had been made chief judge of all Egypt (680-681), but found the duties too tedious, probably because of his advanced age, and asked to be relieved of the judgeship of al-Qâhira. This was granted and he remained judge of Fusţâţ (681-785) until he died.

Taqî al-Dîn Ibn Bint al-A(azz succeeded Wajîh al-Dîn al-Bahnasî as judge of Fusţâţ (685-686) and worked for the deposition of the judge of al-Qâhira, Shihâb al-Dîn Ibn al-Khuwayyî (in office 681-686). He was successful in so far as

Ibn al-Khuwayyî was transferred to Damascus, but he was unsuccessful in gaining full jurisdiction over Egypt, because Burhân al-Dîn al-Sinjârî was chosen to replace Shihâb al-Dîn. However, al-Sinjârî died in office after only a few months, and Ibn Bint al-Aʿazz had his wish. His first term as *qâḍî al-quḍât* of Egypt (686-690) ended when the new sultan, al-Ashraf Khalîl, appointed Ibn Salʿûs his *wazîr*. The new *wazîr* greatly disliked Ibn Bint al-Aʿazz and had him deposed from the judgeship as well as from every other post he held. There are several different reasons given for the *wazîr's* dislike of Ibn Bint al-Aʿazz, depending on the source. Al-Nuwayrî says that during the reign of al-Ashraf's father, al-Malik al-Manşûr Qalâʾûn, Ibn Bint al-Aʿazz had shown a preference for al-Malik al-Şâliḥ ʿAlî, the brother of al-Ashraf, over al-Ashraf Khalîl himself. After Ibn Salʿûs became *wazîr*, he told the new sultan about this, so he deposed Taqî al-Dîn from the chief judgeship.[51] Al-Asnawî says that Ibn Salʿûs and al-Ashraf had been friends prior to the latter's assumption of the sultanate, and that Ibn Bint al-Aʿazz, who was then chief judge, said nasty things about Ibn Salʿûs to Sultan Qalâʾûn and the sultan prevented Ibn Salʿûs from meeting with his son Khalîl.[52] Al-ʿAynî, quoting al-Yûsufî, supplies a different story. He says that Ibn Salʿûs was the *şâhib al-dîwân*[53] of al-Ashraf in Damascus. When Ibn Salʿûs sent greetings to Ibn Bint al-Aʿazz, the latter asked the messenger, "Who is Ibn Salʿûs?" When he was told that he was al-Ashraf's *şâhib al-dîwân*, he referred to him in a derogatory manner, and when Ibn Salʿûs learned of this he became angry and never forgot it.[54] All three sources were contemporaries of the events, and it is difficult to trust one more than another, although al-ʿAynî's account is the longest and most detailed. Still another version is supplied by Ibn Ḥajar al-ʿAsqalânî who places the blame for the enmity between the two on the fact that Ibn Salʿûs recommended someone for an office, and Ibn Bint al-Aʿazz had opposed it.[55] In any case, the important point is that Ibn Salʿûs had a long standing grudge against Taqî al-Dîn Bint al-Aʿazz, and once in power Ibn Salʿûs made several attempts to humiliate and destroy Ibn Bint al-Aʿazz.

At first the *amîr* ʿAlam al-Dîn al-Shujâʿî interceded with the sultan to have Taqî al-Dîn made chief judge of Damascus.[56] When Ibn Salʿûs heard of this he became afraid that Taqî al-Dîn would retain too powerful a position, so the *wazîr* arranged for some people to testify against Ibn Bint al-Aʿazz in regards to his sinful character and the like, and even that he was really a Christian.[57] The sultan believed this, and the *wazîr* jailed him and even wanted to have him beaten.[58] He also fined him 120,000 dirhems.[59]

Soon after this, Baydarâ the *nâʾib* was persuaded to intervene on Taqî al-Dîn's behalf and he was freed from jail.[60] He was forced to reside in a *zâwiya* outside al-Qâhira until he completed paying what he owed, and then he was able to gain a teaching post at al-Nâşiriyya *madrasa* near the tomb of al-Shâfiʿî.[61] Sometime after that, perhaps in 691,[62] he was brought before the sultan and the chief judges again, but some *umarâʾ* intervened and asked the sultan if they could judge Ibn Bint al-Aʿazz instead. The sultan agreed, and in this next *majlis* Taqî al-Dîn denied all the charges against him, including that he was a Christian or descended from Christians. He was then acquitted, the sultan was informed, and Ibn Bint al-Aʿazz was freed.[63] In 693 he went on the pilgrimage, not returning to Cairo until he had learned of the deaths of al-Ashraf Khalîl and Ibn Salʿûs and the establishment of the new *dawla*.[64] He was returned to the chief judgeship, where he remained until his death in 695. Like his father he died a fairly young man at the age of fifty-seven after a very successful career, despite his harsh treatment at the hands of Ibn Salʿûs.

He was followed by Ibn Daqîq al-ʿÎd (in office 695-702) who enjoyed a high reputation for piety and scolarship. He resigned several times, but was always persuaded to return.[65] We have mentioned earlier the dispute between him and the *amîr* Mankûtimur over a deceased merchant's will. Ibn Daqîq al-ʿÎd became so distressed by this pressure that he locked himself in his house and sent word to the sultan that he had resigned. When the sultan heard what had happened he censured Mankûtimur and finally persuaded the judge to come to the citadel to talk about the problem. When he arrived the sultan went to him and sat next to him. He pleaded with him to stay and he finally relented.[66] Ibn Daqîq al-ʿÎd died in office at the age of seventy-seven.

All the remaining judges except two, who retired with pensions, were deposed from the chief judgeship of Egypt and never returned to it, although several of them became chief judge of Damascus. These judges constitute about one half of the Shâfiʿî judges of the Baḫrî period. Muḫyî al-Dîn Ibn ʿAyn al-Dawla (judge of Fusţâţ, 665-676) was one of the two judges who shared the Shâfiʿî judgeship of Egypt following the death of Tâj al-Dîn Ibn Bint al-Aʿazz. He became partially paralyzed and was unable to write. One of his secretaries let this be known, and he was deposed in 676, two years before his death.[67] There is some question about how the term of Ṣadr al-Dîn Ibn Bint al-Aʿazz (in office 678-679) ended. One source says that he resigned,[68] while others claim that he was deposed at the accession of the new sultan.[69]

Shihâb al-Dîn Ibn al-Khuwayyî was judge of al-Qâhira (681-686) at the same time that Wajîh al-Dîn al-Bahnasî was judge of Fusṭâṭ (681-685). Taqî al-Dîn Ibn Bint al-Aʿazz took over al-Bahnasî's post at the latter's death and worked to gain both halves of the jurisdiction for himself. He saw his chance when Ibn Zakî, Shâfiʿî judge of Damascus, died in 686 and he worked to have Ibn al-Khuwayyî appointed to that post.[70] He was successful. Ibn al-Khuwayyî became chief judge of Damascus and received a number of teaching posts there at the same time; he served until his death seven years later.[71] Jamâl al-Dîn al-Zarʿî (in office 710-711) served only a brief term while Badr al-Dîn Ibn Jamâʿa was out of favor. When he lost his high office, he was made *qâḍî al-ʿaskar* and given a number of teaching posts until the chief judgeship of Damascus became available. He was transferred there two years later, and also received a few teaching posts. He had only a brief tenure of one year in Damascus, at which time he was replaced by Jalâl al-Dîn al-Qazwînî, but he managed to keep one teaching post and the office of *shaykh al-shuyûkh*. He lost the judgeship because he was so bold as to ask the managers of the *awqâf* of the *madâris* for an accounting of their financial activities.[72] He eventually lost even those two posts in 726 and returned to Egypt where he became *qâḍî al-ʿaskar* along with the professorships of several *madâris*. He held these offices until he died of a stroke in 734.[73]

Jalâl al-Dîn al-Qazwînî (in office 727-738) would also return to Damascus as chief judge after his humiliating deposition from office in the purge of 738. He was deposed because of the misconduct of his son in the handling of *awqâf*. The background and circumstances of this scandal are given in some detail by al-Maqrîzî and al-ʿAynî.[74] The cause of this scandal was al-Qazwînî's son, Jamâl al-Dîn ʿAbd Allâh. He was greedy and frivolous, took bribes and generally lived above his means; he even bought horses, hired jockeys, and staged races. Jamâl al-Dîn was exiled to Syria twice because of the petitions brought to the sultan against him, but through the mediation of his father and the *amîr* Baktimur al-Sâqî,[75] his first exile lasted only about a year. He was exiled a second time, but the father appealed to the sultan personally, and his son returned.[76] However, the son had not learned his lesson. He had a house built on the Nile, near that of his father, for which the judges of the provinces were assigned the supplying of marble and other things. He went to great lengths in constructing it, even summoning artisans from Syria to work on it. The cost came to more than 500,000 dirhems. When the sultan heard about this he rebuked the judge for his son's actions, especially since Jamâl al-Dîn had to borrow the money for the construction, but the father explained that living in Cairo was not suitable for them, and they needed to live (outside Cairo) on the Nile. Incredibly enough, it was not long before Jamâl al-Dîn bought a house in Cairo, which he renovated at great expense. His father was also being criticized at this time for appointing *nuwwâb* only after consultation with his children. It was alleged that in order to become a (deputy) judge, it was necessary to pay a bribe of 5,000 (dirhems) or more.[77] The complaints against the family became so intense that the sultan deposed al-Qazwînî from the chief judgeship of Egypt and sent word that he should return to his former post as chief judge of Damascus; he also ordered him to make his son pay all his debts. In addition he was required to produce the taxes due for the *waqf* of *al-turba* al-Ashrafiyya which amounted to 230,000 dirhems. In order to do this he had to sell all his properties as well as those of his children and their furniture, but at only one quarter of the value. Then he sold Chinese goods and vessels for 40,000 dirhems; cooking utensils for 600 dirhems; pearls, jewelry, gold and silver brocades for more than 120,000 dirhems; a house in Cairo for 35,000 dirhems; and his son ʿAbd Allâh sold eleven slave girls for varying amounts. Finally, he was able to discharge his debt to the orphans and others, and he was allowed to depart for Damascus to take up his new duties.[78] He died in Damscus the next year.

What is interesting here is not only the huge sums of money involved, but also that the sultan delayed so long before taking decisive action against al-Qazwînî. He finally acted only under great pressure and numerous complaints. We have mentioned earlier his personal fondness for the judge and his exile to Syria was comparatively mild punishment. We should not forget that at a much earlier period Sultan Baybars had imprisoned the Ḥanbalî *qâḍî al-quḍât* Shams al-Dîn Ibn al-ʿImâd over a much milder financial indiscretion, and that al-Qazwînî's fellow Ḥanbalî judge was beaten to pay back money that he owed. Finally, we see here a clear example of the enormous wealth which the Shâfiʿî chief judge could acquire, although some of it, at least, was gained illegally.

Bahâʾ al-Dîn Ibn ʿAqîl was chief judge for only eighty days (759) in the middle of ʿIzz al-Dîn Ibn Jamâʿa's long term of office (738-766). He had become chief judge through the instigation of the *amîr* Ṣarghitmish, and when the *amîr* was imprisoned, Ibn ʿAqîl also lost his post, and returned to teaching until he died in 769.[79] Ibn Jamâʿa was followed by Bahâʾ al-Dîn al-Subkî (in office 766-773). He was deposed by the sultan at the instigation of some court notables *(akâbir al-dawla)*, because he refused to allow the sale of some *awqâf* lands.[80] Afterwards, he remained in Egypt for a while. He was good friends with the amîr Mankalî Bughâ, who tried to get him to accept the post of chief judge of Damascus. He refused, much to the *amîr's* chagrin, and opted instead for the post of *amîn al-ḫukm*. He found its duties tedious, and passed them off to an aide. Eventually he became chief judge of Damascus, in which office he died in 777.[81]

Burhân al-Dîn Ibn Jamâʿa served two terms as chief judge (773-779; 781-784). Halfway through the first term he resigned, because several *umarâʾ*, including the *nâẓir al-jaysh*, opposed one of his judgements.[82] Another source blames his resignation on the interference of some unnamed people at the court *(ahl al-dawla)* in a legal affair.[83] Ibn Jamâʿa obviously resented the interference and resigned. The sultan tried to get him to return, but he refused initially, agreeing only after he had imposed some conditions on the sultan, probably his help in keeping the notables and *umarâʾ* at bay.[84] He tried to resign several more times, but was always persuaded to remain.[85] In 779 he left the chief judgeship of Egypt to go to Jerusalem to be *khaţîb* and to teach.[86] There is some question in the sources whether he voluntarily resigned in disgust at the struggle for the sultanate[87] or whether he was deposed through the instigation of the *amîr* Ţashtamur and Sirâj al-Dîn al-Bulqînî, who worked for the installation of Badr al-Dîn al-Subkî (in office 779-781).[88] In another place we are told that Burhân al-Dîn spoke rudely to Ţashtamur following the deposition of al-Ashraf Sha⁽bân II, blaming him for the dissension; Ţashtamur remembered this insult, and eventually worked for Ibn Jamâ⁽a's deposition.[89] The end of his second term falls in the Burjî period, and is thus beyond the scope of our topic. Badr al-Dîn al-Subkî held the chief judgeship for the three years between Ibn Jamâ⁽a's two terms (779-781), and he would return for two more terms in the Burjî period (784-789; 791-792). Al-Subkî lost his post when the *amîr* Baraka[90] and the future sultan Barqûq decided to bring back Burhân al-Dîn Ibn Jamâ⁽a, but the reasons behind this decision are lacking.[91]

The two judges who finally retired with a pension were Badr al-Dîn and ⁽Izz al-Dîn Ibn Jamâ⁽a. Badr al-Dîn served three terms as chief judge: 690-693, 702-710, and 711-727. His first term was as a replacement for Taqî al-Dîn's Ibn Bint al-A⁽azz. Ibn Jamâ⁽a had been friendly with Taqî al-Dîn's enemy, Ibn Sal⁽ûs, who, when he became *wazîr*, summoned Ibn Jamâ⁽a to take over the chief judgeship.[92] When the sultan al-Ashraf Khalîl was killed and Ibn Sal⁽ûs jailed and beaten to death in 693, Ibn Jamâ⁽a lost the judgeship to Ibn Bint al-A⁽azz, but he was allowed to keep several teaching posts. Later the same year he became chief judge of Damascus at the death of Shihâb al-Dîn Ibn al-Khuwayyî.[93] He returned to the judgeship of Cairo in 702 after the death of Ibn Daqîq al-ʿÎd, but was deposed because of his support for Baybars II when al-Malik al-Nâṣir Muḥammad returned from Kerak.[94] This deposition lasted only about a year, and he returned to office until he asked to be discharged in 727 because of eye trouble and old age; he was then eighty-eight years old. His request was granted, and he was given a pension of 1,000 silver dirhems per months and ten ardebs of wheat, but he still kept one teaching post.[95] He died six years later in 733.

The other member of this family to retire with a pension was Badr al-Dîn's son, ʿIzz al-Dîn. He held office from 738-766, except for those few months in 759 when he was replaced by Ibn ʿAwîl. ʿIzz al-Dîn Ibn Jamâʿa was not very knowledgeable in *fiqh*, and the real legal difficulties were handled by his *nâʾib*, Tâj al-Dîn al-Munâwî. When al-Munâwî died in 765, Ibn Jamâʿa was incapable of continuing on his own, so he resigned.[96] Various *umarâʾ* urged him to continue in office, but he was adamant. He was left with the office of *nâẓir* at the mosque of Ibn Ṭûlûn as well as the teaching posts of *fiqh* (!) and *ḥadîth* there, plus 1,000 dirhems per month from the treasury.[97] He died the next year at the age of seventy-three.

In conclusion, it is not surprising to see that such a large proportion of the chief judges died in office. Usually, this high post was reached after many years, and in spite of the political maneuvering which often played a part in the appointment process, a certain amount of judicial knowledge was generally required. On the other hand, the same political machinations which could bring one man to the chief judgeship could force another man from it. Resignation from office was not common, except with the Ḥanafîs for a brief period, but threat of resignation was sometimes used with a resultant strengthening of the judge's position. Retirement from office with a pension was a luxury reserved for only two Shâfiʿîs; otherwise, a chief judge, even if he had become feeble, normally stayed at his job until he died.

Chart III

Reasons for End of Tenure

	Died in Office	Resigned	Deposed	Retired
Ḥanbalîs	5	0	2	0
Mâlikîs	9	0	2	0
Ḥanafîs	9	4	5	0
Shâfiʿîs	6	0	8*	2
Total	29	4	17	2

N.B. The above table indicates the reasons for the terminations of the judges' last tenure as chief judge. Threats of resignation and the reasons for the end of earlier terms of office as chief judge are not included.

*Ṣadr al-Dîn Ibn Bint al-Aʿazz is included under this classification, but it is an open question whether he resigned or was deposed.

ENDNOTES

[1]Unless otherwise stated the data on age and terms of office have been drawn from Salibi's "Listes". Excessive documentation on these points is unnecessary, since all the sources usually give the same information. I shall revert to a more detailed system of notation only in those cases where there is a serious conflict in the sources.

[2]Sulûk, I, 602.

[3]For biographical details, see Shadharât, V, 428-29 and Ibn Rajab, II, 331-37.

[4]Wiet, Manhal, no. 1170.

[5]Sulûk, I, 602-603. See also Yûnînî, II, 470-71; Ibn al-Furât, Târîkh MS, fols. 209a-b; al-Nuwayrî, BN 1578, fols. 48a-b.

[6]Al-Yûnînî, II, 470.

[7]Sulûk, I, 603.

[8]This group was known as Ḥashwiyya. The name originally was used for a group of *muḥaddithûn* who recognized certain anthromorphic *aḥâdîth* as genuine (EI-2, III, 269). The editor of Sulûk says its refers to Ẓâhirîs who believed in *tajsîm* (Sulûk, I, 603).

[9]Sulûk, I, 603; al-Yûnînî, II, 471.

[10]Al-Nuwayrî, BN 1578, fol. 98b.

[11]Rafʿ, I, 91-92; Durar, I, 239-40.

[12]Sulûk, II, 442-43.

[13]Al-ʿAynî (Ahmet III 2911/c34, fol. 65b) places the blame on the father, whereas al-Maqrîzî and Ibn Ḥajar blame the son

(see two previous notes). In any case, it was the father who suffered.

[14]Raf‘, I, 92.

[15]Ibn Shukr was deposed along with the Ḥanafî and Shâfi‘î chief judges in Rabî‘a II, but the circumstances are obscure. Ibn Kathîr (XIII, 288) and following him al-‘Aynî (BN 1543, fol. 231a) say that they were deposed because of (their) hesitation in bestowing the robe of honor on Sultan al-Malik al-Sa‘îd. However, these depositions occurred during the short reign of Salâmish, at a time when it might have been more likely to see such hesitation rewarded instead of penalized. Even Ibn Kathîr does not have much confidence in this explanation, and says, "wa-allâhu a‘lam." See also al-Yûnînî, IV, 7; Sulûk, I, 657. Ibn Shukr was returned to office at the same time as the Ḥanafî chief judge, sometime during Ramaḍân, 679 (al-Yûnînî, IV, 52), when the Shâfi‘î Ṣadr al-Dîn Ibn Bint al-A‘azz was deposed and replaced by Taqî al-Dîn Ibn Razîn, who had held office previously. According to Ibn Kathîr (XIII, 292) all these installations occurred in Ramaḍân, 679.

[16]Raf‘, II, 406.

[17]Al-‘Aynî, Ahmet III 2912/4, fol. 283b.

[18]Al-Nuwayrî, Leiden Or. 20, fol. 55b-56a.

[19]Ibid. Al-‘Aynî (Ahmet III 2912/4, fol. 283b) simply says he was returned to office after a few days. See also Sulûk, II, 103.

[20]Durar, IV, 292 and III, 202. See also A‘yân, fol. 347b; Raf‘, I, 406.

[21]Raf‘, I, 406.

[22]Durar, III, 202.

[23]Sulûk, III, 19, 21.

[24]Manhal (Ms, fol. 478b) calls him *ḍa‘îf*.

[25]Sulûk, III, 285; Inbâ’ al-ghumr, I, 197.

26 Raf', II, 384-85.

27 Ibid., p. 249.

28 Sulûk, III, 443.

29 Ibid., p. 517.

30 Raf', I, 37; al-'Aynî, Ahmet III 2911/c34, fol. 65a; Sulûk, II, 442.

31 Ibn Kathîr, XIV, 212; Raf', I, 37; Durar, I, 48.

32 Durar, III, 157; Raf', II, 401; A'yân, fol. 33b.

33 Sulûk, II, 813.

34 Ibn Abî al-Wafâ', Jawâhir, I, 391; Manhal MS, fol. 547a.

35 Durar, III, 245; Sulûk, II, 851.

36 Durar, III, 245.

37 Durar, II, 91; Raf', I, 184.

38 Al-Nu'aymî, Dâris, I, 516.

39 Durar, II, 91.

40 Manhal, I, 189-90; Raf', I, 51; Durar, I, 96-97. See also Ibn Kathîr, XIV, 85 and Sulûk, II, 86.

41 Sulûk, II, 611.

42 Raf', I, 203.

43 Ibid.; Durar, II, 128-29.

44 Ibn Ṭûlûn, Quḍât, p. 190.

[45]Raf⁽, I, 90.

[46]Inbâʾ al-ghumr, I, 152.

[47]Rafʿ, I, 55; Ibn Ṭûlûn, Quḍât, p. 202.

[48]Ibn Ṭûlûn, Quḍât, p. 201.

[49]Rafʿ, I, 90.

[50]Sulûk, III, 436-47.

[51]Al-Nuwayrî, BN 1579, fol. 96a.

[52]Al-Asnawî, I, 50-51.

[53]According to Rabie (Financial System, p. 155), "he was a kind of auditor, who had to countersign every account or register signed by the *nâẓir*." The *nâẓir* "was the responsible chief of each *dîwân*" (ibid., p. 154). We cannot be sure which *dîwân* is meant in the source, but probably it refers to the control of finances in general.

[54]Al-ʿAynî, Ahmet III 2912/4, fol. 158a.

[55]Rafʿ, II, 328.

[56]Sulûk, I, 772.

[57]Ibid.; Rafʿ, II, 328.

[58]Sulûk, I, 772.

[59]Al-ʿAynî, Ahmet III 2912/4, fol. 158b.

[60]Sulûk, I, 773; al-Nuwayrî, BN 1579, fols. 96a-b. This is the same Baydarâ whom Taqî al-Dîn had helped when the *amîr* was *wazîr*. See also Ibn al-Şuqâʿî, Tâlî, no. 88.

[61]Ibid., p. 785. The description of the rest of this incident is based on al-ʿAynî, Ahmet III 2912/4, fol. 158b. It seems that both sources are discussing the same *majlis*.

[62] Sulûk, I, 773.

[63] Al-ʿAynî, Ahmet III 2912/4, fols. 158b-159a; Rafʿ, II, 328.

[64] Al-ʿAynî, Ahmet III 2912/4, fol. 167a; al-Asnawî, I, 152. See also Rafʿ, II, 329.

[65] Wâfî, IV, 194.

[66] Sulûk, I, 848-49.

[67] Wâfî, Ahmet III 2920/7, fol. 153a.

[68] Shadharât, IV, 367.

[69] Ibn Kathîr, XIII, 292; Sulûk, I, 683.

[70] Al-Nuwayrî, BN 1579, fols. 63b-64a.

[71] Ibn Kathîr, XIII, 337: Ibn Ṭulun, Quḍât, p. 79.

[72] Durar, II, 256.

[73] Ibid.; Ibn Kathîr, XIV, 167-68; Aʿyân, fol. 201b.

[74] Sulûk, II, 439-42; al-ʿAynî, Ahmet III 2911/c34, fols. 63a-b.

[75] Durar, II, 19-21. Only Sulûk (II, 440) speaks of a second exile.

[76] Sulûk, II, 440.

[77] Al-ʿAynî, Ahmet III 2911/c34, fol. 62a.

[78] Ibid., fols. 63a-64a.

[79] Rafʿ, II, 285.

80 Raf(MS, fol. 110a.

81 Inbâ) al-ghumr, I, 11, 184.

82 Durar, I, 39; Raf(, I, 32.

83 Sulûk, III, 241. Al-Maqrîzî says that Burhân al-Dîn prevented some judicial scribes from *al-tawqî(*, and a few people of the court pressed him to permit it. Burhân al-Dîn became angry at their objection. Perhaps this means that the scribes were signing or placing their own signatures on verdicts or official documents, thus assuming judicial responsibilities. Still another source (Inbâ) al-ghumr, I, 95) says it was specifically the *umarâ)* who were pestering Burhân al-Dîn over the matter of some scribes.

84 Inbâ) al-ghumr, I, 95.

85 Durar, I, 40.

86 Inbâ) al-ghumr, I, 239.

87 Ibid.

88 Ibid., pp. 239-40.

89 Raf(, I, 33-34. All three versions are supplied by Ibn Ḥajar al-(Asqalânî, and he has obviously contradicted himself. In Inbâ) al-ghumr (I, 239) he states that Ibn Jamâ(a resigned, while in Raf((I, 33) he clearly states that he was deposed. The other story, Inbâ) al-ghumr, I, 239-40) does not exactly say that he was driven from office by Ṭashtamur, but it certaibly implies a conspiracy, which resulted in the judge's deposition. Al-Durar al-kâmina (I, 40) says that he was dismissed from office.

90 Baraka ibn (Abd Allâh (d. 782; Inbâ) al-ghumr, II, 23-24).

91 Raf(, I, 34.

92 Sulûk, I, 771.

93 Ibid., p. 803; Durar, III, 368.

94 Al-Asnawî, I, 386; Ibn Ṭûlûn, Quḍât, p. 81.

[95]*Sulûk*, II, 283; Ibn Ṭûlûn, *loc. cit.*

[96]*Durar*, II, 490-91. According to al-Maqrîzî (*Sulûk*, II, 893), Tâj al-Dîn al-Munâwî actually became chief judge in 754, when Ibn Jamâʿa was allowed to resign and make the pilgrimage to Mecca. Ibn Jamâʿa nominated this son-in-law of his as his successor. However, there were complaints against al-Munâwî, and Ibn Jamâʿa was forced to resume his duties very shortly thereafter. In fact, al-Asnawî (II, 467) says his appointment lasted only one day. There is considerable doubt that he was even formally installed in the chief judgeship, because he is not mentioned in *Rafʿ*, and this brief appointment does not appear in *Durar* (III, 470).

[97]*Sulûk*, III, 99.

CHAPTER VII

Conclusion

The existence of judicial arbitrators for the Muslim community goes back to the very beginnings of Islam. Government appointed judges were established under the Umayyads and a hierarchy emerged under the ʿAbbâsids. A major innovation emerged in the early Baḥrî Mamlûk period when a chief judge was established for each of the four generally recognized schools of law. Although it seems that the Shâfiʿî chief judge enjoyed a certain pre-eminence, the other three schools of law gained an enhanced status at this time. This judicial reorganization probably was not so much a radical departure from the previous system, but rather should be seen as the product of an evolutionary process which had begun with the establishment of four professorships of *fiqh* at al-Ṣâliḥiyya *madrasa* during the late Ayyûbid period.

The careers of the chief judges did not vary much from one *madhhab* to another. All the judges held teaching posts before, during, and, usually after their terms as chief judge. However, there is no evidence that an aspirant for the chief judgeship had to have held a set number or type of posts before being considered for that office. A large number of the individuals under study had served as deputy judges under their predecessors before rising to the higher judicial post. Many a deputy judge fortified his relationship to his superior by marrying the latter's daughter, while other deputies enjoyed some sort of blood relationship to a chief judge. A blood or marital relationship to a chief judge and experience as a deputy judge, alone or in combination, seem to have been important factors behind the selection of a candidate for the chief judgeship. On the other hand, friendship with or patronage by an important Mamlûk or court official was also important for such a candidate. The goal of anyone interested in becoming chief judge was to become known well enough in court circles so that when a vacancy occurred his name would be proposed as the new *qâḍî al-quḍât*. The three factors of nepotism, *nâʾib* succession, and patronage seem to have been of considerable significance in such appointments. Merit, that is to say excellent qualifications or a pious reputation, does not seem to have counted for much by itself. Although many of the chief judges came from important families of *ʿulamâʾ*, such connections did not guarantee access to high office, and many sons of chief judges never held any important posts. The factors I have mentioned were important considerations in selecting a chief judge, but the evidence points to personal initiative as a matter of prime importance for any would-be judge. The majority of Cairene chief judges were born and raised within the Mamlûk empire, but a good number of these were Syrians and not Egyptians, let alone native Cairenes. In addition, many came from outside the Mamlûk territories. This willingness and ability to move from place to place in an attempt to improve one's career is another example of the importance of personal initiative for an aspirant to the chief judgeship.

Since attaining the chief judgeship often involved many years of effort, it is not surprising to see that most of the chief judges clung to their offices until they died. Others lost the chief judgeship through political intrigue or, having attached their fortunes to those of an important Mamlûk or notable, lost it when that individual lost power or influence.

At the beginning of this study I said that a discussion of the careers of the chief judges was important not only to study the activities of these judges within the framework of Mamlûk society and politics, but also to assess their role and functions as officers of an Islamic state. Clearly the primary function of the chief judges was to administer the law among the massess of the populace, both personally and through subordinates. Although these activities are not always very well documented, the existence of a judicial bureaucracy is unmistakable, and it could have served no other purpose. These judicial responsibilities also involved dealings with the Mamlûk oligarchy, and the record of these activities is more fully documented.

It was at such times that the chief judges were under the greatest pressure to uphold the highest standards of the *sharî'a*, both in letter and spirit. Unfortunately, the judges were often found lacking. In many cases they readily acceded to the plots of the Mamlûks at the expense of Islamic institutions like the *awqâf*, although in numerous cases the judges did impose the letter of the law on these arrangements. On the other hand, we must remember that the judges had only moral power with which to oppose the designs of the Mamlûks. This was occasionally a adequate weapon, but we have seen numerous instances when a chief judge lost all or part of his jurisdiction in an unsuccessful attempt to oppose a Mamlûk sultan. Finally, we must not forget that many of the chief judges were themselves corrupt, either accepting bribes or, more often, abusing the trust which they enjoyed as superintendents of *awqâf* for their own enrichment. Many judges strove to fulfill the highest ideals as the chief judicial officers of an Islamic state by strictly adhering to the details and spirit of the *sharî'a,* but they often suffered for this devotion and were too often unable or unwilling to oppose the Mamlûk oligarchy. Many chief judges even compounded the difficulties of the Islamic community by adding their own varieties of corruption and fraud to the baser designs of the Mamlûks.

BIBLIOGRAPHY

A. Primary Sources

Al-Adfuwî, Kamâl al-Dîn Ja'far. Al-Ṭâli' al-sa'îd. Cairo: al-Dâr al-mişriyya li-al-ta'lîf wa-al-tarjama, 1966.

Al-Asnawî, Jamâl al-Dîn 'Abd Allâh. Ṭabaqât al-shâfi'iyya. Baghdad: Maṭba'at al-irshâd, 1390-91/1970-71. 2 vols.

Al-'Aynî, Badr al-Dîn Maḥmûd. 'Iqd al-jumân fî târîkh ahl al-zamân. Photographic copies of MSS Ahmet III 2912/4 and 2911/c34.

__________. 'Iqd al-jumân. Hand copy of Dâr al-Kutub MS 1584.

__________. 'Iqd al-jumân. Bibliothèque Nationale MS Arabe 1543.

Ibn 'Abd al-Ẓâhir, Muḥyî al-Dîn 'Abd Allâh. Al-Rawḍ al-zâhir fî sîrat al-malik al-ẓâhir. Riyâḍ, 1976.

__________. Baybars I of Egypt. Edited and translated by S.F. Sadeque. Pakistan: Oxford University Press, 1956.

Ibn Abî al-Wafâ', Muḥyî al-Dîn 'Abd al-Qâdir. Al-Jawâhir al-muḍî'a fî ṭabaqât al-ḥanafiyya. Hyderabad: Majlis dâ'irat al-ma'ârif al-'uthmâniyya, 1332/1913.

Ibn al-Dawâdârî, Abû Bakr. Kanz al-durar wa-jâmi' al-ghurar. Vols. 9-11. Cairo: al-Ma'had al-almânî li-al-âthâr, 1960-71.

Ibn al-Furât, Najm al-Dîn Muḥammad. Târîkh. Beirut: American University press, 1936-38. 3 vols.

__________. Târîkh. Photographic copy of (Vienna) Flügel MS 814.

Ibn Ḥajar al-ʿAsqalânî, Shihâb al-Dîn Aḥmad. Al-Durar al-kâmina fî aʿyân al-miʾa al-thâmina. Cairo: Dâr al-kutub al-ḥadîtha, 1966-67. 5 vols.

__________. Inbâʾ al-ghumr bi-abnâʾ al-ʿumr fî al-târîkh. Hyderabad: Majlis dâʾirat al-maʿârif al-ʿuthmâniyya, 1967- 4 vols. to date.

__________. Rafʿ al-iṣr ʿan quḍât miṣr. Cairo: al-Hayʾa al-ʿâmma fî shuʾûn al-maṭâbiʿ al-amîriyya. 1957- . 2 vols. to date.

__________. Rafʿ al-iṣr. Bibliothèque Nationale MS Arabe 2149.

Haarmann, Ulrich. Quellenstudien zur frühen Mamlukenzeit. Freiburg: Schwarz, 1970. (Islamkundliche Untersuchungen.1.)

Ibn ʿImâd al-ʿAkarî, ʿAbd al-Ḥayy. Shadharât al-dhahab. Cairo: Maktabat al-qudsî, 1931-32. 8 vols.

Ibn Kathîr, ʿImâd al-Dîn Ismâʿîl. Al-Bidâya wa-al-nihâya fî al-târîkh. Cairo: Maṭbaʿat al-saʿâda, 1932-39. 14 vols.

Ibn Rajab, Zayn al-Dîn ʿAbd al-Raḥmân. Dhayl ṭabaqât al-ḥanâbila. Cairo: Maṭbaʿat al-sunna al-muḥammadiyya, 1952. 2 vols. in one.

Ibn al-Ṣâbûnî, Jamâl al-Dîn Muḥammad. Takmilat ikmâl al-ikmâl fî al-ansâb. Baghdad: Majma al-ʿilmî al-ʿirâqî, 1377/1957.

Ibn al-Ṣuqâʿî, al-Muwaffaq Faḍl Allâh. Tâlî kitâb wafayât al-aʿyân. Ed. and trans. by J. Sublet. Damascus: Institut Français, 1974.

Ibn Taghrî Birdî, Abû al-Maḥâsin. Les Biographies du Manhal Sâfî. Summary outline by Gaston Wiet. Cairo, 1932.

__________. Al-Manhal al-ṣâfî. Cairo: Dâr al-kutub, 1956- . I vol. to date.

__________. Al-Manhal al-ṣâfî. Photographic copy of MS Ahmet III 3018.

Ibn Ṭûlûn, Shams al-Dîn. Quḍât dimashq. Damascus: al-Majma' al-'ilmî al-'arabî, 1956.

Al-Jazarî, Shams al-Dîn Muḥammad. La chronique de Damas d'al Jazarî, années 689-698 H. Paris: Librairie Ancienne Honoré Champion, 1949.

__________. Jawâhir al-sulûk fî al-khulafâ' wa-al-mulûk. Photographic copy of Bibliothèque Nationale MS Arabe 6739.

__________. See also Haarman, Quellenstudien.

Lakhnawî, 'Abd al-Ḥayy. Al-Fawâ'id al-bahiyya fî tarâjim al-ḥanafiyya. (Cairo): Maṭba'at al-sa'âdah, 1324/1906.

al-Maqrîzî, Taqî al-Dîn Aḥmad. Histoire des sultans mamlouks de l'Egypte. Translated by M. Quatremère. Paris: Oriental Translation Fund, 1837-45. 2 vols.

__________. Kitâb al-sulûk li-ma'rifat duwal al-mulûk. Cairo: Maṭba'at lajnat al-ta'lîf wa-al-tarjama wa-al-nashr, 1934-73. 4 vols.

__________. Al-mawâ'iẓ wa-al-i'tibâr bi-dhikr al-khiṭaṭ wa-al-âthâr. Bûlâq: Dâr al-ṭibâ'a al-miṣriyya, 1853. 2 vols.

Al-Nu'aymî, Muḥyî al-Dîn 'Abd al-Qâdir. Al-Dâris fî târîkh al-madâris. Damascus: Maṭba'at al-taraqqî bî-dimashq, 1948.

Al-Nuwayrî, Shihâb al-Dîn Aḥmad. Nihâyat al-arab fî funûn al-adab. Photographic copies of Bibliothèque Nationale MSS Arabes 1578 and 1579.

__________. Nihâyat al-arab. Photographic copies of Leiden Or. MSS 19b and 20.

Al-Qalqashandî, Shihâb al-Dîn Aḥmad. Ṣubḥ al-a'shâ fî ṣina'at al-inshâ'. Cairo: Wizârat al-thaqâfa wa-al-irshâd al-qawmî, 1963. 14 vols.

Al-Ṣafadî, Khalîl ibn Aybak. A'yân al-aṣr wa-a'wân al-naṣr. Photographic copy of MS Emine Hazine 1217.

__________. Al-Wâfî bi-al-wafayât. Istanbul, Damascus, and Wiesbaden, 1931- . 9 vols. to date.

Shâfi(ibn (Alî. Kitâb ḥusn al-manâqib al-sirriyya al-muntaza(a min al-sîrat al-ẓâhiriyya. Riyâḍ: Maṭâbi(al-qûwât al-musallaḥa al-su(ûdiyya, 1396/1976.

Al-Subkî, Tâj al-Dîn (Abd al-Wahhâb. Ṭabaqât al-shâfi(iyya. (Cairo): al-Maṭba(a al-ḥusayniyya al-miṣriyya, 1906. 6 vols.

Al-Suyûtî, Jalâl al-Dîn (Abd al-Raḥmân. Ḥusn al-muḥâḍara fî akhbâr miṣr wa-al-qâhira. Cairo, 1897. 2 vols. in one.

Al-(Umarî, Shihâb al-Dîn Aḥmad. Al-Ta(rîf bi-al-muṣṭalaḥ al-sharîf. (Cairo): Maṭba(at al-(âṣima, 1894.

Yâqût ibn (Abd Allâh al-Ḥamawî. Kitâb mu(jam al-buldân. Leipzig: F.A. Brockhaus, 1866-73. 6 vols.

Al-Yûnînî, Quṭb al-Dîn Mûsâ. Dhayl mir)ât al-zamân. Hyderabad: Majlis dâ)irat al-ma(ârif al-(uthmâniyya, 1954- . 4 vols. to date.

__________. Dhayl mir)ât al-zamân. Ahmet III MS 5803.

Al-Zâhirî, Khalîl. Kitâb zubdat kashf al-mamâlik. Paris: Imprimerie nationale, 1894.

B. Secondary Sources.

Ashtor, E. Histoire des prix et des salaires dans l'orient medieval. Paris: S.E.V.P.E.N., 1969.

Ayalon, David. "Names, titles, and 'nisbas' of the Mamlûks," Israel Oriental Studies, V (1975), 189-232.

__________. L'Esclavage du Mamelouk. Jerusalem: The Israel Oriental Society, 1951.

__________. "The Great Yâsa of Chingiz Khân. A Reexamination," Studia Islamica, XXXIII (1971), 97-140; XXXIV (1972), 151-180; XXXVI (1972), 113-158; XXXVIII (1973), 107-156.

__________. "Studies on the Structure of the Mamlûk Army," Bulletin of the School of Oriental and African Studies, XV (1953), 203-28, 448-76; XVI (1954), 57-90.

Baqlî, Muḫammad Qandîl. Fahâris kitâb ṣubḫ al-aʿshâ. Cairo: ʿÂlam al-kutub, 1972 (?).

Brockelmann, Carl. Geschichte der arabischen Litteratur. 2 vols. and 3 supplements. 2nd edition. Leiden: E.J. Brill, 1945-49.

Coulson, N.J. A History of Islamic Law. Edinburgh: Edinburgh University Press, 1964.

Encyclopaedia of Islam. Edited by Thomas Houtsma et al. 4 vols. and supplement. Leiden: E.J. Brill, 1913-38.

Encyclopaedia of Islam. Edited by J.H. Kramers et al. 2nd revised edition. 4 vols. to date. Leiden: E.J. Brill, 1960- .

Escovitz, Joseph H. "A Lost Arabic Source for the History of Early Ottoman Egypt," Journal of the American Oriental Society, XLVII (1977), 513-18.

__________. "A Study of al-Durar al-kâmina as a Source for the History of the Mamlûk Empire," Unpublished M.A. thesis, McGill University, 1974.

__________. "Vocational Patterns of the Scribes of the Mamlûk Chancery," *Arabica*, XXIII (1976), 42-62.

Gabrielli, Giuseppi. "Indice alfabetico di tutte le biografie contenute nel Wâfî bi-l-wafayât di al-Şafaḍî," *Rendiconti della Accademia dei Lincei*, Ser. V, XXII (1913), 547-77, 580-620; XXIII (1914), 191-208, 217-65; XXIV (1915), 551-615; XXV (1916), 341-98.

Gaudefroy-Demombynes, M. *La Syrie à l'époque des Mamelouks*. Paris: Geuthner, 1923.

Gottheil, R.J. (ed.). *The History of the Egyptian Cadis...by...al-Kindi*. Paris, 1908.

Guest, R.W. *The Governors and Judges of Egypt*. Leiden: E.J. Brill, 1912.

Humphrey, R.S. "The Emergence of the Mamlûk Army," *Studia Islamica*, XLV (1977), 67-99; XLVI (1977), 147-82.

Lane-Poole, Stanley. *A History of Egypt in the Middle Ages*. London: Methuen and Co., 1901.

Laoust, Henri. *Essaie sur les doctrines sociales et politiques de Takî-d-Dîn Aḥmad ibn Taimîya*. Cairo: Institut Français d'Archéologie Orientale, 1939.

__________. "Le Hanbalisme sous les Mamlouks Bahrides," *Revue des Etudes Islamiques*, XXVII (1960), 1-71.

Lapidus, Ira. *Muslim Cities in the Later Middle Ages*. Cambridge, Mass.: Harvard University Press, 1967.

Little, Donald P. "An Analysis of the Relationship between Four Mamlûk Chronicles for 737-745," *Journal of Semitic Studies*, XIX (1974), 252-68.

__________. "Coptic Conversion to Islam under the Baḥrî Mamlûks, 692-755/1293-1354," *Bulletin of the School of Oriental and African Studies*, XXXIX (1976), 552-69.

__________. "Did Ibn Taimiyya have a Screw Loose?" *Studia Islamica*, XLI (1975), 93-111.

__________. "The Historical and Historiographical Significance of the Detention of Ibn Taymiyya," International Journal of Middle Eastern Studies, IV (1973), 311-27.

__________. An Introduction to Mamlûk Historiography. Montreal: McGill-Queen's Press, 1970.

__________. "The Recovery of a Lost Source for Baḥrî Mamlûk History," Journal of the American Oriental Society, XLIV (1974), 42-54.

__________. "Al-Ṣafadî as Biographer of His Contemporaries," in Essays on Islamic Civilization Presented to Niyazi Berkes. Edited by D.P. Little. Leiden: E.J. Brill, 1976.

Mandaville, Jon. "The Muslim Judiciary of Damascus in the Late Mamlûk Period." Unpublished Ph.D. dissertation, Princeton University, 1969.

Murâd, Hasan Q. "Miḥan of Ibn Taymiyya: A Narrative Account Based on a Comparative Analysis of Sources." Unpublished M.A. thesis, McGill University, 1970.

Northrup, Linda S. "Muslim-Christian Relations during the Reign of the Mamlûk Sultan al-Malik al-Manṣûr Qalâʾûn (678/1279-689/1290)." Unpublished M.A. thesis, McGill University, 1974.

Petry, Carl. "Geographic Origins and Residence Patterns of the *ʿulamâʾ* of Cairo in the Fifteenth Century." Unpublished Ph.D. dissertation, University of Michigan, 1974.

Petry, Carl and Stanley Mendehall. "Geographic Origins of the Civil Judiciary of Cairo in the Fifteenth Century," Journal of the Economic and Social History of the Orient, XXI (1978), 52-74.

Popper, William. Egypt and Syria under the Circassian Sultans, 1382-1468 A.D.: Systematic Notes to Ibn Taghrî Birdî's Chronicles of Egypt. Berkeley, California: University of California Press, 1955-57. 2 vols.

Rabie, Hassanein. The Financial System of Egypt: A.H. 564-741/A.D. 1169-1341. London: Oxford University Press, 1972.

Salibi, K.S. "The Banû Jamâʿa, a Dynasty of Shafiite Jurists in the Mamlûk Period," Studia Islamica, IX (1958), 97-109.

__________. "Listes chronologiques des grands cadis de l'Egypte sous les Mamelouks," Revue des Etudes Islamiques, XXV (1957), 71-112.

Sauvaget, Jean. "Noms et surnoms de Mameloukes," Journal Asiatique, CCXXXVIII (1950), 31-58.

Schimmel, A. "Kalif und Kadi im spätmittelalterlichen Aegypten," Die Welt des Islams, XXIV (1942), 1-128.

Sourdel, Dominique. Le Vizirat Abbaside de 749 à 936 (132 à 324 de l'Hegire). Damascus: Institut Français, 1960. 2 vols.

Sublet, Jacqueline. "La Folie de la princesse Bint al-Ashraf," Bulletin d'Etudes Orientales, XXVII (1974), pp. 45-50.

Tyan, E. Histoire de l'organization judicaire en pays d'Islam. Leiden: E.J. Brill, 1960.

INDEX